Cross-Cultural Transactions in
Multi-Ethnic Literatures of the U.S.

Cross-Cultural Transactions in
Multi-Ethnic Literatures of the U.S.

edited by

Anil Raina
Manju Jaidka
Somdatta Mandal
Vijay K. Sharma

PRESTIGE

Published by
PRESTIGE BOOKS
3/28, East Patel Nagar
New Delhi 110 008

Printed at Chaman Offset Press, New Delhi 110 002

CONTENTS

Foreword

In August 1997 MELUS-India came into being when a small group of academics got together at the Department of English, Panjab University, Chandigarh, to float a new literary association. Strictly speaking, it was not *new* but an offshoot of the parent organization in the USA, a body called MELUS (the Society for the Study of the Multi-Ethnic Literature of the United States) which had a very interesting beginning. The story handed down tells us that "MELUS was conceived in anger and brought forth into the academe in words of defiance" in 1972, in the corridors of a New York hotel which was the venue for the annual convention of the MLA. The main sessions of the Convention, all of them dealing with "White Male American Literature," were accommodated within the given space and time, but a session on Afro-American Literature was presented a day *before* the Conference, in the corridor of the hotel. Apparently the organizers were of the view that Afro-American literature was of an inferior status and deserved a different treatment. Not surprisingly, the outrage among a sizable section of the participants was great. It was seen as blatant racism and something had to be done about it. Indeed, something WAS done about it. The following year, in 1973, at the MLA convention in Chicago, MELUS took birth. Within one year a hundred members were enrolled. That was the beginning of MELUS; the rest is history. MELUS has increased steadily in numbers. MELUS has also expanded beyond the US, into Europe and India. There is talk of MELUS Chapters being set up in other countries, too.

Like its parent body, MELUS-India, the Society for the Study of the Multi-Ethnic Literature of the United States (India Chapter), wishes to provide a common forum for intellectual exchange, and establish an international network of scholars who share mutual interests. We, the founder members of this Society, are united in our wish to expand the conventional horizons of "American" Literature, to promote an attitude that cuts across boundaries, de-centers the given canon and facilitates a multi-layered, multi-perspective approach to the study of literature. As academics from India, one of our goals is to encourage comparative analyses and re-examine our own multi-ethnic literatures. So, on the one hand, while we look outward, establishing literary connections with the United States and the whole wide world outside, on the other hand we look at our own literatures, too, and place them in a global perspective.

In this direction this anthology is a small beginning, but a beginning nevertheless! It puts together selected papers from the MELUS-India International Conference held at Hyderabad in January 2000, which was attended by more than one hundred participants from India and abroad. The theme of the conference was "Cross-Cultural Transactions: Representations of Race, Gender, and Culture in Multi-Ethnic Literatures of the U.S." The essays collected here cover a wide range of topics on related themes, from broad-based critical approaches to specific scrutiny of selected texts. To use the quilting metaphor which is popularly exploited in American Studies, what we present here in this volume is a quilt made of different hues, shades and textures. Each piece, each fragment, each essay is unique in its own individual character, and yet it is part of a larger whole. If one focuses on race, another deals with gender issues, a third with individual dilemmas, all of them representing different facets of the study of literatures of America, reaching far beyond, to connect with literatures beyond the U.S. borders. Roughly, one could divide the essays into four broad categories—those focusing on background or survey studies, Afro-American, Native American, and Asian American studies. There is an essay each on Jewish-American fiction, on Chicano, and even on popular, mainstream literature. Two essays explore new ground with a comparatist approach, drawing parallels between American literary texts and specific Indian texts from regional languages. The editors hope that this will be a significant thrust of MELUS-India in the coming years.

The first essay of the collection is by Sandra Gilbert, the internationally known author of *The Mad Woman in the Attic.* In what was her keynote address, "Widow," she focuses on the elegiac tradition in literature that cuts across all boundaries of time and space. Grief is universally felt and understood, it knows no frontiers. Beginning with a highly personal experience of loss, Sandra Gilbert moves on to critically examine the tradition of mourning across different cultures, citing studies of grief and mourning, illustrating from literary texts by Sylvia Plath, Ted Hughes, Robert Lowell, Wallace Stevens, *et al*. The dirge appears in various forms through diverse cultural contexts despite the sameness of the essence, the underlying pain and sorrow.

Cultural diversity is the subject of the second essay by Sukalpa Bhattacharjee who gives a pan-ethnic, Asian-American perspective on multiculturalism. Multiculturalism in cultural discourse helps us understand the various constructions of cultural identity in multi-ethnic and multi-racial societies as in America. Referring to the doctrine of 'other-ising' and the politics of inclusion and exclusion, Bhattacharjee believes that a fusion of horizons is possible through a dialogic encounter.

Over the last couple of decades, the Afro-American sensibility has been a popular focus of attention in the study of American Literature in India. Not surprisingly, the MELUS-India 2000 conference had a sizable number of papers devoted to Black literature, and to the problems of race and colour. Alice Mills, a participant from France, has here contributed a paper on "Black Woman Power in Afro-American Theater," highlighting the emergence of the female voice of colour. Beginning with a reference to the scholarly works of Franklin Frazier, Melville Herskovits and others, Mills examines how Afro-American theater has participated in the debate concerning black women's power within their community and how, successive generations of black playwrights have carried on the discussion beyond the dialogue of their characters.

Anu Celly examines Nella Larsen's semi-autobiographical portrayal of Helga Crane, the protagonist of *Quicksand,* with a perspective which pays credence to her entrapment amidst a paradigm of cultural determinism as well as psychic interiorization of conflict that debars her from the wholeness of life. Helga does not come across as a stereotype of the black woman—the Mammy, the Loose Woman or the Conjure Woman, found so often in the works of antebellum Southern American writers—but as a superb creation, representing the existential predicaments of "a black world distilled," conceptualizing the authorial perception of the actualities of identity crisis fraught with oscillation, frustration and despair faced by an entire generation of Afro-Americans in contemporary America. A similar theme in Toni Morrison is explored by Rajyashree Khushu-Lahiri in "Politics of Race and Gender in Toni Morrison's *Paradise*" which delineates the underpinnings of race and gender in Toni Morrison's novel, highlighting the effect that living in a historically racialized society has had on the African-American people, how black women are subjected to double oppression—on the basis of their colour as well as sex.

Meenakshi Paul focuses on communication through an absence of speech as a strategy in Toni Morrison's work. She is concerned with the various forms of "articulate silence": non-verbal communication of gesture, totem, subtle social behaviour, encoded music and metaphor, encrypted song and genealogy, cultural legend, and words not extended cognizance to. Silence becomes almost deafening when it is used to express submerged concerns of race and gender, the unsaid revealing all that is said. An example of how this works is Morrison's *Beloved*, which charts the movement of silences from the weak and the limited to the employment of silence for healing and regeneration.

Riju Gopal discusses the response to the reclamation of racial beauty in the sixties with special reference to Toni Morrison's charged and painful recognition of a tragic fact that lies at the center of *The Bluest Eye*. She highlights how Morrison's novel written at a time of great social upheaval in the lives of the black people during 1965-69, focuses on the grotesque fact that the demonization of an entire race could harbor inside the most delicate member of a racialized male-dominated society: the female child. Still dealing with the question of race and colour in the essay that follows, Manohar Samuel examines multiculturalism in Afro-American Poetry to show how African-American women poets express their present predicament and envision their future through their poems which afford a rich insight into the nature of American society and culture and some of the intricate problems that are inherent in the system.

In recent years, along with the study of the Afro-American, it is noticeable that Chicano and Native American literature have also found favour with academics in India. This trend is evident from some of the papers anthologized here. Krishna Sen's meticulously documented essay, "The Dialectic of History: Rudolfo Anaya's *Bless Me, Ultima,*" undertakes a much needed survey in this field and is concerned with the portrayal of the self against a given culture and history. What is the relationship between them? Against a broad ideological perspective, Sen's paper places literature of the minority communities in America, in general, and Rudolfo Anaya's work in particular. Although it is located in specificities of time and space, the history that informs Anaya's ethnic *bildungsroman* has many facets, many layers, and several different standpoints, reaching out in divergent directions.

Three of the remaining essays take up specific studies of Native-American literature. Mahesh Nivargi's is a brief textual analysis of D'Arcy McNickle's *Runner in the Sun,* placing it in the oral tradition. He sees this novel, which is often taken as a storybook for juvenile readers, as a significant contribution to modern Native American literature, heralding the revival of a tradition that had fallen into neglect, carrying a distinct message of hope and survival in the face of all odds. Nila Das, in "Experiments in Cultural Politics," re-reads Thomas King's *Green Grass Running Water* (1993), and Paula Allen's *Woman Who Owned the Shadows* (1983) to illustrate how recent Native American novels are experiments at living through the ideal/ideology, not necessarily in the usual forms of either/or choice of value polarities and the clash of binary cultural opposites. Her essay probes new inroads to cultural politics that examine the exclusively historical and the transhistorical. Further narrowing the focus of attention to pinpoint on an Indian reservation, Rajendra Karmarkar makes an in-depth study of an episode from Alexei Sherman's *Indian Killer* to muse on the twin problems of ethnicity and identity.

Equally important in the salad bowl of multi-ethnic literature is the Asian-American contribution. Somdatta Mandal turns to popular cinema, looking towards Hollywood to examine whether stereotypes of the Chink, the coolies, cooks, launderers, still exist in American mainstream media or whether they have been done away with after the emergence of a whole new brand of Asian-American directors who could successfully dispense with the myth of the "erotic Oriental" and her objectification as a sexual mannequin. Mandal's paper, "Is Charlie Chan Really Dead? The Evolution of Asian American Characters and Images in American Mainstream Media," comes to the conclusion that Hollywood has not been able to do away with its sinister villains, dragon ladies, comical servants or its wily asexual detectives—all alien "others."

Shukla Saha speaks of the gender issue in Maxine Hong Kingston's *The Woman Warrior*. Her paper looks back at an earlier one in this collection as she discusses the role of silence in bringing out specific female dilemmas. Whereas in the earlier essay silence is discussed as a device in Afro-American fiction, Saha uses a similar approach to Asian American literature to tackle questions of double marginalization because of gender and ethnic background. In Himadri Lahiri's "On Their Immigrant Mothers' Trails: Chinese-American Daughters' Search for Identity in Amy Tan and M.H. Kingston," the focus remains on Chinese-American contribution as it explores the trans-cultural experience in Asian-American women writers from two different perspectives: the mother's and then the daughter's. The essays by Saha and Lahiri analyze ethnic and gender concerns of women characters in immigrant communities through the works of Amy Tan and Maxine Hong Kingston. Located in a culturally hybrid "third space," the daughters, despite their differences, identify themselves as women with their mothers and simultaneously affirm their own cultural location in the social reality of contemporary America. They pursue the older generation's story of disruptions and continuities, and unearth "buried plots" and silent voices. Their narratives, mediated by gender considerations, are largely dependent on memories and imagination, and reveal the contours of a marginalized but dynamic society in the process of being formed.

Short fiction of Indian origin is the concern of Rebecca Haque in "Women of the South Asian Diaspora: Chitra Banerjee Divakaruni's *Arranged Marriage* and Ginu Kamani's *Junglee Girl*." Haque focuses on the way Divakaruni and Kamani develop brief, succinct images of women caught between the old world and the new world values. How women cope with cross-cultural sexual relationships, how they try ultimately to achieve self-esteem and autonomy denied to them within their own somewhat insular and bigoted community, and how they attempt to find and fuse a viable self-image within the mainstream United States culture are of crucial importance in the short stories.

R.G. Kulkarni and S.S. Kumar bring the study of multiethnic literatures of the United States into the interior of peninsular India, making comparative studies of American writers from the margin with Indian writers from regional languages. Kulkarni undertakes a comparative study of Richard Wright's autobiography, *Black Boy,* and the Marathi Dalit writer Pralhad Sonkamble's autobiography, *Athavaninche Pakshi* to study the thematics of social awareness, class consciousness, racial prejudices, and caste discrimination as they are presented in these first-person narratives. S.S. Kumar compares the Jamaican troubadour wanderer of the Harlem Renaissance, Claude McKay, with Bharathidasan, the revolutionary poet of the Tamil Renaissance, concentrating on their portrayal of oppressed women characters. The two writers, contemporaries both (1891-1964), from antipodal locations, have much in common despite the vast distance separating them.

Jewish-American fiction is represented in this anthology with Eami Mathew's essay which analyses the ways that lead an innocent child into the underworld of experience. Ward Minogue, the hope of an immigrant Jewish family in Bernard Malamud's *The Assistant*, is a little noticed and invariably ignored character who represents the modern American youth of an ethnic minority. Mathew studies the role of social, domestic, educational, and religious institutions in shaping the individual's character.

And, finally, the inimitable Mark Twain, who has long been a part of the canon, also gets included in this collection. K.S. Saji, in his paper on the character of Huckleberry Finn seeks to read *The Adventures of Huckleberry Finn* as a subversive narrative of the White-Black power equation. Saji takes up the well-known classic as an example of how the American has problematized his own identity while struggling to establish his ideas, images, and imaginings in the new geographical space. Huck stands out as the true representative of the American spirit characterized by a total scorn of WASP standards and a fierce sense of identification with his black companion, Jim.

As is apparent, the present anthology covers a wide variety of topics and themes. It has been brought out to commemorate the January 2000 MELUS-India International with the hope that students and scholars of American literature will find much here to read and appreciate.

The Editors would like to acknowledge with gratitude the warm co-operation of all the contributors and are grateful to Prestige Books for undertaking the publication of this book.

Anil Raina
Manju Jaidka
Somdatta Mandal
Vijay K. Sharma

Widow*

SANDRA GILBERT
University of California, Davis

April 21, 1964. 2 AM. When the phone rang, Elliot and I were sublimely asleep, striped pajamas and flowered night gown drifting side by side in silky syrupy billows of sleep, the kind of luxurious sleep perhaps known only to the parents of very small, very demanding children, in this case three under four, the youngest just a month old.

The wonderfully weighty and serious brass marital bed we'd bought for a song in the late fifties was flanked by rickety orange-crate nightstands, on which we'd precariously stood the kind of electrified oil lamps that went with our *fin de siecle* bed. But an up-to-date white princess phone sat next to the lamp on Elliot's side.

He picked up the phone, only dropping it once.

"Well, I'm a widow," my mother said. Her voice was high, shrill, with a metallic edge. Pressed close to the safety of Elliot's shoulder, I could hear her hysteria beginning to leak out of the receiver. "I knew it would happen. Ah, but I didn't think it would be so soon. I'm a widow, I'm a widow, I'm widowed."

My father had been ill for what I then, still in my mid-twenties, considered a long time. Three years earlier a heart murmur, left by a childhood bout of rheumatic fever, had turned out to be the sign of a damaged mitral valve that had started to deteriorate badly. My father was a relatively young man—only fifty-four when this problem was diagnosed—but the doctors

---

* This paper was originally written for the Hyderabad conference where it was delivered as the keynote address. A different version of it has subsequently appeared in the summer 2001 issue of *Critical Inquiry*.

were gloomy about his prospects. They said his heart was sick, couldn't pump properly. Without the artificial mitral valve cardiologists had only recently devised, they said he'd certainly die of heart failure within a few years. And so far the valve replacement surgery was eighty percent successful, meaning, in those early days of cardiac operations, that it had a mortality rate of twenty percent. My father, who had a master's degree in civil engineering, didn't like such odds.

"They just called me, he had a heart attack, he was trying to push the button for the nurse, they just called me right now, they must have just found him." I could still hear my mother's rapid, metallic voice—a Sicilian voice on the verge of a scream—spilling out of the receiver.

"Oh I'm so sorry, mother," my husband said, also speaking rather loudly but very slowly, as if by speaking in a loud calm slow way he could calm her also. "But here's your daughter, let me put Sandra on."

"I'm a widow, Sandra, a widow now," my mother cried into the phone as I sat up in bed gripping the receiver with one hand and the bedclothes with the other. "A widow!" Her voice finally broke into the wail that had been building since her first minute on the phone.

Only that afternoon I had visited my father in the hospital, where he'd spent the last two weeks with what we were told was a cardiac infection. He was gaunt, pale, and clammy in his white hospital gown—but I imagine he thought, we all thought, this El Greco look was only temporary, it was the way a person looked who had to take endless diuretics in order to get down to what his doctors called "dry weight" so his heart could pump more efficiently. Then, when the person recovered—for surely this unpleasant episode through which he was passing wasn't the promised end—and left the hospital and drank the proper fluids, surely then he'd resume his usual shape, like one of those Japanese paper flowers that unfold and thicken when you put them in water.

"I can't wait to get out of here, Sandra," my father had said on that last afternoon. He'd seemed to have so much excess nervous energy that his fingers were twitching on the starchy hospital counterpane, plucking at the crisp white cotton.

"Maybe you can go home tomorrow, daddy," I'd said, hopefully. (But I really believed it.)

"I've got to get out of here!" he'd repeated, his fingers still twitching.

Maybe a year later, when I reread *Henry V* for an exam, I understood what had been happening. "*'For after I saw him fumble with the sheets, and play with flowers . . . I knew there was but one way,'* says the hostess, describing the death of Falstaff. "*He fumbled with the sheets and he plucked at the counterpane, as the dying often do.*"'[1]

"I knew it would happen but I didn't think it would be so soon," my mother lamented again, "I'm a widow. So soon! So soon!"

What did I do when she and I finally got off the phone? Snuggled down next to Elliot probably, burrowed into the warmth of our bed like an animal going to cover. By now we'd turned on the lights. Outside the blackest part of the night hung gloomily beyond the windows, the after midnight blackness when there were no cars on the long avenue outside our big shabby elderly house. It was warm and still in the lamplight; I could hardly see the wallpaper roses that looped around our room but I must have felt that, like Elliot, they were holding me close, safe in my coupledness, safe in my milky young maternity—though yes, there was some secret sickening knowledge they were holding at bay, too.

At that moment my father's death had little reality for me. It was implausible, ridiculous. A fifty-seven-year old man, nervily alert and twitching with energy, what could it mean to say such a man had *died?* Why was my mother keening on the phone? I was stony-hearted, numb.

The death became more real to me a day later, when I saw him in his coffin at the funeral "home" just up the hill from our house, although at first the body laid out in the stuffy "parlor," surrounded by reeking masses of flowers, didn't look very much like my real father but instead like a wax effigy of the man I'd known all my life, and an angry effigy at that. There was a hard twist to the mouth, as if someone had just erased a reproachful grimace, and a blankness to the brow, as if the same kind soul had smoothed away a scowl.

To my mother, though, my father must have looked perfectly real and plausible. All day she sat near his body, next to his eighty-year-old Russian mother, who also sat there all day. As if by mutual agreement they sat one on each side of the polished mahogany casket where the effigy of my father lay, humiliatingly exposed to prying eyes in all his stony almost-anger.

Every once in a while my grandmother, round and small in swathes of black, would get up and go to the head of the coffin and stroke my father's forehead and kiss it, as if she were trying to comfort him, as if she were the one who had been smoothing away his scowls. It was her right as a mother, her gesture seemed to say, to pet him this way. Her strokes were tiny yet not tentative, quick tiny capable touchings like the urgent licks a cat gives her kittens, and as she stroked I could see that she was almost inaudibly muttering something to herself, probably one of the Russian prayers I had heard her say so often during my childhood.

When my grandmother would go to the head of the coffin to comfort my father with her quick touches, my mother would often also rise and go to the coffin—to *speak* to him. "Alex, Alex*ei*," she would cry, in the high metallic voice of Sicilian keening that we had first heard on the phone that night, "Alex"—giving the first syllable theatrical weight—"*Oll*ex"—as if by addressing him so dramatically she could best communicate with him, "*Oll*ex, you were too young, it was too soon, I wasn't ready . . ." and then maybe some words in Sicilian that I didn't understand.

"*I* wasn't ready." "*I'm* a widow."

Why did she emphasize herself that way, I wondered, why did she keep reiterating the fate of the *I* who was doing the lamenting rather than the sorrowful end of the *he* who was the subject of the lamentation?

While my mother half-shrieked at my dead father—melodramatically, it seemed to me—my little, black-shawled grandmother stood silently at the head of the coffin, still quickly, urgently stroking his forehead or now and then dipping her lips toward his brow to give him a tiny kiss in a gesture that looked almost like *sipping*, as if grandma were sipping or tasting what was left of her beloved only son.

My grandmother was making these stroking-kissing-sipping movements as I entered what I sardonically considered the "so-called parlor" of the "so-called home." A wave of sickly perfume from the masses of "so-called floral tributes" surrounding the coffin seemed to break over my head, shocking and frightening me with its hint of vegetable decay.

Like most young people of my generation, my century, my country, I'd had hardly any experience of death. Panicky and embarrassed, I stared at my grandmother, who was kissing and stroking my father as if licking her young. Perhaps kissing was the thing to do.

"Oh daddy." I approached the coffin nervously, leaned gingerly toward my father, looking yet not looking at his angrily twisted mouth, his bizarre pallor, and let my mouth rest a minute on his grayish forehead.

Stone. Shock of stone, taste of cold stone even through closed lips. Ice on the tongue, steel in the throat.

I was astonished. How could grandma be kissing, stroking, sipping at *that*? What was *that?* Surely *it* was nothing to do with me, not my warm funny father, not the jokey ex-altar-boy who used to begin our dinner preparations hovering in the doorway of our closet-sized Jackson Heights kitchen, martini glass in hand, lowering his chef's apron over his head, and hilariously intoning "*In nomine patris et filius et spiritus sanctus*." Oh in the name of the Father and the Son and the Holy Ghost, this was not *that* father.

Yet my mother too seemed to recognize this effigy, this *thing*, as something to which she was related, leaning toward *it* and crying hysterically *at* it, "Alex, Alex*ei*, it was too soon, I wasn't ready."

Why "*I* wasn't ready"? Why not "*you* weren't ready"? Stony-hearted and shocked by the stone of my father's body, I was utterly alienated from my mother's grief and, worse, the sense of doom implicit in her "*I* wasn't ready," with its assertion that death had somehow happened to *her* as well as, or even *rather than*, my father. Maybe in fact the shock of the kiss that had seemed to coat my lips with some kind of toxic ice had alienated me from my father's death too, as much as from my mother's lamentations. In a few weeks I would write a poem in which I struggled to measure the distance between me and the fearful thing I had encountered in the coffin dominating that "so-called parlor."

"I am far away from you," it began, and then a stanza later went on to formulate what I now realize was numbness, repression, denial:

> I am astonished by my calm.
> Have you really left me no pain?
> The enormous sky, floodlit by thunder,
> recalls your cold home—
> the comforting grass,
> the black socket of stone
> in which you are fixed
> like a blind eye, directionless.

Death had sealed my real father away from me, closed his eyes to me and lured him off in a "directionless" direction I couldn't and wouldn't recognize.

But now I think I know that death had opened for my mother, opened and become not only a plausible but an inescapable part of her just as it had, in a different way, for my grandmother. My grandmother kissed and stroked her son as if by proffering enough caresses she could take him back into the heat of her own life, the body that had given him birth, and by incorporating his death into herself console him, redress the insult to his heart, even reconceive and rebear or repair him. My mother cried out again and again to my father because she didn't imagine him as a "blind eye, directionless": his eyes were open to her as hers were to him, she was *with* him in his death, addressing him directly as, in her *dialogue* (not monologue) of lamentation, he directed his dead gaze back at her. In her mind, he answered her apostrophes of "Alex, Alex*ei*, I wasn't ready" with a silent prosopopoeia, a speech of absence that she heard as presence.

Maybe, then, my mother's "I'm a widow" wasn't, as I crankily felt at the time, a narcissistic self-dramatization or, worse, self-promotion, a personal claim that disregarded the suffering of the dead man, but instead an acknowledgment of the "reality of death" for the one who has lost the *other* and in particular for the woman who has lost a man. According to the OED the word *widow* is from the Indo-European *widhwe*, meaning "to be empty, to be separated," to be "divided," "destitute" or "lacking." Death has entered the widow, this etymology implies, and she has entered death, for she is filled with vacancy and has dissolved into a void, a state of lack or non-being that is akin to, if not part of, the state into which the dead person has journeyed, fallen, or been drawn.

What my mother knew, then, what she was saying as, keening, lamenting, she cried "I'm a widow" with that metallic edge of amazement at discovering herself in a new *place*—the place of death—was what I wasn't to discover until more than a quarter of a century later, when *my* husband died and death so surprisingly opened its dark doors to me too.

Not that a poet need necessarily be herself a widow to try to grasp the widow's special relationship to loss, the bereaved wife's sense of death's plausibility. In 1961, a few years before my father died, Sylvia Plath had drafted a poem on which I was to brood repeatedly over the years, as I thought about my mother's grief. Perhaps it was Plath's early, traumatic loss of her own father—or perhaps, even more likely, it was what evidently became her embittering intimacy with her own mother's mourning—that caused this acolyte of the thesaurus and the dictionary to focus the piece (simply entitled "Widow") so intensely on the dreadful etymology of the very word we use to define a woman whose husband has died.

"Widow. The word consumes itself—" is how Plath's poem begins, "consumes itself," perhaps precisely in the sense of vacating itself or emptying itself out, and she goes on to describe the word as a "dead syllable, with its shadow/Of an echo."[2]

"Wid" or *widh O* is what she must have been thinking of. And thinking, too, that *widh* leads to the French *vide,* meaning "empty" or indeed, in an English word that chimes with it, "*void.*" *"Vide—Oh!"* says the poet. Or *"Void, oh,"* maybe even *"Shad-ow"* or *"Shade-oh!"* Yet the shade, says Plath also, is *with* the widow, in her and on her, as she enters the "dead syllable" of her newly empty life, "with its shadow/Of an echo." For "Death is the dress" the widow "wears," adds Plath, "her hat and collar," as if the death of the husband had annihilated, *nullified*, the wife too. Did all those growing-up years with a widowed mother, years haunted by depression and deprivation, teach this poet that?

In the fifth stanza of her bleak meditation, Plath confronts the metaphysical implications of such philology even more grimly, more head-on.

> Widow: that great, vacant estate!
> The voice of God is full of draftiness,
> Promising simply the hard stars, the space
> Of immortal blankness between stars
> And no bodies, singing like arrows up to heaven.

For the author of "Ariel," that mad gallop in verse, life had to be all forward motion, all urgency and drive. Esther Greenwood, the heroine of *The Bell Jar*, wanted to shoot off like a set of arrows into the future. Widowhood must have seemed at the very least "Ariel's" "stasis in darkness," at worst the "O-gape of complete despair" that settles over "The Moon and the Yew Tree," a piece (written a few months after "Widow") in which, as if in an echo of the dead echoes that must have shaped her mother's grief and perhaps her own, the poet encounters a place inhabited by "[f]umy, spiritous mists," a place "Separated from my house by a row of headstones." (172-73)

"Fumy, spiritous mists": the widow both longs and fears to confront such manifestations of the lost one who may be reaching toward her from the realm of the dead. Plath's "Widow" ends, eerily, with an examination of such ambivalence, zeroing in on the way the widow, "a shadow-thing" herself, yearns toward the disembodied shade her husband has become.

"A bodiless soul could pass another soul" in the "clear air" of "immortal blankness between stars," the poet worries, "and never notice it—

That is the fear she has—the fear
His soul may beat and be beating at her dull sense
Like blue Mary's angel, dovelike against a pane
Blinded to all but the gray, spiritless room
It looks in on, and must go on looking in on. [164-65]

As the anthropologist Nigel Barley has observed, in many cultures around the world, it is "above all the dead that feel desperate grief and loneliness."[3] They miss us, need us, and struggle to "look in on" us, perhaps in the sense of paying us desperate visits—like, say, Hamlet's father—as they "go on looking in on" the kingdom of the living from which they've been banished. *"I am thy father's spirit,/Doomed for a certain term to walk the night."* So Hamlet learned. Doomed to look "in on, and . . . go on looking in on" our unattainable lives. So Plath may have decided. Thus, doomed to look "in on" and perpetually "go on looking in on" the life that seeks unavailingly to go on looking back at them, such shades invade Plath's widow with the shadow of their own emptiness, draining her soul of its own being so that ultimately she herself becomes an incarnation of *nothing*: a "gray, spiritless room."

"Spiritless," though? Surely my mother—keening, calling—was if anything fuller of animation than usual. "Alex, Alex," she cried, as if in "waking" the dead with her shrieks of dismay she suddenly understood herself to be somehow living, now, not for the one that was herself—*had been* herself—but for the two that she had become, a double self that incorporated the being of my dead father into her own being. Yes, death opens to the widow, becomes plausible in ways I didn't understand as I listened, horrified—even vaguely scandalized—to what I considered my mother's half-mad dialogue with my dead father. But the speech I heard wasn't coming from a "spiritless" place. Surely some of the emptiness Plath attributes to the "great vacant estate" of the widow as she follows the etymology of the word to a dark only half-legitimate root in *vide-oh!*—surely some of this emptiness isn't what the widow herself experiences when death opens its door to her, surely it's what her culture tells her and those around her that she's experiencing or *ought* to be experiencing.

Standing by my father's coffin, keening her lament to his dead *being*, my mother wasn't gray or vacant. She was a cage crowded with a thousand birds shrieking their grief and anger—hers *and* his. Reproaching my husband for his untimely death, as I was to do a little more than a quarter of a century later, I myself wasn't a gray and spiritless room either—more, rather, a chamber of rage and despair—mine *and* his.

Surely, after all, it's the society that defines the maiden as an empty cipher, a virginal blankness, and the matron as a *femme couvert*—a woman concealed or enclosed in the blanket of her husband's authority—surely it's this society that asserts the widow's emptiness, and not the widow herself. *Man and wife is one being,* says the ancient English law, *and* he *is that being.* "By marriage," wrote the eighteenth-century jurist William Blackstone, "the very being or legal existence of a woman is suspended, or at least it is incorporated or consolidated into that of the husband, under whose wing, protection, and cover she performs everything, and she is therefore called in our law a *femme couvert.*"

And Blackstone was merely rephrasing a concept that had governed the lives of women since the middle ages. Sometimes, in fact, both in England and America, marriage was called "civil death." But if the husband is dead, then the wife must be dead too. Or at least she must be a gray spiritless room, a vacancy yearning toward numbness, annihilation.

This is how William Carlos Williams portrays the widow in his sensitive and lovely "Widow's Lament in Springtime," a lyric written for his mother not long after his father's death.

> . . . Thirtyfive years
> I lived with my husband.
> The plumtree is white today

with masses of flowers . . . .
but the grief in my heart
is stronger than they
for though they were my joy
formerly, today I notice them
and turn away forgetting.
Today my son told me
that in the meadows,
at the edge of the heavy woods
in the distance, he saw
trees of white flowers.
I feel that I would like
to go there
and fall into those flowers
and sink into the marsh near them.[4]

I would like to sink into that marsh: does this notion of the widow's helpless passivity—her nullity—explain the vexed, now nearly non-existent but always terrifying Indian practice of *sati*? In *Sati: Widow Burning in India*, an incisive exploration of this custom, the Bombay journalist and writer Sakuntala Narasimhan has noted that since in traditional Hindu culture "a woman's salvation lay in the service of her husband, it followed that she lost her *raison d'etre* the moment her husband died [so that] widowhood came to be seen as the worst calamity that could ever befall a woman . . . the ultimate degradation because it practically invalidated her continued existence."[5] In some Indian languages, adds Narasimhan, "the word for widow is an insult and a curse . . . in Tamil euphemism, a widow is referred to as a woman 'who does not live anymore' (even if she is alive)'." (40) Shades of the Indo-European *Widh*-oh, or of Plath's implied *vide—oh!* the moan of the daughter-onlooker observing the "great vacant estate" of widowhood!

Is the lady for burning, then, because she's useless as used-up stationery, nuller than yesterday's news? I now realize that Plath's poem actually begins with a reference to *sati*:

Widow. The word consumes itself—
Body, a sheet of newsprint on the fire
Levitating a numb minute in the updraft

Over the scalding red topography
That will put her heart out like an only eye.

But as commentators on the concept of *sati* have observed, the woman bent on such self-immolation is not, strictly speaking, a *widow* but still a *wife*, since she's determined to die with her husband rather than endure what Plath (and the transcultural precepts that must have helped shape Plath's thought) defines as the "vacancy" of widowhood. Writes the anthropologist Lindsey Harlan, in a study of "Sati Tradition in Rajasthan," "when a woman utters her sati vow, she places herself in the context of a vivid temporal fiction. Time is condensed, so that she becomes a *sahagamini*, 'one who goes (*gamini*) together (*saha*) with one's husband.'"[6]

In *this* death-narrative of female grief, then, the lady's not for burning because she *is*, already, burning. Adds Harlan, the "Rajput *sativrata's* death is thought to be a manifestation of her goodness, her *sat* . . . which is a moral heat . . . It is said that when [she] learns of her husband's death, this heat begins to consume her body. So the woman who has taken a sincere *vrat* of *sati* quite literally becomes too hot to touch." Not only too hot, though, but also too eerily potent. "During the period between the *sati vrat* and the sati's death, a woman is considered extremely powerful. Because she has renounced life, she has in a sense progressed beyond life. She possesses special powers, among them the power to curse . . . the power to establish prohibitions," and ultimately, when she is transformed into a *satimata*, a kind of saint, the power "to protect her earthly household" from her special place in eternity. (81)

But from a western perspective, too, there's something alarmingly apocalyptic in the burning rage and grief of the bereft wife. Consider, after all, the paradoxically empowered and exultant lament that Richard Wagner wrote for Brunhilde, the warrior woman who is the heroine of his great *Ring* cycle. Remember, here, that Brunhilde is an *ex*-Valkyre: once, along with her Valkyrie sisters, she was an immortal who collected the bodies of heroes dead in battle, but she lost her divinity when she defied her father, the god-king Wotan, and was thereby condemned not just to mortality but to the humiliations as well as the pleasures of human love. Now, though, as she commands the lighting of her husband, Siegfried's funeral pyre, she sings in triumph of her ecstatic re-entry into the other world of the gods—and the dead.

> Greetings, Grane, my horse.
> Do you know, friend,
> Where I am leading you?
> In the blazing fire
> Lies your master, . . .
> Feel how my breast also burns. . . .
> To be wed
> In the most powerful Love!—
> Hi-ho! Grane!
> Greet our friend!
> Siegfried! Siegfried!
> Let my greeting bless you.[7]

And of course we know what's going to happen. We know that the sheer fire of Brunhilde's grief is going to consume the world and, most terribly, Valhalla, the heavenly home of the father god who had cursed her. *Gotterdammerung*, the name of the last opera in Wagner's *Ring*, means "the twilight of the gods," but this is no gentle, gray-blue evening; *this* twilight issues in an explosion of female passion, a vengefully blazing sunset.

Is it the power—not the emptiness—of the widow that unnerves the world, not just her rage and grief but the sudden, mysteriously privileged access to the other world that such rage and grief bestow? Did I sense something alarmingly uncanny in my own mother's keening, her weird address to what I myself merely perceived as the absence graven on my father's icy forehead? "In most 'traditional' cultures . . . as in our own," writes the classicist Gail Holst-Warhaft in a fine study entitled *Dangerous Voices: Women's Laments and Greek Literature,* "women and men are perceived and expected to mourn in different ways." Men, she argues, tend to defuse and politicize grief in public eulogies or else, as I myself have written, in ceremonial elegies.[8] Thus, although both women and men "weep for their dead . . . it is women," declares Holst-Warhaft, "who tend to weep longer, louder, and *it is they who are thought to communicate directly with the dead through their wailing songs*."[9] [emphasis added]

Not that widowers don't also grieve, often in deeply personal, intimate language. (And the word "widower" here should really stand for any man who mourns a dead beloved.) C.S. Lewis's *A Grief Observed*, one of the twentieth-century's classic bereavement texts, is a record of one man's sorrow at his wife's death—his insight that "grief . . . feels like fear," or "like suspense . . . like waiting," giving "life a permanently provisional feeling" as the survivor merely endures "pure time, empty successiveness" while hopelessly anticipating the impossible return of the lost one who has passed to the other side of silence.[10] And before Lewis mourned the death of the wife so tellingly named "Joy," Thomas Hardy struggled to get beyond the wall of silence, to "communicate directly with the dead" through the "wailing songs" he included in his *Poems 1912*, another classic text of modern grief. In "After a Journey," he even convinced himself that he was really *seeing* the specter of his dead wife Emma: "Hereto I come to view a voiceless ghost," he began, adding in a direct address to the bodiless Emma,

> Where you will next be there's no knowing,
> Facing round about me everywhere,
> With your nut-coloured hair,
> And gray eyes, and rose-flush coming and going.

And as David Gewanter has pointed out, the first draft of this poem is even more explicit in its determination to cross the border between the living and the dead that separates the poet from his wife. "Hereto I come to *interview* a ghost" (emphasis added) was Hardy's initial assertion, as, in Gewanter's formulation, he called "out to a nearby but unseen spirit, asking it to pull him onward" but also to manifest it(*her*)self to him.[11]

Douglas Dunn, Peter Davison, Paul Monette, Ted Hughes, Donald Hall: these are only a few of the more recent male poets who have elegized lost beloveds, and especially the most recent of these writers—Monette, Hughes, Hall—have at times strained with a passion very like Hardy's to address the invisible dead, if not exactly to "interview" them. But weren't Hardy's elegies for Emma innovative precisely because they swerved significantly from much masculine grief-work, at least as it has come down to us through a literary tradition in which a man mourns in highly structured, eloquently styled and clearly resolved modes (the public eulogy, the pastoral elegy), and usually in fact mourns for another *man* rather than for a woman? Unresolved—*never* resolved—struggles to get beyond the grave, Hardy's poems take on at least certain qualities of the female-authored lament as opposed to the male-crafted elegy, reminding us that the English word *widower* is a back-formation on our word *widow*, and one of the few such formations in a language where *actress* is generated from *actor*, *poetess* from *poet,* and so on.

In spousal loss, women are primary, men secondary. What change of title, after all, is required for a widow*er? He* was Mr. John Doe before the death of Jane and will continue thus ever after. The widow, though, was Mrs. *John* Doe before her husband's demise, but after his death reverts to a part (but not the whole) of her single, unadorned self, or so Emily Post admonishes her to do: *John* having departed this earth, his widow must now be Mrs. *Jane* Doe, unless a Bill or Joe Doe or Smith or Jones comes along to replace the lost John.

In Samuel Beckett's *Krapp's Last Tape*, the gloomily aging protagonist, musing on his mother's death following a "long viduity," becomes so obsessed with the word "viduity" that he looks it up in "an enormous dictionary":

> Krapp: (reading from dictionary) State—or condition—of being—or remaining—a widow—or widower. (Looks up. Puzzled.) Being—or remaining? . . . (Pause. He peers again at dictionary. Reading.) 'Deep weeds of viduity.' . . . Also of an animal, especially a bird. . . the vidua or weaver-bird. . . . Black plumage of male. . . . (He looks up. With relish.) The vidua-bird![12]

"Black plumage of male": the vidua-bird of Krapp's ruminations, and the relish with which Krapp contemplates his finery, should remind us too that when widower's weeds aren't borrowed from a historically female tradition of lamentation they draw on other, historically masculine funeral traditions.

Maybe the most famous utterance of a widower-poet, after all, was the seventeenth-century "Exequy" that Bishop Henry King produced after the death of his much-loved young wife, a highly stylized and prayerful statement that the twentieth-century British poet Peter Porter copied generations later in an "Exequy" of his own, for *his* much-loved young wife. Unlike Hardy, or those writers like, say, Monette and Hall, who have followed in Hardy's "falteringly" confessional footsteps, King is lavishly ceremonial. And clearly he expects neither reply nor "interview" from the "Matchless, Never-to-Be-Forgotten Friend" in whose honor he writes:

> Accept, thou shrine of my dead saint,
> Instead of dirges, this complaint;
> And for sweet flowers to crown thy hearse,
> Receive a strew of weeping verse.

Unlike Hardy, King speaks not to a ghost but to a structure, a "shrine." And though Porter doesn't distance his dead wife quite so thoroughly, he is certainly frank about his adoption of the ritual flourishes that marked his carefully chosen precursor's verse:

> This introduction serves to sing
> Your mortal death as Bishop King
> Once hymned in tetrametric rhyme
> His young wife, lost before her time.

And maybe the distinction between the ceremonial mode of these exequys and the more personal genre of lamentation lies in the etymologies of the words that define the genres themselves. *Exequy*, meaning "funeral rite," very likely originates in the Indo-European *sekw*, "to follow," while *lamentation*, meaning "an expression of grief," probably comes from the Indo-European *la*, meaning "to mutter," "to lull," to "sing a lullaby," or even "to talk." So the exequy is a ritual of *following* and in fact *distancing;* it is public, performative, oratorical, while the lamentation is intimate, private, oral, informal. The widower, in his "black plumage," often stands apart from his loss, enshrining it in solemn measures, while the widow more frequently mutters or croons a lullaby to the lost one.

Yet don't the genres of exequy and lament ultimately refer not just to loss and not primarily to the *dis*embodied ghost but to the body itself—the corpse of the departed whose washing is usually, in most cultures, the business of women? In traditional Greek villages, Holst-Warhaft tells us, "At the wake, when females related . . . to the deceased surround the coffin, squabbles may break out over both singing and sitting positions." (46) (Can this be why my mother and my grandmother sat one on each side of my father's coffin, warily balancing each other?)

"The women," adds Holst-Warhaft, "demonstrate their closeness to the deceased not only through . . . song or spoken testimony, but by direct physical contact, touching and caressing the hair or head of the corpse or holding the forehead." (46) (Does this explain the kissing, even the apparent *sipping* my Russian grandma did? The keening and caressing my Sicilian mother did?) But when "the male relatives enter to pay their respects, their behavior is strikingly different. They remain in small groups on the margin . . . or wait at the entrances [for in] 'contrast to the linguistic, emotional and tactile intimacies of the women, men (including the priest) maintain a purely *visual* relation to the dead.'" (emphasis added)[13] (Is it possible, then, that even Hardy's yearning toward "interview," with its overtones of expressive, "female" lamentation, comes from a "male" orientation to the visual?)

Perhaps it's because in so many cultures women are so physically as well as psychically close to the dead that, according to Holst-Warhaft, one anthropologist has found in some settings "'an underlying fear of laments as magic songs," sinister lullabies. Perhaps these female cries and whispers of loss seem to "open up perilous channels of communication between the living and the dead'" as the lamenter becomes a "medium through whom the dead speaks to the living" a "shaman who leads the living to the underworld and back." (47)

Holst-Warhaft gives as an example of such a risky song the famous Irish "Lament for Art O'Leary," "composed by

O'Leary's widow, Black Eileen, for the second burial of her husband, who died in 1773 . . . shot on the run as an outlaw." In the stanzas quoted here, Eileen discovers and begins to lament O'Leary's death.

My friend and my love!
Of the blood of Lord Antrim
And of Barry of Allchoill,
How well your sword suited you,

. . . .

My friend you were forever!
I knew nothing of your murder
Till your horse came to the stable
With the reins beneath her trailing,
And your heart's blood on her shoulders

. . . .

I struck my hands together
And made the bay horse gallop
As fast as I was able,
Till I found you dead before me
Beside a little furze-bush. . . .
Your heart's blood was still flowing;
I did not stay to wipe it
But filled my hands and drank it.

My love you'll be forever!
Rise up from where you're lying
And we'll be going homewards.
We'll have a bullock slaughtered,
We'll call our friends together,
We'll get the music going.

I'll make a fine bed ready
With sheets of snow-white linen,
And fine embroidered covers
That will bring the sweat out through you
Instead of the cold that's on you! (7-8)

Not only disturbingly tactile and erotic but scandalously oral, the "drama of Eileen's ride . . . leads to an act that fills us with horror [her drinking of O'Leary's blood] and breaks the boundaries between the living and the dead," notes Holst-Warhaft, "enabling the lamenting woman to call up her husband and invite him to feast and lie with her again." (8)

Even today, women poets who have been widowed dramatize moments of transgressive communion with the dead that bear a striking similarity to Eileen's fierce address to her murdered husband. Plath, after all, drafted "Widow" from the position of a daughter, terrified by what she experienced as the "vacancy" of her mother's "estate," just as Williams composed his "Widow's Lament in Springtime" from the position of a son, (re)constructing his mother's grief. But two recent American writers, Tess Gallagher and Ruth Stone, speak specifically as widows themselves. The impassioned elegies for Raymond Carver that Gallagher collects in *Moon Crossing Bridge* (and note the boundary breaking, the border *crossings*, implied by that title) record moments of strange conjugal dialogue, silent but full of meaning. "Three nights you lay in our house," recalls Gallagher in a lyric entitled "Wake," "Three nights in the chill of the body," but

> In the room's great dark
> I climbed up beside you onto our high bed. . .
> There was a halo of cold around you
> as if the body's messages carry farther
> in death. . . . We were dead
> a little while together then, serene
> and afloat on the strange broad canopy
> of the abandoned world. (5)

Two equally erotic elegies by Ruth Stone are perhaps even more shocking in the powerful candor of their dialogue not just with the dead but in a sense with death itself. In her openly necrophiliacss "Habit," for example, Stone confesses to her husband, twenty years dead, that

> Every day I dig you up
> And wipe off the rime
> And look at you. . . .
> Your eyelids pull back from their sockets.
> Your mouth mildews in scallops. . . .
> I hold your sleeves in my arms;

Your waist drops a little putrid flesh.
I show you my old shy breasts. [*Cheap*, 15]

And in "Becoming You" Stone's fantasy of devouring her dead husband—of quite literally *incorporating* him into herself—even more directly recalls Eileen's drinking of O'Leary's blood. Burning with an intensity that parallels Brunhilde's passion, this piece is marked by a frankness that might be terrifying were it not so loving:

I think about territory
And how you invaded my skin.
Now, I shall grow
Until I encompass you.
There in your box,
Barefoot in your best suit. . . .
I am everywhere growing larger . . .
As, taking my time,
I come on digesting you. [14]

Is it possible that in her voracious desire to cross the bridge between the living and the dead and incorporate her husband's ghost into her own being the widow-poet seems to become a kind of shaman? Meditating on Chinese culture in her classic memoir *The Woman Warrior: Memoirs of a Girlhood among Ghosts,* Maxine Hong Kingston describes her mother—not a widow but a one-time doctor—as having a special prowess in confronting ghosts "because she can eat anything. . . . All heroes are bold toward food." Perhaps there's a thin and blurry line between (in Stone's words) "encompassing" and "digesting" the dead so as to sustain them in one's own life and devouring them in order to defeat the ghostly dangers they pose. Kingston tells the ancient tale of "Wei Pang, a scholar-hunter of the Ta Li era of the T'ang dynasty (A.D. 766-779)" who defeated a spirit that had taken on the form of a "shining twinkling sphere" by shooting it "with three true arrows," ordering his servant to cook morsels of the thing "in sesame oil," and cheerfully devouring it.

But maybe, then, if she's thought to be capable of a special access to the supernatural, the widow has to be defined as "empty"—*vide-Oh! Shade-Oh!*—because she's less dangerous that way. Brunhilde burns up the world and brings down the gods. Eileen O'Leary crosses threatening borders between life and death. Even contemporary women like Gallagher and Stone seem to have strange powers to speak to ghosts. My own mother frightened me, shrieking beside my father's coffin! Perhaps onlookers shiver at the widow's uncanny access to the other world in the same way that culture shudders, more generally, at woman's power, as if woman's power to give birth must be matched by an equal power to take the gift of life back into herself.

Think of the "black widow" spider, devouring her mate in a paroxysm of necrophiliac abandon. Or think, for that matter, of Juana la Loca, Renaissance Queen of Spain and Flanders, whose mind supposedly "snapped under the strain of [her husband's] death" so that she "would not be parted from his coffin." Do some of us secretly believe that grief induces spasms of perverse desire in bereft women? As if in imitation of Juana, the infamous nineteenth-century Princess Belgiojoso, whom Mario Praz was to call a "'cracked vessel' [suffering] from profound nervous disorders," was found in 1848 to have kept "in a cupboard" of her villa "the embalmed corpse of her young secretary and lover . . . who had died of consumption a short time before."[14] And the perhaps misunderstood Principessa herself had a number of fictional mimics, ranging from the protagonist of Rider Haggard's *She* to the subject of William Faulkner's "A Rose for Emily"—grievously erotic (and apparently *neu*rotic) women who fetishistically possessed and were possessed by the bodies of dead beloveds. Have such women been culturally defined as heiresses of the black widow spider's cunning—and "her" murderous desire?

At the same time, though, almost as troublesome as the "black widow's" apparently monstrous desire may be the possibility that the unnervingly self-possessed widow feels *no such desire*! What if, like the infamous "merry widow" she is just, cheerily, *for* and *in* herself, *of* herself, *to* herself? In other words, what if the widow is utterly delighted to be relieved of that burden called "a husband" and freed, instead, to be a seductress of whom it might be said that (as Oscar Wilde put it about one of his more lubricious female characters) "Her hair has gone quite gold from grief"?

Indian widows are admonished to wear white, sleep on straw mats rather than in beds, and avoid meats and spices—any food that might "heat the blood" and, by implication, stir desire. The purity of the dead man's wife must be guarded with caution this custom suggests; otherwise her raging sexuality, awakened in marriage, might be given to some interloper who would take unto himself the libido that was presumably destined for her lawful husband, and only her husband.

As if to comment on the problems posed by mature female sexuality (and the vulnerability felt by men of all ages), Kingston offers in *China Men* a parable of how death came into the world. "The last deed of Maui the Trickster . . . was to seek immortality for men and women by stealing it from Hina [the goddess] of the night," she explains. So "Maui dived into the ocean, where he found great Hina asleep. Through her vagina like a door, he entered her body. He took her heart in his arms. He had started tunneling out feet first when a bird, at the sight of his legs wiggling out . . . laughed. Hina awoke and shut herself, and Maui died."[15]

In her grief and fury, the widow wants only to speak to the dead one, to sustain and preserve him. But from the perspective of those outside her grief, her desirous speech is both awesome and awful. If she seeks to absorb her dead husband, perhaps she is as mad as Juana, as perverse as the Princess Belgiojoso and Faulkner's Emily! And maybe she can swallow up life too—like Hina, like Brunhilde! But at the same time, suppose she just wakes up from the long dream called "marriage," "shut[s] herself," and goes back to dreams of her *own*, perhaps disturbingly fierce pleasures.

Those of us still safe in our dailiness fear all aspects of such voracity just as men all too often fear female power. In a psychoanalytic commentary on Lindsay Harlan's examination of the sati tradition in Rajasthan, Karen McCarthy Brown has observed that when the *sativrata* "mounts the funeral pyre [she] takes the body of her husband into her lap, in a breastfeeding posture," at which point her body supposedly "explodes into flames." Thus, argues Brown, as "he feeds on her, she eats him up and, most important, devours herself as well. The nurturing woman and the devouring woman become one through a process in which fire transforms the [potentially] rapacious, willful bad mother"—the mother who curses and destroys—"into a self-devouring good mother." And even if this primarily psychocultural analysis doesn't sufficiently decipher the complex meanings that the very notion of *sati* has taken on in India over the centuries, in a western context it helps explain some of the ambivalence associated with the status of the widow as a grieving woman who seems to have been simultaneously emptied of her former social role and filled with a new power to mediate between the ordinary human world of the living and the mysteriously *in*human world of ghosts.

But in her liminal position—her scary stance betwixt and between the quick and the dead—the widow takes on some of the morbid glamour that the great American modernist Wallace Stevens attributed to the earth mother in "Madame La Fleurie," one of his most eccentric and moving late poems. In this grim text, the once cheerful skeptic of "Sunday Morning" offers readers a "handbook of heartbreak" in which he elegizes a dead friend who has been swallowed up, like Maui, by the death mother:

> He looked in a glass of the earth and thought he lived in it.
> Now, he brings all that he saw into the earth, to the waiting parent.
> His crisp knowledge is devoured by her, beneath a dew. . . .
> He does not lie there remembering the blue-jay, say the jay.
> His grief is that his mother should feed on him, himself and what he saw,
> In that distant chamber, a bearded queen, wicked in her dead light.[16]

A powerfully transgressive and indeed *phallic* (bearded!) mother: is that what the widow becomes in the misty places of the cultural unconscious? Must we therefore define her as empty precisely because we fear she's full? Or worse, has she, in her fearsome fullness, become coextensive with death itself?

The ferocious conclusion of Robert Lowell's "Mr. Edwards and the Spider" actually makes such a claim. Throughout this brilliant monologue Lowell has, of course, drawn on imagery from the writings of Jonathan Edwards (his early *Of Insects*, his triumphant sermon entitled "Sinners in the Hands of an Angry God") to replicate the impassioned evangelism of America's most eloquent Puritan. The piece opens, in fact, with a paraphrase of the young Edwards' observations of spiders who "die/Urgently beating east to sunrise and the sea," then gradually develops a link between spiders who die with "no long struggle" and sinful souls with "abolished will." Yet in the poem's final stanza Lowell himself utterly transforms the spider image, explicitly sexualizing death (in a way Edwards did not). The Puritan preacher's formulation of an angry God's ultimate threat to the sinner is followed by the twentieth-century poet's own explosive interpretation of the darkness implicit in that threat, as Lowell links the infamous viduity of the "hourglass-blazoned spider" to the horrific blaze of consciousness that is eternal hellfire:

> . . . picture yourself cast
> Into a brick-kiln where the blast
> Fans your quick vitals to a coal—
> If measured by a glass,
> How long would it seem burning! Let there pass
> A minute, ten, ten trillion; but the blaze
> Is infinite, eternal: this is death,
> To die and know it. This is the Black Widow, death.[17]

Lowell's leap away from Edwards' original text is as disquieting as it is dazzling. For even while the poet himself may well have intended simply to surface the misogynistic madness to which Edwards himself was heir, that brief, sudden last sentence is thickened, darkened, made weighty by countless cultural hints that what widowhood itself supposedly means (*to mourn and know it)* might at any moment dissolve into an awareness of obliteration (*to die and know it)* inexplicably fostered by the raging murderousness of the one who grieves (*to kill and know it*).

"I'm a widow, a widow, it's too soon, Alex, it's too soon," my mother told my father, wailing beside his coffin. Listening to her, I was embarrassed, bewildered, oddly anxious. Did I fear that shadows had already invaded and nullified her? Or did I secretly suppose that her uncanny keening signified the sudden immanence of "the Black Widow, death"?

Notes

1. *Henry V*, II, iv, 15-17.
2. Plath, *The Collected Poems* (New York: Harper & Row, 1981), pp. 164-65. Further page references to Plath poems will appear in the text.
3. Nigel Barley, *Grave Matters: A Lively History of Death around the World* (New York: Henry Holt, 1997), p. 31.
4. Williams, *The Collected Poems of William Carlos Williams*, Vol. I, 1909-1939, ed. A. Walton Litz & Christopher MacGowan (New York: New Directions, 1986), p. 171.
5. Sakuntala Narasimhan, *Sati: Widow Burning in India* (New York: Doubleday Anchor, 1990), p. 36. Further page references will appear in the text.
6. Lindsey Harlan, "Perfection and Devotion: Sati Tradition in Rajasthan," in John Stratton Hawley, ed., *Sati, the Blessing and the Curse: The Burning of Wives in India* (New York: Oxford, 1994), p. 85. Further page references to this and other essays in *Sati, the Blessing and the Curse*, will appear in the text.
7. Cited and discussed in Dorothy M. Figueira, "Die Flambierte Frau: Sati in European Culture," in Harlan, p. 64.
8. See Sandra M. Gilbert, "American Sexual Poetics of Walt Whitman and Emily Dickinson," in Sacvan Bercovitch, ed., *Reconstructing American Literary History* (Harvard University Press, 1986), pp. 123-154, esp. 143-148.
9. Gail Holst-Warhaft, *Dangerous Voices: Women's Laments and Greek Literature* (London and New York: Routledge, 1992), pp. 1-2. Further page references will appear in the text.
10. Lewis, *A Grief Observed* (New York: Bantam, 1976; 1st pub.1963), pp. 1, 38.
11. David Gewanter, "'Undervoicings of Loss' in Hardy's Elegies to His Wife," *Victorian Poetry*, 29, 3 (Autumn 1991): 196-97. In this

illuminating essay, Gewanter also shows how thoroughly absorbed the poet was in a dialogue with his dead wife's journals, both a "diabolical," angry diary entitled "What I think of my Husband" and a more "breathless and sentimental memoir" entitled "Some Recollections." (See Gewanter, 193-94 and passim.)

12. Beckett, *Krapp's Last Tape and other Dramatic Pieces* (New York: Grove/Evergreen, 1960), p. 18.
13. Holst-Warhaft is here drawing on work done by anthropologists Anna Caraveli-Chaves and Nadia Seremetakis, who have studied women's laments on the Greek island of Mani. (See Holst-Warhaft, pp. 45-46.) Later, in a discussion of "The Ritual Nature of Ancient Lament," she notes that evidence for "the differing behaviour of men and women during the prosthesis [wake] and at the tomb comes from a limited but persuasive combination of archaeological and literary sources. In vase paintings, men are rarely depicted close to the body, but appear in formal procession with right arms raised in a conventional gesture of mourning. Around the bier of the dead man, whose head is clasped by the chief mourner, the women stand, their arms raised, sometimes beating their heads, or pulling out their hair in what [one analyst] refers to as 'wild ecstasy.'"
14. See Mario Praz, *The Romantic Agony* (Oxford & New York: 1970), pp. 123-24, 178, n. 80.
15. Kingston, *China Men.*
16. Stevens, *The Collected Poems and Prose* (New York: Library of America), pp. 431-32.
17. Lowell, *Selected Poems* (New York: Farrar Straus, 1976), pp. 17-18.

Beyond Multiculturalism: A Pan-ethnic Asian American Perspective

SUKALPA BHATTACHARJEE
G.C. College, Silchar

Multiculturalism, in the context of the United States had been brought into cultural discourse to understand the various constructions of cultural identity in a multi-ethnic and multiracial America. But multiculturalism in a broader sense generally refers to the doctrine that "cultural diversity should be recognized as a permanent and valuable part of political societies."[1] And so, by recognizing cultural diversity as a permanent aspect of political societies, Multiculturalism in the United States has not succeeded in projecting the ongoing processes of social construction of collective identities. The different theories of Multiculturalism virtually work out the different possibilities of the doctrine of otherising, based on the politics of inclusion and exclusion. One significant aspect of the politics of Multiculturalism is "the façade of welcoming non western *others* into putatively interdisciplinary and cross cultural exchange, a continual tendency to stigmatize and ghettoize non western cultures precisely by way of ethnic, national labels."[2] Multiculturalism appeals as a kind of cultural globalization to non-western countries with its apparent liberal democratic contents. This is why Multiculturalism has become an obsession with literary authors and critics who claim to 'decentre' the hegemony of the west.[3] But actually, Multiculturalism with its agenda of exclusion has denied cultural pluralism because 'difference as exclusion actually denies difference.' Mutual recognition in the Taylorian sense[4] or 'fusion of horizons' on the Gadamerian lines has not been able to be a part of the multiculturalism politics, especially in the United States. A 'fusion of horizons' can operate "through developing new vocabularies of comparison by means of which we can articulate these contrasts."[5] The evolution of a democratic Multiculturalism requires the assignment of transitive, transformatory and emancipatory meaning to cultural differences, rather than confixing it to 'exclusionary' mode. Thus, Multiculturalism cannot liberate oppressed *classes*—both in the sense of economic classes and the classroom as a space for pedagogical practices.[6] Universality remains a far cry.

Therefore, transcending the limits posed by exclusivist, national and global policies like Multiculturalism involves what Barthes has described as 'going beyond the sentence',[7] which is one of the ways of resisting cultural and political closure. The possibilities of a 'fusion of horizons' which would appropriate a non-dialectical form of closure lies in a process of articulation of subjects of exclusion, whose dialogic encounter would emerge as relocation and reinscription beyond the essentialism of western theoretical productions. Contrarily, Pan-ethnicity to an extent has been able to appropriate the logic of multinational capitalism in Multiculturalism.[8] The politics of localization and globalization makes it necessary to have a workable notion of how social groups are unified by a common culture and at the same time the need to "identify genuine cultural differences (and similarities) across groups."[9] Pan-ethnicity makes an adjustment of the multiplicity of racial, ethnic and national boundaries, within a larger world of global 'civic friendship. ' Pan-ethnicity assumes a conglomerating form with chunks of identities coming together in a contingent fashion. Further, it acts as a search for common grounds for living together between diasporic, racial, and other identities. What looms large through such a construction of pan-ethnicity is the possibility of a moment of difference and alterity that gives it a dynamic and changing character. Pan-ethnic identity deploys on foreignness, a mixness of various identities that articulate their sameness and difference in a language that preserves the sense for itself. Pan-ethnic discourse leads to a political, economic, and ideological intention and imagination that is capable of decentring symbolic power relations within which they are embroiled. One is aware that there is an ongoing metropolitan debate on the construction of pan-ethnic identities—an irresolution between belonging to an ethnic community or polity and a sense of belonging together in the new world order. It has been a new global experience that produces a shared identity across cultures by expanding the latitudes of race ethnicity and other specific markers. It has a surge to move beyond the limits of subjecthood to emerge into subjects-in-the-making or a class of non-subjects. This further destabilises the need for a privileged/under privileged voice but alters it to a decentred narrative of hope and despair.

This dynamics makes the Asians of the East to appropriate the Western symbols, especially the symbol of the 'Frontier.' Asians have dispersed, migrated and have spread across the globe. They have settled especially in the United States where they are a significant population. The social significance of the Asians in America is that they are neither black nor white and hence beyond the binary construction of difference. The Asians in America exhibit complex manifestation of the East-West encounter and complicate the either/or definition of the colour lines of the twentieth century. The 'East' and the 'West' in their mutual encounter of inclusion and exclusion suggests the carving out of a 'third space' of 'neither/nor' and as 'both/and'.[10] The politics of inclusion and exclusion mostly operates through a discriminatory discourse that marks and unmarks identity. As racial others, Asians in America occupying this 'third space' disrupt and conform to the hegemonic dualisms. Racial and ethnic categories have been used in the United States to distinguish groups in relation to a white majority, both for the purposes of exclusion and inclusion. Asian Americans, as a racial or ethnic category in the United States were defined first with respect to their legal status. After the 1990s, "Asian American" is gaining common usage as a pan-ethnic category, relative to other groups—first is the relationship of Asian Americans with Asians who have emigrated from Asian countries of origin and settled in other regions and second, the relationship to other Asians throughout the world. Interestingly the formal classification of Asians in America "as a racial group by the federal government coincided with the self-identification of Asian Americans as a pan-ethnic group in the 1970s and 1980s."[11] Within the United States, the terms nationality, race and ethnicity are sometimes overlapping but are also quite distinct. Given a civic culture, nationality is based on citizenship; race is imposed by the dominant group and is meant to distinguish people of colour with the white majority. The construction of Asian-American pan-ethnicity in this context has been a projection of the 'other' from the settled American point of view, a telescoping of American identity into others. One can mention here that ethnicity has been used mainly as a self-definition of "white ethnics," "not necessarily related to or based on a majority group. "[12] It may be mentioned here that, 'ethnic nationalism' makes a distinction between 'ethnos' and 'state' and allows people to imagine a different—often conflicting type of community.[13] Asians in America categorised as 'Asian-American' and 'American Indian' view the need for a pan-ethnic unity, as the "polar alternatives of traditionalism and assimilation—both still pursued—have proved unsatisfactory as adaptive responses to contact with Whites."[14] The way Indians and Asians view themselves has been significantly influenced by the way outsiders view them and lump them as broad categories with an ethnocentric 'myopia.' Within the confines of race, class and gender politics of exclusion, Asians in America and Ameri-Indians have tried to maintain independent self-definitions, challenging controlling images and replacing them with ethno-cultural stereotypes. The civil rights and ethnic studies movements of the late sixties have also inspired other ethnic minorities of the United States who shared solidarity with the blacks. Ethnic and minority movements within the Asian countries have also inspired the Asian minorities in the United States. Grounded in the U.S. black power movement and in anticolonial struggles of Third World countries, ethnic antihegemonic projects have been unified by a common goal of articulating cultural resistance. Given the historical distortions and misrepresentations of Asians in America in mainstream media, most cultural projects produced by Asian Americans and Ameri-Indians perform the important tasks of correcting histories, shaping legacies, creating new cultures, constructing a politics of resistance, and opening spaces for the forcibly excluded. Therefore one significant way of producing such cultural resistance has been through the construction of cultural stereotypes, which traces a community's ethnic identity and appropriates the strong modern subject of the 'West.' These cultural stereotypes reveal heterogeneity rather than regulating ideas of cultural unity or integration. Such a cultural project also seeks to destabilize the dominant racial discourse that constructs 'Asians' as a homogeneous group conforming to types such as 'yellow peril'; and 'Oriental Mastermind.' The myth of the United States is deconstructed by the 'cultural nationalism' of the Asians, which has been crucial for their struggle for self-representation.

There is a lot of ambiguity reflected in the attempt for self-representation in the growing body of Asian literature in English translation and Asian-American literature. Cultural projects in literature and pedagogical practices constitute the deconstructing of the myth of the benevolent United States which offers a lot of promises to men and women of Asia. For example, Carlos Bulosan's *America Is in the Heart* (1943/1973), is one of the core works of Asian American literature that challenges the narrative of the United States as a land of opportunity. Rejecting the myth of the United States also involves an interrogation of ideological racism through a system of promoting and controlling racist images. John Okada's *No-No Boy* (1957) is a strong indictment of the racist hysteria. Asian American literature of the 1970s has been mainly male centred, as gender is only a part of a larger pattern of unequal social relations. Reacting to such gender discriminations, Asian American feminists have tried to expose Asian American sexism. Maxine Hong Kingston's *The Women Warrior* (1977) and Amy Tan's *The Joy Luck Club* (1989) are two such texts which make a critique of the Asian American community's patriarchal structure. These divergent positions of Asian American men and women should be however understood from the more complex relationality of the categories of oppression. It is only when Asians and Asian Americans recognize the intersections of race, gender and class, that the transformation of the existing hierarchical structure can take place. It is in the unifying function of culture and literature, that the greatest importance has been attached. An 'imagined community' not bounded by colour, race, gender and class, but crucially by a shared struggle against all pervasive and systemic forms of domination is what constitutes the liberating spirit of the 'third space' between the Western and Non-Western dichotomy. The system of drawing boundaries and arbitrarily isolating the immigrants' history and culture of the homeland under the rubric 'Asian Literature' has been questioned. Asia has been understood in relation to multicultural America and vice versa, focusing not only on the period after the immigrants' arrival in the United States, but linking the immigrants to his ethnic roots. Eric Wolf suggests a more collaborative enterprise between Asian studies and Asian American studies, forging new paradigms. Methodology, that would not look at Asian identities and the Unites States "as fixed entities opposed to one another by stable internal architecture and external boundaries" and that which would not interfere with "our ability to understand their mutual encounter and confrontation," should be adopted.[15] Ethnic groups are formed and changed in encounters among groups and therefore ethnicity is the basis of a pan-ethnic experience. Rey Chou has indicated that Asian literature is increasingly defined in terms of ethnicity rather than nationality. Asian literatures are taught in American Universities not for their 'intrinsic value.' She states that, it is "in terms of the cultural interventions which Asian literatures, in alliance with other minor literatures, bring to American society as a politically constituted community, that answers should and will be sought in decades to come."[16] A desire for a Pan-ethnic bonding through a recognition of mutual ethnic differences and heterogeneity has become a typical characteristic of self-expression for Asians especially those in the United States, in the new global order. Wayne Chang's commercial film *Chan is Missing* (1981) indirectly conveys the message that Chinese Americans, like other Americans or Asian Americans are heterogeneous. Ethnicity has been given preference over nationality. Doak[17] observes that many people in Japan envisage a natural ethnic body as a national community, and it is through 'ethnic nationalism' that the Japanese people are imagining an alternative community to oppose the state. The most significant agenda of the Asian Movement in the contemporary times is a redefinition of the Asian experience within the United States as 'Amerasia,' which is also a campaign carried out by the Asian-American studies programmes at various universities.

These cultural and academic interventions also produce their extremities. One can notice a celebratory impact of such contestation over identity in its ludic expressions. A text like David Shambaugh's *Beautiful Imperialist: China Perceives America 1972-1990*[18] expresses the professional point of view of China's America watchers while it strikes at the roots of individuals' acculturation to American conditions in terms of their cognitive dissonance. Shambaugh shows full agreement with an experienced and senior American official who said, "None of these individuals can put themselves in the place of a United States decision-maker; they lack the sociological-anthropological training necessary for them to transcend their own system and view the United States as American world." Another mode of intervention could be something like that of Jack Goody, who in *The East in the West*[19] problematises the contingent and inscriptive character of Asian American ethnic identities, while at the deep cultural level he dissolves the apparent differences between civilization. The Asian-American imagination could perhaps transcend the limits of multiculturalism as a doctrine of exclusionivist politics by problematizing the question of cultural identity on the one hand and dissolving the differences through a dialogic encounter. Only then a "fusion of horizons" could be made possible.

Notes

1. S.N. Eisenstadt and B. Giesen have discussed the doctrines of multicultural exclusivism in "The construction of collective identity" in *Archives of European Sociology*, XXXVI (1995).
2. Rey Chow in "Introduction: On Chineseness as a Theoretical Problem" *boundary* 225; 3, 1998 quotes from the section "Chinese film in the age of interdisciplinarity" in *Primitive Passions: Visu-*

ality, Sexuality, Ethnography and Contemporary Chinese Cinema (New York: Columbia University Press, 1995).

3. See Rey Chow, "In the Name of Comparative Literature" in Bernheimer: *Comparative Literature in the Age of Multiculturalism*, 108.
4. See Charles Taylor, "The Politics of Recognition" in C. Taylor, *Multiculturalism and the Polities of Recognition* (Princeton: Princeton University Press, 1994).
5. Hans-Georg Gadamer: *Heideggers Wege: Studien Zum Spatwerk* (Tuhingen: Mohr, 1983) quoted in *Beyond Orientalism.*
6. Bell Hooks has recounted that performance of the text in the classroom involves the use of personal experience with the issues under the construction of identity as difference and difference as exclusion.
7. See Roland Barthes, *The Pleasure of the Text*, trans. R. Miller (New York: Hill 1975).
8. Zizek states that 'true universalism' is yet to come in "Multiculturalism or the Cultural Logic of Multinational Capitalism," *New Left Review*, No. 225, September/October 1997.
9. Satya P. Mohanty makes a study of the epistemic status of cultural identity in *Literary Theory and the Claims of History: Postmodernism, Objectivity, Multicultural Politics* (New Delhi: OUP, 1998).
10. Paul A. Cohen, *Discovering History in China* (New York: Columbia University Press, 1979). Due to their racial ambiguity, Asians in America or Asian Americans have been constructed historically to be 'like black' or 'like white' or as neither black nor white.
11. Gen Le Espiritu, *Asian American Panethnicity: Bridging Institutions and Identities* (Philadelphia: Temple University Press, 1992).
12. Jorge del Penal, "Impact of Ethnic Data Needs in the United States" in *Statistics of Canada and the U.S. Bureau of the Census: Challenges of Measuring an Ethnic World* (Washington D.C.: U.S. Government Printing Office, 1993).
13. Doak, "Ethnic Nationalism and Romanticism in Early Twentieth Century Japan" in *American Historical Review*, 102, 1997. Cited by Ellehiro Azuara in *Pacific Historical Review*, 1998. Chandra Mohanty has called such a community, an "imagined community."
14. Richard W. Trottier, "Charters of Panethnic Identity: Indigenous American Indians and Immigrant Asian-American" in *Ethnic*

Change ed. Charles F. Keyes (London: State University of Washington Press, 1981).

15. Eric R. Wolf, *Europe and the People without History* (University of California Press, Berkeley, 1982).
16. Rey Chou, "The Politics and Pedagogy of Asian Literatures in American Universities," *Differences: A Journal of Feminist Cultural Studies*, No. 23, 1990.
17. Doak, "Ethnic Nationalism and Romanticism in Early Twentieth Century Japan," *American Historical Review*, 102, 1997.
18. David Shambaugh, *Beautiful Imperialist: China* (Princeton: Princeton University Press, 1993).
19. Jack Goody, *The East in the West* (Cambridge: Cambridge University Press, 1996).

Black Woman Power in Afro-American Theater

ALICE MILLS
Université de Caen

The media generally tend to echo the theories of those American sociologists, historians and politicians who give credit to the idea that black men's high rate of delinquency in the United States is linked to black women's position of authority within their families. The current view of American political conservatives is that all unmarried or divorced mothers, regardless of their ethnic origins, are responsible for the disintegration of traditional family values leading to the rise of criminality. The single black mother's high visibility designates her as the prototypical bad example. Her situation, unlike that of other single mothers, has been officially studied and analyzed for more than fifty years. For this reason, before we turn to black theater's depiction of the character of the strong woman, it seems useful to recall briefly the theories which have popularized the notion of the excessive power of black American women.

Franklin Frazier's *The Negro Family in the United States*, published in 1939 was the first well-known scholarly work in this vein. Frazier strove to show how slavery, migration to the cities, fathers' desertion of their families and simple habituation to the fact of illegitimacy had generated truncated family structures which were totally dependent on maternal authority and thus a source of imbalance for the black community. Frazier's intent was not to incriminate the black woman, but both intellectuals and politicians subsequently used his work to back their own theories of her castrating tendencies.

Frazier's publication was countered in 1941 by Melville Herskovits' *The Myth of the Negro Past*. Herskovits maintained that the family and the couple in the contemporary African American community were continuations of traditional African structures. His intention was to promote a positive view of the black family, but his work, based as it was on the traditional African matriarchy, incidentally reinforced the image of the black woman as excessively powerful.

In *Beyond the Melting Pot* (1963), Nathan Glazier and Daniel Patrick Moynihan again took up Frazier's thesis, in particular, the idea of the black woman's excessive authority and its negative consequences for the black couple, the black family and also, most importantly, for the black man.

In 1965, during the Johnson presidency, the subject was brought to the front of the national political scene with Moynihan's study, "The Negro Family: A Case for National Action," commissioned by the Labor Department.[1]

In 1968, the black sociologist, Andrew Billingsey, published *Black Families in White America*, which amongst other things criticized the Moynihan report and questioned its methodology and the statistics used in support of his theory of a black matriarchy. Billingsey also stressed the black family's resilience and its ability to adapt, thus opening the way for the success in 1976 of Herbert Gutman's *The Black Family in Slavery and Freedom*.[2]

More importantly, the 1970s and 1980s witnessed the rise of black female voices determined to define for themselves their own roles and their own identities and to escape the burden of the official theories. Among the defining works of this period are Toni Cade's anthology, *The Black Woman* (1970), Joyce Ladner's *Tomorrow's Tomorrow* (1972), *Black Women in White America* (1973) edited by Gerda Lerner, Michele Wallace's *Black Macho and the Myth of the Superwoman* (1978), *Women, Race and Class* (1981) by Angela Davis, *All the Women Are White, All the Blacks Are Men, But Some of Us are Brave* (1982), edited by Patricia Bell Scott, Gloria T. Hull and Barbara Smith, and *When and Where I Enter* (1984) by Paula Giddings. *Reading Black, Reading Feminist* (1990) edited by Henry Louis Gates brought together many of the essays on the subject written by prestigious African American women intellectuals.[3]

Finally, we should also undoubtedly acknowledge the impact of the enormous success of black women novelists over the past two decades. Toni Morrison, Alice Walker, Paule Marshall, and Maya Angelou, among others, have largely contributed to the now infinitely more complex public image of the role and identity of African American women. Their success, however, cuts both ways because, while it increases black women's prestige, it also reinforces the idea of their inordinate power, be it only literary.[4]

The purpose of the present essay is to examine how African American theater has participated in the debate concerning black women's power within their community and how, beyond the dialogue of their characters, successive generations of black playwrights have carried on the discussion.

Langston Hughes was one of the first African Americans to write for the black theater, a theater which, according to Webster Smalley, "hardly existed" (viii) prior to the 1930s. As early as 1935, that is, before the publication of the first sociological texts on the subject, Hughes created female characters endowed with extraordinary forcefulness. He continued over the next twenty years to use and develop this type of character, but, unlike the learned sociologists and historians, he invariably presented the black women's strength as an asset to her community. Strong black women are the source of dynamism and creativity in Hughes' plays; they give Harlem its particular rhythm. Their authority and fits of anger are invariably accompanied by an equal amount of playfulness, wit and laughter. Their violent outbursts do not create divisions in the community but actually help to unite it; and this union not only takes place between the actors on the stage but also in the theater itself, where the audience loudly congratulates each of the female protagonist's victories, be they verbal or otherwise.

By turns jovial or boiling over with anger, these enormous women—Hughes frequently compares them to elephants—raise innumerable progeny on next to nothing and seem to survive partly because they are able to laugh about their situation. Instead of whining and bemoaning their fate, they dance and sing around the church organ and the jukebox in an affirmation of their will to live and of their desire to attract the attention of men. No matter how enormous they are, these women have lost none of their sex appeal, and in spite of the official wisdom of the psychologists and historians,[5] the men around them fall under their spell. In *Simply Heavenly (*1953*)*, Melon points out that the imposing Mamie is "large but shapely" and Ham in *Little Ham* (1935) confides to his friends: "You know I believes I does like that big old fat girl . . . the bigger the woman, the bigger boss I bes." (59)

Men are at the center of the Hughesian woman's preoccupations, and one thing is certain: whether the man in question is the father of her numerous children, her lover, or even her son, he must be kept under her control and scolded as severely as he is loved. The women in the overpopulated ghetto freely share advice on keeping one's man in line and openly discuss their latest domestic quarrels, complete with embellishments. Fully aware that actions speak louder than words, Hughes' heroines periodically and publicly dress down their worthless sons and rake their no good husbands over the coals. One is left with the impression that, from scene to scene and from play to play; Hughes' heroines lend each other the same knife and the same gun with which they threaten, punish and generally make their men respect the rules which they have dictated. Although they all share the same heavy-handed approach to the art of love, each one, according to her personality, brings her own subtle differences to bear. Mam uses insults and Tiny, the flat of her hand. Geraldine shoots her lover's rearend full of buckshot, Arcie chases after hers with a knife, and Laura (*Tambourines to Glory*, 1949) actually catches and stabs hers. The pious Essie would never use a knife herself, but she keeps one to lend to her friends in case of need. Only Madam Bell, terrified by the idea of the electric chair, decides against cutting her man.

Hughes' male characters are undismayed by these displays of aggression. In fact, the ritual beatings which they receive constitute an indispensable element of their personal prestige and are proof of how much they are loved. Where others might be tempted to fear for their safety and flee, they perceive expressions of caring and tenderness:

Melon: "Oh you act so cute and you switch so coy, Mamie, I was meant to be your playboy. I dial your phone, hear you yell, 'damn Sam,' which means you know I am your honey lamb. (*Simply Heavenly* 150)

In Hughes' theater, the woman protagonist's excessive power never provokes a feeling of embarrassment or indignation. Her most impudent actions and shameless lies invariably stimulate laughter. Who could be more appealing than Laura, a preacher who uses her church both to attract men and as a means of selling, at an exorbitant price, the "water from the Jordan" straight from her kitchen faucet? But not only is Hughes' heroine funny, she is also a fountain of poetic justice and the source of important lessons. Thanks to her, the evil are punished and the weak are protected. The delinquent find in her a worthy adversary, experienced enough to defeat them but too merciful to destroy them completely. She acts as a conscience for all of the characters, reminding them of their duties and responsibilities. Far from causing destruction and provoking failure among her fellow blacks, Hughes' matron, in her alternating explosions of violence and kindness, is a model of the broader world and prepares them to confront it. Many of the most positive aspects of ghetto culture[6] are brought to light by her inimitable liveliness, her love of a good time and her extreme generosity, whose limitlessness is perhaps best illustrated by her willingness to display publicly her personal quarrels and family disputes.

One can argue that Hughes had effectively "deconstructed" official history well before it had become the fashion to do so. In the sense that his heroines are masters of humor, of the spoken word and of exaggeration, Hughes' female characters are as evocative of Esu Elegbara, African mythology's marvelous trickster, as they are of anything suggested by the American scholars and politicians. They share the trickster's exuberant sexuality entirely free of any feelings of guilt, and their fecundity is as abundant as it is joyous. Indeed Esu, the lord of conflicts and reconciliations, finds worthy representatives in Hughes' female characters. Their physical appearance itself is consistent with that of the legendary African figure who, because of his function as the mediator of opposites, is by turns represented as minuscule or enormous, as male or female.

Hughes' female character becomes a fixture of African American theater. Over the years, sometimes mellower, sometimes more exacerbating, she issues forth from the pen of many playwrights. The stormy Vera in Martie Charles' *Black Cycle* is a 1971 version of Madam Bell in *Little Ham*; without a second thought, she breaks up with the man who has set her up as a hairdresser. Irene in Alice Childress' *Mojo* seems to repeat Tiny's marriage proposal to Ham and even takes it one step further:

> Teddy (Irene's husband): you say "I wanta be married . . . marry me." I married you . . . didn't see you no more for a year and a half . . . then you pop up with some paper (. . .) you want a divorce. I sign the paper (. . . One year later you come walking in on me (. . .) and you say "Teddy I got to take you to court and charge you with adultery, 'cause it's proper for the man to be the guilty one." (9)

Periodically, black theater shows the entire community joining to check the overwhelming energy and ambition of the domineering female. The church members in Baldwin's *The Amen Corner* rebel against Sister Margaret's authoritative zeal just as they do with Laura in Hughes' *Tambourines to Glory*. As in Baldwin's play, the father joins forces with the son in order to resist the mother's orders in Ted Shine's *Herbert III*. In Lorraine Hansberry's *A Raisin in the Sun* (1959),[7] each member of the family succeeds in opposing his own dream against Lena Younger's dictates.

But, as a general rule, at least through the end of the 1950s, these domineering women are able to practice timely enough self-effacement to win back the love and friendship of all concerned and, thus, to continue to occupy center stage. Starting in the 1960s with playwrights like James Baldwin, Ed Bullins, Jimmy Garrett and later on with August Wilson,[8] the powerful woman begins to lose, if not her talent for repartee, at least some of her good-naturedness, her sense of humor and, most importantly, her love for children and for the black man. The character, thus despoiled of many of the attributes of the trickster, becomes more neutral and even less feminine, because the trickster, who exaggerates all things, also accentuated its feminity.

A comparative study of Hughes' *Tambourines to Glory* and Baldwin's *The Amen Corner* is all the more interesting for the fact that the heroines of the two plays have enough in common to allow us to discern the first stages of the metamorphosis of the powerful woman's image.

Laura in *Tambourines to Glory* and Margaret in *The Amen Corner* are both forced by solitude and poverty to take refuge in religion. Animated with an exceptional sense of organization, a decided taste for despotism and unusual energy, each of them, assisted by a sister's total devotion, becomes the minister of her church. Their authority over the faithful is associated more or less overtly with divine right and would be limitless were it not for the arrival of a man whose presence provokes a feminine response from both "Sister" Laura and "Sister" Margaret. From that point on, confusion reigns in the relations of each of the ministers with her congregation. One of the important aspects of the male character's role in both plays is to bring attention to the excessive nature of the women's authority. In the end, the death of the two men causes the congregation to realize that it must free itself from the absolute power of its spiritual guide.

These many points in common do not prevent the two plays from following different paths to different conclusions and from communicating messages varying with the different dramatic approach of each of the two authors. Where Hughes casts a good-humored, benevolent eye on his heroine's antics, thus implying approval, Baldwin questions his with a gravity bordering on condemnation. It is, therefore, not surprising that the excessive nature of each of the characters takes a different direction. For Laura, who belongs to the tradition of the trickster, life should be an adventure and, if possible, an amusing one. Her prodigality is a match for her abandon. The laughing, pranksterish side of her personality lends even her most impudent acts and shameless machinations a wacky and jovial character. Conversely, Margaret is more the product of a puritanical tradition. Her growing authority leads her to impose the most draconian prohibitions on the behavior of her faithful flock, and any even mildly pleasureful activity is banned. She forces her son to lead the life of a recluse and won't allow herself the company of her husband. In *The Amen Corner*, Margaret's virtue is rigid, austere and unpleasant; in *Tambourines to Glory*, Laura's low blows and dirty tricks are comical.

Each heroine is headed towards the fall, which corresponds to her particular lack of balance. Laura yields to the passion of her senses at the expense of her dignity. Margaret, who denies all sensuality and adventure, dries up and becomes asexual, mutilated and unwhole. She chokes on her own intolerance. In the long run, her refusal to yield to pleasure and tenderness destroys her following more surely than Laura's impassioned violence does hers.

Their spouses' deaths also reflect the two women's personalities. Buddy is knifed by Laura; Luke, Margaret's husband, slowly succumbs after twenty years of emotional and physical isolation. These male roles complement and accentuate the heroines' roles. They not only reveal the main protagonists' character, they are also the vehicle for the playwright's message. Buddy, in Hughes' *Tambourines to Glory*, is the devil incarnate. In killing him, Laura commits an act, which paradoxically, sanctifies her. By slaying the dragon she earns the title of saint, which she had already so impudently assumed. Introduced by Baldwin at the beginning of *The Amen Corner* as a cowardly drunk, Luke progressively becomes the bearer of a truth that threatens Margaret's prerogatives. Her power over her congregation, far from being a sign of her courage, is simply a trick that allows her to avoid the dangers of the secular world. Hughes ends his play with a note of triumphant feminity; Baldwin ends his with a vision of feminity that can achieve glory only through self-denial and submission to men.

It is interesting to note, parenthetically at least, that LeRoi Jones' and Jimmy Garrett's theatrical works in the 1960s make a non-negotiable demand for the punishment of black women. The latter are condemned without a trial by a movement which claims to be both black and revolutionary but which adopts conventional white attitudes when it comes to dealing with black women.[9]

By 1965, Ed Bullins had already begun to doubt the black revolution and, with *Clara's Ole Man*, put a surprisingly energetic and physically forceful woman back into the limelight. Because Bullins belongs to a generation of playwrights well removed from Hughes and his generation, his characters' moral substance has considerably evolved. Where Hughes' matron plays the role of protector and adoptive mother for the young girls of the ghetto, Big Girl in *Clara's Ole Man* becomes her protegee's tyrannical lover. With Bullins, an important and decisive step has been taken. The strong woman no longer seduces men; she becomes their sexual rival. She has become virile (isn't she the "old man?") to the point of assuming the unattractive role of the jealous husband. She breaks up the party rather than being the life of it as was Hughes' fun-loving matron. Not that Bullins' strong woman is totally devoid of generosity—she rooms, boards, and sympathizes with both a retarded sister and an invalid aunt and offers asylum to neighborhood adolescents. But Big Girl's generosity is self-serving. She has no sympathy for anyone who is not incurably inferior to her. The verbal and physical blows she delivers are no longer part of a lover's ritual but are meant to destroy potential rivals (in particular her girl-friend's admirer) and to humiliate loved ones. She never allows her flair and sense of humor to blossom into joyful creativity but employs them at the expense of her community's best people.

Big Girl has retained the trickster's verbal skills, his flamboyant style, and his penchant for conflicts and lies. She also quite obviously possesses his sexual ambiguity. But the trickster's charm, benevolence, and fecundity have deserted her. The official position of the scholars and politicians (critical of the black woman for having too many children and being unable to raise them properly) is undoubtedly relatively well intentioned compared to the view advanced by Bullins' theater. His spokeswoman is both sterile and sterilizing (she is involved in her young friend's abortion) and rules over a world of idiots, cowards, and senile fools.

Nonetheless, Bullins never seeks to pass judgment on his heroine who, in fact, is a relatively faithful reflection of the spirit of his theater, a disenchanted space where the sensitive are crushed and only the hardened survive. The playwright tends to legitimize Big Girl's behavior, which she has learned in response to a truly wretched existence. Still, her intolerance of all but weaklings bodes ill for the future of her community.

The character of Ma Rainey in August Wilson's *Ma Rainey's Black Bottom (*1984) also extends the tradition of the domineering woman. "Ma the boss" flattens anyone foolish enough to quarrel with her and, in providing protection for aging musicians, a stuttering nephew and a young woman who might be her mistress, is both generous and destructive in the manner of Bullins' Big Girl. Because of her relationship with the young woman, Ma crushes Levee, a talented young musician who is attracted to the girl. Like Big Girl, Ma surrounds herself with the weak and the deficient, those who are either too old or too young. She may be "the mother of the blues," but she has no children of her own, she has little sense of humor (in Wilson's theater the gift for verbal repartee is usually a male attribute). We are far from the Hughesian character whose laughter and vitality enliven the entire community.

The Ma Rainey character is ambiguous in many ways. Through her art she gives a great deal to her community and to the world, but, by stifling their creativity whenever possible, she also deprives her people of other talented artists. In shutting herself off from any idea of sharing talent and celebrity, she suffocates those around her. She is unwilling to admit even the existence of another singer, let alone an influence on her own career, and replies "Bessie what?" when one of her musicians mentions Bessie Smith. Like Big Girl, she brags that she owes nothing to anyone.

Her claim to absolute originality, her refusal to depend on anyone else, or even, for that matter, to recognize the other's existence, seems more typical of the heroines created by male playwrights than of those created by women authors.[10] The latter generally tend to show heroines whose exploits, as well as their daily lives, are a continuation of family and community traditions. Gratitude becomes an end in itself, a motivator, rather than a weakness.

Women playwrights tend to replace the notion of rivalry with one of sharing. As early as 1959, Lena Younger, in Lorraine Hansberry's *A Raisin in the Sun*, proudly proclaims her debt to five previous generations, and the idea of a shared experience common to all women "of color" takes on major importance in the work of Ntozake Shange.

In *For Colored Girls Who Have Considered Suicide* (1975), all of the joys and sufferings of each of the heroines find an echo or a continuation in those of the others. In no way can a woman character, approached from the inside in Shange's play, become an image of mere strength and authority. The moments of doubt and weakness common to all human beings are integral to her heroines' personalities. As a result, the character of the domineering woman as such ceases to exist—the formidable Lady in Red takes and rejects men at will, but she cries in her solitude. In the end, Shange's "ladies," emotionally and physically battered by their men, are willing to abandon their solitude only for each other.

In Gayl Jones' *Chile Woman* (1974), the heroine is so little attached to her individual identity that she constantly trades it for those of other women, thus employing the technique of modified repetition, one of the distinguishing marks of the trickster who much prefers endless variations on a theme to the conclusion of any discussion. A character clearly and uniquely defined in terms of authority cannot exist in a theater where everything is fluidity and the cohabitation of opposites.

With Gayl Jones, everything is measured against the time of collective memories which defy conventional time and outlive individual existence. Thus, Crazy Woman is insane today because she was beaten as a slave. The old drunken slattern in the bar is a little girl in Africa. "I am a Congo Chile," affirms Blues Singer in a discourse first sketched by Langston Hughes' heroine in *Don't You Want to be Free?* (1937): "I am the child they stole from the sand, three hundred years ago in Africa's land" (273). Gayl Jones' female characters share with Shange's heroines the need to bond and become one with other women, but their penchant for laughter and their love of men is like Hughes' heroines.

An interesting case is the happy-go-lucky trickster-like figure, Henrietta, in Karen Jones Meadow's *Henrietta* (1985). The heroine carries on the Hughesian tradition in her outrageous, but comical, behavior with the man who worships her. Her final decision to stay with him, a destitute inner-city figure, rather than to leave the ghetto and to bond with a successful woman friend to whom she is deeply attached, makes her an unusual character for the period.

A recent trend in African American theater is to put forward male characters who apologize to the wives who have deserted them for their past behavior. The apology may sound credible when it comes from LeRoi Jones/Amiri Baraka's heroes since their treatment of black women in the 1960s was particularly brutal, but the hero's constant smiting of his breast in Nubia Kai's *Harvest the Frost* (1984) looks more like political correctness than like a reasonable desire for atonement. As far as the audience can tell, Renson, a faithful, devoted and hard-working husband and father, is guilty of only two things. The first is not to have paid enough attention to the emotional needs of his wife of 30 years upon discovering her affair with another man, but to have acted distant and hurt. The second is to have treated his grown-up daughter like a child by offering her shelter, love, and money after her separation from her violent husband. In some ways the play mirrors the philosophy of black revolutionary theater where women were made to feel guilty for their mysterious ancestral crimes against black men, beaten for those crimes and then expected to find this treatment fair.

In Kai's play, Renson and, to some extent, his father, who is slapped by his son's run-away wife, take on the roles of penitents. One has to wonder how these characters will be perceived when the current American fad for public apology and chastisement dies. But after all, a woman character bossing and slapping men is nothing new, and it can come out all right in the end if balanced by wisdom, laughter, and generosity. As Gayl Jones' heroine says, "If I mistreat you, honey, I don't mean you no harm."[11]

Notes

1. Paula Giddings observes that, in fact, Moynihan was less severe in his evaluation of black non-traditional family structure than E. Franklin Frazier had been and that "as far as matriarchy was concerned, Moynihan's report stated there was nothing inherently wrong or pathological about a woman headed household, only that it was not the norm in the society and thus subject to disadvantage." But she added that his report "was (. . .) particularly untimely, leaving Blacks with no option but to challenge it" (*When and Where I Enter* 328).
2. See also R. Staples' "The Myth of the Black Matriarchy" (1970) and *The Black Woman in America: Sex, Marriage and the Family* (1973), E. Herzog's "Social Stereotypes and Social Research" (1970), W. Ryan's "Blaming the Victim" (1971), and J. Jackson's "Black Women in a Racist Society" (1972).
3. The past few years have seen renewed scholarly interest in the relationship between black men and black women. Charles Murray's *The Bell Curve: Intelligence and Class Structure in America* (1994) was only indirectly linked to it but deserves to be mentioned because of the violent opposition it aroused. Recent publications on the subject include: *The Decline in Marriage Among African Americans* edited by M. Belinda Tucker and Claudia Mitchell-Kernan (1995), *Race, Gender and Power in America: The Legacy of the Hill Thomas Hearings* by Anita Faye Hill (1995), *African American Women Speak Out on Anita Hill-Clarence Thomas*, edited by Geneva Smitherman (1995), *Entitled to Good Loving: Black Men and Women and the Battle for Love and Power* by Audray B. Chapman (1995), *Black on Black Crime: Facing Facts—Challenging Fictions* by P. Ray Kedia (1995), *Compelled to Crime: The Gender Entrapment of Battered Black Women* by

Beth Richie (1995), *The Assassination of the Black Male Image* by Earl Ofari Hutchinson (1996), *The Matrifocal Family: Power, Pluralism and Politics* by Raymond T. Smith (1996), *How to Love a Black Man* (1996) by Ronn Elmore, and *The Spirit of a Man: A Vision of Transformation for Black Men and the Women Who Love Them* by Iyanla Vanzant (1996). The *International Herald Tribune*, March 26, 1998 carried an article by Richard Morin entitled "As Marriage Rates Fall, Black Women Despair."

4. See John Domini's article, "Roots and Racism: An Interview with Ishmael Reed," 5 April 1977, and *The Assassination of the Black Male Image* by Earl Ofari Hutchinson, 1996.
5. See W. Grier and P. Cobb's *Black Rage*, 1968.
6. In "Wings of Gauze, Women of Color and the Experience of Health and Illness" (1993), Linda Dumas points out that older residents call "home" what outsiders refer to as the "ghetto."
7. Can we really justify, however, placing Lena Younger, one of the central characters in *A Raisin in the Sun*, in the same class as Hughes' matrons? Her unwavering rectitude, constant seriousness and infallible sense of responsibility do not favor such a categorization. Nonetheless, her quick repartee, her opposition to abortion and her encouragement of her grandson's pranks certainly evoke certain aspects of the trickster.
8. August Wilson, however, occasionally allows a minor character to reflect the Hughesian tradition. Thus, in *Seven Guitars* (1996) when Hedley says, "Louise, you a woman need a man," she replies, "I don't need none that bad. I got me a thirty-two-caliber pistol up there. That be all the man I need." (19) But more often Wilson's women characters make the deliberate choice of deserting their families. In *Fences*, Troy, a typical Wilsonian hero, is deserted by two of his women, after his mother has abandoned him and his father. His son, in turn, will be deserted by his mate.
9. See L. Jones' *Experimental Death Unit* and *Madheart*; and J. Garret's *And We Own the Night*.
10. For an interesting discussion of black female characters created by African American women playwrights, see *Not a Man's Story, Not a White Story: Contemporary African American Women's Playwrighting*, Beatrix Taumann's doctoral dissertation at Friedrich-Alexander-Universität Erangen-Nürnberg, to be published by Köngshausen & Neumann.

11. Some of the ideas expressed in the present article have been published in French in "Complexité de l'autorite de la femme noire américaine." Cf. Mills (1997).

Bibliography

Baldwin, J., *The Amen Corner*, in *Black Theater USA, 45 Plays by Black Americans*, Hatch ed., NY, Free Press, 1974.

Baraka, A., (Jones, L.) *Song*, in *New Plays from the Black Theater*, King, W., Chicago, Third World Press, 1989.

.... *Madheart* in *Four Black Revolutionary Plays*, Indianapolis, Bobbs-Merril, 1969.

.... *Experimental Death Unit*, in *Four Black Revolutionary Plays*, Indianapolis, Bobbs-Merril, 1969.

Bell-Scott, P. , Hull, G.T. and Smith, B. eds., *All the Women are White, All the Blacks Are Men, but Some of Us Are Brave*, NY, The Feminist Press, 1982.

Belinda-Tucker, M. and Mitchell-Kernan, C., eds., *The Decline in Marriage among African Americans*, NY, Russell Sage, 1995.

Billingsley, A., *Black Families in White America*, London, Prentice-Hall, 1968.

Bullins, E., *Clara's Ole Man* in *Five Plays by Ed Bullins*, Bullins, E. ed., Indianapolis, The Bobbs-Merrill Company, 1968.

Cade, T., ed., *The Black Woman, An Anthology*, NY, New American Library, 1970.

Chapman, A., *Black Men and Women and the Battle for Love and Power*, NY, Henry Holt & Co. Inc., 1995.

Charles, M., *Black Cycle* in *Black Drama Anthology*, King, W. and Milner, R., eds., NY, Columbia University Press, 1972.

Childress, A., *Mojo*, NY, Dramatic Play Service, 1971.

Davis, A., *Women, Race and Class*, NY, Vintage Books, 1981.

Dickerson, B., *African American Single Mothers*, Newbury Park, Sage, 1995.

Domini, J., "Roots and Racism: An Interview with Ishmael Reed," in *The Boston Phoenix*, April 5 1977, p. 20.

Dumas, L., "Older Women of the Project: The Socio-medico Consequences of Urban Change" in *Wings of Gauze, Women of Color and the Experience of Health and Illness,* Blair, B. and Cayleff, S.E., eds., Detroit, Wayne University Press, 1993.

Elmore, R., *How to Love a Black Man*, NY, Warner Books, 1996.

Frazier, F., *The Negro Family in the United States*, Chicago, University of Chicago Press, 1939.

Garrett, J., *And We Own the Night* in *Black Theater*, Summer 1968.

Gates, H.L., Jr., *Reading Black, Reading Feminist*, NY, Meridian, 1990.

Giddings, P. , *When and Where I Enter, the Impact of Black Women on Race and Sex in America*, NY, 1984.

Glazier, N., and Moynihan, D., *Beyond the Melting Pot*, Cambridge, The MIT Press, 1963.

Gutman, H., *The Black Family in Slavery and Freedom*, NY, Pantheon, 1976.

Hansberry, L., *A Raisin in the Sun*, NY, New American Library, 1959.

Herskovits, M., *The Myth of the Negro Past*, Boston, Beacon Press, 1958.

Herzog, E., "Social Stereotypes and Social Research," *Journal of Social Issues*, 26, 1970, pp. 109-125.

Hill, A.F., *Race Gender and Power in America: the Legacy of the Hill-Thomas Hearings*, Oxford, Oxford University Press, 1995.

Hughes, L., *Little Ham*, *Simply Heavenly*, *Tambourines to Glory* in *Five Plays by Langston Hughes*, Smalley, W., ed., Bloomington, Indiana University Press, 1968.

______. *Don't You Want to Be Free?* in *Black Theater USA, 45 Plays by Black Americans*, Hatch, ed., NY, Free Press, 1974.

Hutchinson, E.O., *The Assassination of the Black Male Image*, NY, Simon and Schuster, 1996.

Jackson, J., "Black Women in a Racist Society" in *Racism and Mental Health*, Willie, C., Kramer, B. and Brown, B., eds., Pittsburgh, University of Pittsburgh Press, 1972.

Jones, G., *Chile Woman*, NY, Strubert Playbook Series, 1974.

Jones, L. (See Baraka, A.)

Jones-Meadow, K., *Henrietta* in *The National Black Drama Anthology, Eleven Plays from America's Leading African American Theaters*, King, Jr., W., ed., NY, Applause Books, 1995.

Kai, N., *Harvest the Frog* in *The National Black Drama, Anthology, Eleven Plays from America's Leading African American Theaters*, King, Jr., W., ed., NY, Applause Books, 1995.

Kedia, P. R., *Black on Black Crime: Facing Facts—Challenging Fictions*, Bristol, Wyndham Hall Press, 1995.

King, E. and Mitchell, C.A., *Black Mothers to Sons*, NY, Peter Lang, 1995.

Ladner, J., *Tomorrow's Tomorrow*, NY, Anchor, 1972.

Lerner, G., ed., *Black Women in White America, A Documentary History*, NY, Vintage, 1973.

Mills, A., *Complexité de l'Autorité Féminine dans le Théâtre Afro-Américain* in *La Femme Noire Américaine, Aspects d'une Crise d'Identité*, Dubost T. and Mills, A., eds., Caen, Presses Universitaires de Caen, 1997.

Moynihan, D.P. , *The Negro Family, A Case for National Action*, Washington DC, Government Printing Office, 1965.

Murray, C., *The Bell Curve: Intelligence and Class Structure in America*, NY, The Free Press, 1994.

Richie, B., *Compelled to Crime: the Gender Entrapment of Battered Black Women*, NY, Routledge, 1995.

Ryan, W., *Blaming the Victim*, NY, Vintage Books, 1971.

Shange, N., *For Colored Girls Who Have Considered Suicide/When the Rainbow is Enuf*, Bantam Book, 1980.

Shine, T., *Herbert III* in *Black Theater, USA*, Hatch, J., ed., NY, Free Press, 1974.

Smalley, W., Introduction to *Five Plays by Langston Hughes*, Smalley, W., ed., Bloomington, Indiana University Press, 1968.

Smith, T., *The Matrifocal Family: Power, Pluralism and Politics*, NY, Routledge, 1996.

Smitherman, G., ed., *African American Women Speak out on Anita Hill-Clarence Thomas*, Detroit, Wayne University Press, 1995.

Staples, R., "The Myth of Black Matriarchy" in *The Black Scholar*, 1, 1970, pp. 8-16.

______. *The Black Woman in America: Sex, Marriage and the Family*, Chicago, Nelson Hall, 1973.

Taumann, B. *Not a Man's Story; Not a White Story; Contemporary African America Women's Playwrighting*, Friedrich-Alexander-Universität Erangen-Nürnberg, 1998.

Vanzant, I., *The Spirit of a Man: a Vision of Transformation for Black Men and the Women who Love Them*, San Francisco, Harper San Francisco, 1996.

Wallace, M., *Black Macho and the Myth of the Superwoman*, NY, Dial, 1978.

Wilson, A., *Fences* in *August Wilson, Three Plays*, Pittsburgh, University of Pittsburgh Press, 1991.

______. *Ma Rainey's Black Bottom*, NY, New American Library, 1985.

______. *Seven Guitars*, NY, Penguin Books, 1996.

Dialectic of Fragmented Identities: The Black Woman's Quest for Self-Realization in Nella Larsen's *Quicksand*

ANU CELLY
Panjab University, Chandigarh

Nella Larsen belongs to a generation of Afro-American writers of the 1920s who gave vent to their literary creativity during the period of intense fermentation in the content and expression of the Afro-American mind as a part of the Harlem Renaissance. As an oft-ignored writer, Larsen's contribution to the world of letters and cultural enrichment suffered at the hands of societal prejudice which cast aspersions on the ingenuity of her writing ability by accusing her of plagiarism, leading her to opt out of a fledgling literary career. Larsen came to be identified with the Black women's tradition of self-expression through meaningful modes of artistic creativity, along with her predecessors like Francis Harper, Ida B. Wells and Harriet Beecher Stowe and her contemporaries like Ann Petry and Jessie Fauset. Larsen's belated acknowledgment as a writer was overshadowed by luminaries like Zora Neale Hurston, Pauline Hopkins, Alice Walker, Maya Angelou, Paule Marshall and others who wrote in the following years. Larsen's meager output by way of two novels, *Quicksand* and *Passing* and one short story, "Sanctuary" may certainly be considered as a significant component of women's writing, although it is regrettable that she did not earn a well-deserved fame in her lifetime. In all her works, she delineates the ever-present dilemma of identity crisis faced by her female protagonists whose 'mulatto' stature unleashes for them a trail of agony, perplexity and misfortune which is unprecedented in its pathos, while being grounded in the reality of contemporary times.

My objective in this paper is to examine the portrayal of Helga Crane, the semi-autobiographical portrait of the female protagonist in *Quicksand,* with a perspective which pays credence to her entrapment amidst a paradigm of cultural determinism as well as psychic interiorization of conflict that debars her from the wholeness of life. Still, Helga does not come across as a stereotype of traditional black women's images including those of the Mammy, the Loose Woman or the Conjure Woman, found so often in the works of antebellum Southern American writers. Rather, she has been termed as a superb creation and the most intriguing character in Renaissance fiction. Helga represents the existential predicaments of "a black world distilled," conceptualizing as she does the authorial perception of the actualities of identity crisis fraught with oscillation, frustration and despair faced by an entire generation of Afro-Americans in contemporary America.

An adroit glance into Larsen's personal life reveals a striking resemblance between the birth and circumstances of both the women, being born of a dark-skinned father who is no more and a Danish mother who remarries a white American. Both Helga and her creator were restless women, forever undertaking a journey to different places in America and Europe, shuttling between careers, immersed in a limbo of self-contempt and a quest for self-definition, while being sucked inadvertently in "a vacuum of unarticulated tradition" (Christian 40). Carole Davies considers the trope of migration in Afro-American women's writings as a metaphorical manifestation of the Black female subject's refusal to be subjugated amidst the dialectical pattern of fragmentation ensuing from her exilic rootlessness on home ground, "Black female subjectivity asserts agency as it crosses the borders, journeys, migrates and so re-claims as it re-asserts" (37).

Right at the outset, Helga appears to have a soul beset with restive discomfiture amidst her job as a school teacher at Naxos, a sleepy town in Southern America. Helga's untapped sensuality and her inner yearning for freedom manifested through her "wayward" and "unrestrained" hair, is countered by her disenchantment with a sense of suffocative drudgery finding expression in "the questioning petulance and tiny dissatisfied drop" on her lips. She feels herself to be "an insignificant part" of the teaching establishment that seems to be making no single contribution to the cause of enhancing the degree of respectability and self-reliance enjoyed by the Negroes who are taught to accept their lot as "heavers of wood and drawers of water." She bemoans the dearth of spirited rebelliousness in the Negro temperament, while resenting her own conformity to the machinery of oppression by continuing to be a part of the system:

> This great community, she thought, was no longer a school. It had grown into a machine. It was now a showplace in the Black Belt, exemplification of the white man's magnanimity, refutation of the black man's inefficacy. Life had died out of it. It was, Helga decided, now only a big knife with cruelly sharp edges restlessly cutting all to a pattern, the white man's pattern. Teachers as well as students were subjected to the paring process, for it tolerated no innovations, no individualism. (28-29)

Helga's intrinsic ferocity makes her distraught with the realization of the Negroes' fatalistic submission to their condition, even while she feels utterly powerless as a woman in effectuating any change even in her own life. Financial constraints prevent her from giving up her job and she feels entrapped with the recognition of a warring self within her which is up against "a formidable antagonist" and "a ruthless force" (37). It is none other than a personification of her desire for freedom and happiness as "she could neither conform, nor be happy in her non conformity," discerning within herself "a lack somewhere . . . a lack of acquiescence" (33). An authorial perception into Helga's psychic torment reveals her aspiration for personal fulfillment and social distinction even as the voice of her "interior dialogization" articulates her disillusionment with anonymity and self-effacement. Helga Crane is an assertive and ambitious individual who feels out of place in an environment which offers her no opportunity for growth and expansion, "If you were just plain Helga Crane, of whom nobody had ever heard, it was presumptuous of you to be anything but inconspicuous and comfortable" (35).

Helga knows that she can gain access to social stature, howsoever superficial, as well as personal luxury, howsoever inane, by virtue of flaunting her appearance, education and refinement of manners; yet, she abhors the idea of gaining counterfeit respectability and spurious happiness. She realizes the fact that society would bestow on her a qualified access to such rewards only in lieu of her willingness to mortgage the independence of her spirit and the truth about her birth and parentage. In the view of Lillie Howard, "Because she can thus never realize an identity which ignores the irrefutable fact of race, Helga Crane is fated to never to know who she is" (232).

The intrinsic honesty of Helga's outlook on life prevents her from making a total surrender to the societal dictum of self-sublimation and acquiescence to convention, and yet, she fails to gather the strength and self-possession to remain completely immune to the need of modulating her personal desires in accordance with socio-cultural injunctions. She fails to find solace in her state of engagement to James who does not enjoy social approval, nor does she revel in Dr. Anderson's condescending approval of her dignified bearing. On the contrary, Helga feels that she must exact retribution, with her "lacerated pride," for the society's unkind treatment of all Negro women, who, like her mother have to resort to marriage on the premise that "even foolish and despised women must have food and clothing, even unloved li'l Negro girls must be somehow provided for" (55).

It may not be a search for her roots that takes Helga Crane to Chicago; rather, it is her desire to find a new opening for her career combined with a metaphysical yearning for a sense of belonging which finds fruition amidst the milling crowds of emigrated Negroes at the metropolis, with a feeling that "she had come home. She, Helga Crane, who had no home" (65). Larsen employs the trope of journey as a metaphorical reflection of Helga's unending quest for selfhood amidst successive surroundings that offer her nothing but a set of self-defeating choices. As Addison Gayle puts it, "The end result of this journey from land, from one's roots, from one's ancestral past means to sever all relationships with the race. . . . It means too, this journey from self, to surrender one's identity, which once lost, is impossible to regain again" (99).

Helga's decision to return to America and take on a job as a companion to Ms. Ross, a Negro who professes to dislike the whites, comes at the heavy price of an expectation for disowning her familial heritage of parentage from a 'white' woman. Helga's attempt to find compensation for the inner vacuity of her spiritual orphancy finds a peripheral appeasement in the "mad rust of white New York" with its façade of recreation and glitter. Helga feels torn apart by a searing need for a "sense of freedom, a release from the feeling of smallness" (89) on the one hand, and, on the other, to find solace in the "goodness, gaiety, wisdom and beauty" amidst the materialistic abundance of a married life. Yet, any prospect of getting wedded to a white-skinned man seems an obnoxious idea, since, "of that white world, so distant, so near, she asked only indifference" (88).

Larsen displays an ethnographic perspicuity in taking up the dilemma of assimilation versus confrontation faced by countless Negro men and women, who, like Helga Crane could not either pick up the courage to perpetrate an absolute rebellion against the condition of discrimination and oppression, nor could they obliterate their self-esteem to the extent of adapting themselves to such circumstances. Helga Crane never does get acclimatized to the socio-cultural scenario of New York, as her sensibility is beset by an inconsolable isolation bordering on self-revulsion. "It was of herself, she was afraid" (91), muses the authorial vision which probes deep into the "double consciousness" of the "souls of black folk" (Du Bois):

> It is a peculiar sensation, this double consciousness, this sense of always looking at one's self through the eyes of others, of measuring one's soul through the tape of a world that looks on in amused contempt and pity. One even feels his twoness—an American, a Negro; two souls, thoughts, two irreconciled strivings, two warring ideals in one dark body, whose dogged strength alone keeps it from being torn asunder. (615)

It's a perplexing phenomena, to be a 'black' and an American at the same time, going by the first-hand account of so many thinking Afro-American individuals, right from Du Bois to Langston Hughes, from Zora Neale Hurston to Toni Morrison.

Larsen portrays the irreconcilable conflict besieging the Negro psyche not with any patronizing platitudes in commiseration with the agony of blacks and mulattos, but, rather, with a subtly ruthless satire on individuals like Anne Ross. She claims to hate the white people even while aping their mores and manners, professes to disdain the vulgarity of Negroes and yet, doesn't hesitate in showing her patriotic championship of the Blacks. Larsen displays an unprecedented honesty in recognizing the traits of hypocrisy and double standards implicit in the consciousness of her own race which prevent them from taking a stand in life, be it that of "conditional integration" (Arna Bontemps 271) or of insular separation.

In case of an individual like Helga Crane, financial constraints combined with her craving for materialistic well-being serve to accentuate her predicament and just when she begins to recognize within her a sense of alienation and rebelliousness against the state of her racial identity and all that it entails, comes a gift of five thousand dollars from her Uncle Peter. Ironically enough, it is accompanied with a declaration of severing all ties with her; yet, it is Helga's need that overtakes her pride, forcing her to accept the cheque. Life poses to her a choice between survival and self-esteem and she chooses former, making use of the money to take a passage to Denmark as she immerses herself in a welter of "leisure, attention and beautiful surroundings" (11). Helga's forthright honesty in relishing the peripheral pleasure of hedonistic self-indulgence overwhelms the perplexity accruing from her unrequited love towards Dr. Anderson. Helga betrays an instinct for self-possession as she revels in "a blessed sense of belonging to herself alone and not to a race" (114). However, Helga's quest for peace and bliss takes her to a land that places a premium on her identity as a 'black' woman.

Helga's sojourn in Denmark with her aunt Fru Dahl and her husband, turns out to be an exercise in spiritual enlightenment, even while her physical self is steeped in a ceaseless sensation of splendor and amusement. Amidst the sophisticated elite of upper class Danish society, she is required to exhibit, like a pet dog, those features of her racial identity which have grown most abhorrent to herself. Not only this, her aestheticized femininity has to be paraded as "a curiosity, a stunt, at which people came and gazed" (126). The desire of a renowned Danish painter, Alex Olsen to paint a portrait of Helga is the manifestation of a patriarchal assumption which seeks to fetishize women as the exotic 'other' as "an object, a conglomerate of attributes, to be predicated and controlled" (Alcoff). Helga's warm and genuine response to Olsen as a human being acquires, in his view, metaphorical overtones of a commercial enterprise, wherewith he professes to discern in her "the soul of a prostitute" (149) which sells itself to the highest bidder.

It is the supreme irony of Helga's fate that she is seldom recognized as a 'person' in her own right throughout the novel, either in the 'black' or the 'white' world. As a spirited spinster or a refined lady, a sensuous woman or a dutiful wife, she is constantly expected to fit into respective image patterns at the behest of socio-cultural norms, be it Harlem or Denmark, Naxos or Chicago, Alabama or the private sanctuary of her mind. Helga betrays symptomatic neurosis and internalization of repression as the sole remedial response to such situations. Hazel Carby considers the socio-cultural context of women's literary signification as 'mulattos' when she says:

> The figure of the mulatto should be understood and analyzed as a narrative device of mediation. After the failure of reconstruction, social conventions dictated an increasing and more absolute distance between black and white ... In response, the mulatto figure in literature became a more frequently used literary convention for an exploration of what was increasingly socially prescribed ... the mulatto figure allowed for movement within two worlds, black and white, and acted as a literary displacement of the actual, increasing separation of the races. (90)

The fragmented horizon of Helga's personal yearnings longs to be cemented with "the irresistible ties of race" which had drawn her father away from the supercilious smugness of her mother's attitude, towards a space of uncompromised personal freedom. Helga, too, rejects another proposal from her ex-fiancé James on her return to America and arrives at the brink of her enlightening insight about the Negroes' need to exorcise themselves of the "skeletons" of slavery and oppression and lead a life of unhindered joy sans insecurity, deriving sustenance from the uninhibited candor and life-affirming sensuality which is typical of their temperament. The authorial vision which dwells at length on Larsen's own irrevocable alliance with "these mysterious, these terrible, these fascinating, these lovable, dark hordes" (162), has shades of autobiographical reflection, which reverberates with the realization that "the true Negro renaissance awaits Afro-Americans' claiming their 'patria,' their nativity." (Huggins, 309)

Helga's vacillating temperament and her inability to sustain a faith in one direction leads her to scuttle between an attempt to retrieve a sense of selfhood from a perplexing process of acculturation to her own race, versus her tormenting moments of attempted assimilation among the 'whites.' The reader is allowed to have a glimpse in the lacerated terrain of her psychic world as she submits herself to the strife and stress of divided loyalties, her peregrinated shift from depleted morale to simulated self-assurance. Helga's inner desolation reaches a point where she starts craving for eternal liberation from the bondage inherent in the "long trouble of body and of spirit," willing herself almost to the cataclysmic moment of self-annihilation. Helga's emotional reconnaissance of Harlem, with its "cramped and cruel environment," counterpoints the unbridgeable gap between the choice of physical emancipation in Europe and spiritual enslavement in America offered to her by her fate as a Negro woman. As pointed out by Barbara Christian:

> In this novel, the tragic mulattos of the abolitionist novels finally reach bitter fruition. Coupled with this devastating theme, Larsen's analysis of the small degree of sensuality that is allowed the lady deviated from the usual novel of upper class convention, for Helga can neither be a lady nor a peasant resigned to "primal uncluttered feelings." Had Helga accepted the role of a lady in Harlem, or a peacock in Denmark, she would have lost a part of herself (53).

It is the world of religious virtuosity from where comes a "creature of God and Man" (194), named significantly, Mr. Pleasant Green, who takes on the role of being Helga's rescuer, exploiting her emotional and physical vulnerability with the promise to be her patron forever. In a moment of frenzied despondence, Helga decides to marry one who appears to her nothing more than "a rattish yellow man," a stark contrast to the earthly and healthy blackness of a groom that she wanted.

However, a zest for moral upliftment through the avenue of community service offers itself as a course of compensation for Helga's unfulfilled aspirations. "An anesthetic satisfaction" (197) mesmerizes her into an obeisance to the requirement of a role model wife to a preacher whose social status would undergo a further enhancement through matrimony. The fierce independence of Helga's spirit is overtaken by her dormant desire for security which springs from her desperate need "to be a mistress in her own house, to have a garden, and chickens, and a pig, to have a husband and to be right with God—what pleasure did that other world which she had left contain that could surpass these?" (200). It is worth noting that a husband comes at the end of her list of priorities.

The inviolable societal dictum that respectability ensues only for women who are married, serves to unleash her physical disintegration, even as spiritual exaltation seems to be a panacea for Helga's soul. Helga's body, on the other hand, seems to be free of her mind, having a life of its own, wherewith it thrives in "a disturbing medley of feelings" (200) arising from her natural vitality which remains irrepressible. Her husband's figure acquires a faceless physical appeal accruing from transient moments of carnal pleasure which fail to requite her inner vacuity, making her feel like "a finicky, showy thing of unnecessary prejudices and fripperies" (202).

Helga permits herself, inadvertently, to be sucked into the "quicksand" of limitless despair and self-abhorrence, wherewith the arrival of four children in quick succession serve to incite her inborn rage against the sexist norms of matrimony which expects optimum servitude and self-abnegation from a woman in her role as a wife and mother. She resents the parochial nature of social convention that augments the delimitation of women's life through the glorified imposition of drudgery in the sphere of domesticity.

Helga's intrinsic wrath against racial injustice surfaces again, too, leading her to loath her own role in the procreation of a fourth child who appears to her like "a little dab of amber humanity which Helga had contributed to a despised race" (209). Helga's critical illness during her fourth delivery acquaints her with the real face of humanity, and human relationships appear to her like superfluous mantles which hide aloofness and lack of concern, be it her mother, Dr Anderson, Olsen, James or most of all, her husband. All of them acquire an air of dehumanized detachment, as the immanent realization of the truth about the Negro condition dawns on her sensibility, making her realize this time around, with stark clarity, the psychological deprivation and physical entrapment which comprises an irrevocable fate for Negroes.

The benign face of religion is unmasked by Larsen as Helga affirms to herself the redundant value of religion which has served to blunt her perception into the reality that her husband's self-proclaimed status as "the white man's God" is nothing but an illusion. There is scathing irony in her admission to herself that she cannot do anything to change "this vicious, hypocritical land" (215) where her children would grow up as Negroes whose life would be a disappointment to be handled by themselves alone. A discreet note of moral sermonizing, here, indicts the lack of solidarity among the colored people to combat the menace of racism without, through the unified solidarity of their cohesive links within.

Tragedy, at the end of the novel, springs from the fact that the consciousness of the woman figure remains besieged by irredeemable loss, even as she begins to see into the essence of life at last. The more deeply she sees into the heart of her ruin and desolation, the more clearly she knows that her life cannot change for the better. The tumultuous upheaval in her conscience remains directed inward, jeopardizing the life of her mind, even as her body as well as her sense of integrity is going to pieces. Helga's inordinate faculty of perception remains asphyxiated within the iron cage of drudgery and delimitation, rendering her passive and helpless in the "quicksand" of spiritual sterility, even as her body is sprouting forth the seeds of humanity in the shape of her children. An element of shame and dread brings forth to her the institutionalization of human relationships, wherewith all the conditions of women's life deemed natural, right from matrimony to motherhood appear repugnant to her. She loses her faith in the sanctity of God and children, of neighbors and husband, all of whom have exacted from her too heavy a price for investing on her an aura of normalcy and well-being.

Yet another time, at a crucial juncture in her life, Helga takes a momentous decision, that of leaving her home, husband, and children, as the alluring dream of freedom beckons her to the world outside, with its clothes and books and probably, an option of self-determination. The implacable determinism of fate, however, claws in at a time when she herself does not dither, restricting her to physical immobility with the conception of a fifth child, even as her soul is burgeoning with the germination of an identity which envisages selfhood as the mere fantasy of a woman who happens to be a Negro.

Works Cited

Alcoff, Linda. "Cultural Feminism Versus Post-Structuralism: The Identity Crisis in Feminist Theory." *Signs* 13 (Spring 1988): 405-36.

Bontemps, Arna. *The Harlem Renaissance Remembered.* New York: Dodd, Mead, 1972.

Carby, Hazel. *Reconstructing Womanhood: The Emergence of Afro-American Woman Novelist.* New York: Oxford Univ. Press, 1987.

Christian, Barbara. *Black Women Novelists: The Development of a Tradition, 1892-1976.* Westport, Connecticut: The Greenwood Press, 1980.

Davies, Carole B. *Black Women, Writing and Identity: Migrations of the Subject.* London: Routledge, 1994.

Du Bois, W.E.B. "Souls of Black Folk." *The Norton Anthology of Afro-American Literature.* Ed. Henry L. Gates and Nellie Y. McKay, 613-74. New York: W.W. Norton & Co., 1997.

Gayle, Addison, Jr. *The Way of the New World: The Black Novel in America.* New York: Anchor, 1975.

Howard, Lille P. "'A Lack Somewhere': Nella Larsen's *Quicksand* and the Renaissance." *The Harlem Renaissance Reexaminned.* Ed. Victor A. Kramer, 223-33. New York: AMS Press, 1987.

Huggins, Nathan I. *The Harlem Renaissance Remembered.* New York: Oxford Univ. Press, 1971.

Larsen, Nella. *Quicksand.* 1928. New York: Collier Books, 1971.

Politics of Race and Gender in Toni Morrison's *Paradise*

RAJYASHREE KHUSHU-LAHIRI
Gujarat University

The aim of this paper is to delineate the underpinnings of the politics of race and gender in Toni Morrison's novel *Paradise*. Her seventh novel, and the first to be published since she won the Nobel Prize for Literature in 1993, *Paradise* deals once again with the experience of the African-Americans living in a historically racialized society, and the victimization of women in a patriarchal society.

The novel opens starkly—"They shoot the white girl first."[1] According to Gay Wachman, in *Paradise* Morrison "ridicules the stereotypes of exclusion by setting the overly race-conscious reader off on a wild goose chase right from the very first sentence. Which of the four young women at the Convent is the white girl the men shoot first? . . . But we are never told which of the women is white."[2] Morrison herself has admitted that she purposely constructed her narrative so as not to answer that question. "I wanted the readers to wonder about the race of those girls until those readers understood that their race didn't matter. I want to dissuade people from reading literature in that way, [because] race is the least reliable information you can have about someone. It's real information, but it tells you next to nothing."[3] This assertion is apparently surprising as it comes from the writer who has been the most eloquent chronicler of the black experience during slavery and after, and who is almost solely responsible for giving African-American women their rightful place in American literature. Moreover, in most of her critical essays, racial questions figure prominently. But, as Paul Gray rightly points out, "there is really no contradiction between what she says now and what she has written in the past. She views her life and work as a struggle against racial categories, or any categories, as a means of keeping groups of people powerless and excluded." [4]

In *Paradise,* Morrison problematizes the whole subject of racism by positing it as a divide between the light-skinned and the dark-skinned blacks, rather than the slave against the free man, and the white against the black. Thus, racial categories presented here may be different, but they are nevertheless real as well as discriminatory, responsible for the great "Disallowing" on which the whole novel hinges. Further, Morrison makes it clear that the categories are a consequence of a historically racialized society in which blacks have been living for generations. The term racism refers to the unequal treatment of people on the basis of some biological and physical characteristics—especially skin colour, and shape of the face. The paradigm case is that of the black people, whose mistreatment by whites in the history of the American society has been so conspicuous, so enduring, so closely tied to biological ideas, and has affected so large a segment of the population of the United States. Because of their skin colour and their history as slaves, African Americans have been regarded as "the depth below the depth." Commenting on Haley's *Roots*, Ishmael Reed observed, "If Alex Haley had traced his father's bloodline, he would have travelled twelve generations back to, not Gambia, but Ireland."[5] Yet the distinction Haley made was driven by a historically racialized society insofar as the extent to which each American individual destiny has been determined by ancestrally derived distinctions. That any person now classified as black or African American might see his or her own life as more the product of African roots—however small or large a percent of one's actual, biological genealogy and cultural experience—than of European roots, reflects this history. Hence, Haley's choice was in effect a structured dilemma, or rather as David Hollinger points out: "Haley's choice is the Hobson's choice of ethno-racial identity in America because it is not a real choice at all."[6] Further, the persistence of the "one drop rule" deprives those with any hint of black skin of any choice in their ethno-racial affiliations, simultaneously placing them in a dilemma. In *Paradise*, Patricia, reminiscing about her mother's light coloured skin observes: "The one drop law the whites made up was hard to live by if nobody could tell it was there. When we drove through a town, or a Sherrif's car was near, Daddy told us to get down, to lie down on the floor of the car, because it would have been no use telling a stranger that you were colored and worse to say you were his wife." (200)

The brutal act described in the opening sentence of the novel occurs in 1976, but Morrison traces its genesis back to the 1870s, the time of the Reconstruction, when nine African-American patriarchs, ex-slaves in Mississippi and Louisiana, joined together and headed west to settle in the Oklahoma Territory. A number of historical factors were responsible for this westward migration. Although Reconstruction was a time when black people, supported by Northern will, achieved a limited measure of political power in the South, it was not a time when the walls of colour caste came tumbling down. The building and maintenance of those walls had been a primary concern of whites of all classes from the moment of the Emancipation. So far as the whites were concerned, their aim during Reconstruction was to maintain as much physical and social separation as necessary to impress upon the black man his inferiority. Thus, a number of states passed Jim Crow[7] laws requiring separate schools and forbidding marriages between blacks and whites. The ideology underlying Jim Crow was racial proscription including disfranchisement, based on the belief in white supremacy. Consequently, the desire for separation was not confined to whites. A Georgia Negro spoke for many black people when he stated in January 1865 that they preferred to live by themselves because it would take years to eradicate the prejudice against them. They went to their own churches and sent their children to black schools.

Seen in this context, the westward migration of the nine black families in search of a haven, a refuge, a paradise—at any rate a more bearable future, has underlying political implications—it is clearly the outcome of racial politics. Of course, the haven they seek is an all black town. A proud community of freedmen, of gunsmiths, seamstresses, cobblers, ironmongers and masons, they were extraordinary people. They had served, picked, ploughed, and traded in Louisiana Territory since the time of the French. And when it was divided into states, they had helped govern it till 1875, after which they were reduced to field labour. And so, armed with advertisements of cheap land for homesteading, they took that history, each other, and their incorruptible worthiness (194) and walked to Oklahoma. On their way to the Promised Land they were turned away by rich Choctaw and poor whites, chased by yard dogs, camp prostitutes and their children, they were nevertheless unprepared for the aggressive discouragement they received from Negro towns already being built. The headline of a feature in the *Herald*, "Come Prepared or Not at All," could not mean them, could it? . . . It stung them into confusion to learn they did not have enough money to satisfy the restrictions the 'self-supporting' Negroes required. In short, they were too poor, too bedraggled-looking to enter, let alone reside in, the communities that were soliciting Negro homesteaders." (13-14)

This was a humiliation that more than rankled, that threatened to crack open their bones, that reverberated through the next hundred years of their collective memory as the "Disallowing." For generations they had believed that the division they had fought to close was the free against the slave, the rich against the poor, and the white against the black.

> Now they saw a new separation, light-skinned against black . . . the sign of racial purity they had taken for granted had become a stain. The scattering that alarmed Zechariah because he believed it would deplete them was now an even more dangerous level of evil, for if they broke apart and were disvalued by the impure, then, certain as death, those ten generations would disturb their children's peace throughout eternity. (194)

They had been "Disallowed" by fair-skinned coloured men," "shooed away" by "blue-eyed gray-eyed yellowmen in good suits," because they were too black (8—rock after the deep, deep level in coal mines)—so black that they must be trashy. And so they were "bound by the enormity of what had happened to them. Their horror of whites was convulsive but abstract. They saved the clarity of their hatred for the men who had insulted them in ways too confounding for language: first by excluding them, then by offering them staples to exist in that very exclusion." (189)

The band of the Disallowed eventually established Haven, where they installed a communal oven in the centre of the town, then lived in willed isolation from the outside world. Haven prospered for decades until World War II after which it atrophied with the residents moving out seeking work in cities, looking for a share in post war prosperity. So, the male descendants of the founding fathers decided to repeat the past. They dismantled the oven, loaded it on a truck, and moved it and their families farther west to start up, from scratch, another Oklahoma town. This town they named Ruby, to honour the woman in their clan who died after the journey having been denied medical attention, as was the custom those days. Morrison gives a poignant account of her death and the shattering effect it has on her two brothers—Deek and Steward Morgan.

> When it became clear she needed serious medical help, there was no way to provide it.
>
> No colored people were allowed in the wards. No regular doctor would attend them. . . .
>
> She died on the waiting room bench while the nurse tried to find a doctor to examine her. When the brothers learned the nurse had been trying to reach a veterinarian, they gathered their dead sister in their arms, their shoulders shook all the way home. . . . After that they understood the terms and conditions of the deal better. (113)

What this meant for the settlers of Haven and Ruby, those "Blue-eyed black people, tall and graceful, whose clear, wide eyes gave no sign of what they really felt about those who weren't 8—rock like them" (193) was that everyone marrying outside the coal black 8—rock bloodlines, "tampering with the gene pool was an outcast. Such a person was no longer welcome in a community as tight as wax, "no longer even represented in a Christmas schoolroom enactment of the Nativity that somehow hybridized the birth of Christ with the trek story and the creation myth of the 8—rock forefathers. And so, willfully isolated, hoping to insulate themselves from "Out There where every cluster of white men looked like a posse," the proud and intolerant 8—rock settlers ironically embrace the values of colourism and racial categories they had tried to escape. At the end of the novel Richard Misner the pastor, reflecting on the brutal attack on the defenceless women of the Convent remarks:

> Whether they be the first or the last, representing the oldest black families or the newest, the best of the tradition or the most pathetic, they had ended up betraying it all. They think they have outfoxed the whiteman when in fact they imitate him. . . . Born out of an old hatred, one that began when one kind of black man scorned another kind and that kind took the hatred to another level, their selfishness had trashed two hundred years of suffering and triumph in a moment of such pomposity and error and callousness it froze the mind. (306)

With the passage of years, Ruby is fissured by ancestral feuds and financial squabbles, not to mention the political ferment of the era, which has managed to pierce the town's isolation. In the wake of "the desolation that rose after King's murder," Ruby succumbs to militancy, and a Black Power Fist is painted on the oven. In view of its leading citizens, these troubles call for a scapegoat. And one readily exists: the Convent, an abandoned mansion about seventeen miles away from the town—or more precisely the four women who occupy it, and whose unattached and unconventional status makes them the perfect targets for patriarchal ire. The animosity that the patriarchs of Ruby harbour towards the inmates of the Convent, is a clear illustration of Simone de Beauvoir's classic thesis that woman has been made to represent all of man's ambivalent feelings about his own inability to control his own physical existence, his own birth and death.[8] As the Other, the woman comes to represent the contingency of life, life that is made to be destroyed. In addition, as Karen Horney and Dorothy Dinnerstein[9] have shown, the male dread of women has historically objectified itself in the vilification of women, male ambivalence of female charms underlies the traditional images of such terrible sorceress—Goddesses as the sphinx, Circe, Kali, Delilah and Salome, all of whom possess duplicitous arts that allow them both to seduce and to steal male generative energy.

Paradise established the two locales—the place where men rule and the one where women try to escape that rule—in a complex and nuanced manner. By the late 1960s the Convent is occupied only by an elderly dying nun and Consolata, her devoted servant and helper of thirty years. And the Convent becomes with Consolata's diffident acquiescence, a sanctuary for young women orphaned or broken on history's wheel, a safe house for the castaway female children, on the road and trying to hide from angry fathers, abusive husbands, dead babies, treacherous boyfriends and rapists. For example, Mavis had accidentally killed her infant twins by leaving them in a car while she shopped for groceries. Terrified of her abusive husband, she stole his Cadillac and lit out for the territory. Next came Grace, wanting to be called Gigi, looking for a man, but good-hearted under a tough exterior. She is followed by Seneca who is heart wrenching with the little gashes she carves into her body. The last to arrive is Pallas, the youngest, unbelieving that her mother and her lover could betray so cruelly. And she is not the only victim of betrayal. Consolata, who has had a passionate affair with Deacon Morgan is also cruelly betrayed by him as he could not endure "a woman bent on eating him like a meal." After the crime he confesses to the pastor that he needed to expunge his "shame," and that he had to "erase both the shame and the kind of woman he believed was its source. An uncontrollable, gnawing woman who had bitten his lip just to lap the blood it shed . . . a Salome from whom he had escaped just in time." (279-80) Deacon and his kind think of the women as bloodsuckers and they must erase the shame of their dependence on such women. These women, who are cultish and strange, seem to be witches to the patriarchs of the town. They were "not women locked safely away from men; but worse, women who chose themselves for company, which is to say not a convent but a coven" (276). They possessed uncanny and supernatural powers of healing and second sight, and of raising the dead—powers that were particularly threatening to the patriarchs of Ruby. The women, for their part, "felt permeated by a blessed malelessness, like a protected domain," a sanctuary in which they were renewed and reinvigorated to face life with courage and fortitude. Throughout the novel, Morrison juxtaposes the values represented by the patriarchs of Ruby against those of the women in the Convent—exclusion versus inclusion, rejection versus acceptance, destruction versus regeneration and healing. And there is no doubt as to where Morrison's sympathies lie.

The violence that men inflict on women and the painful irony of an "all-black town" whose citizens succumb to those very values they have tried to oppose in the past, themselves becoming oppressors, are the central concerns of *Paradise*. Morrison is certainly suggesting that a Paradise is not established so easily, but in critiquing the underlying politics of race and gender in the American society, she is perhaps, by implication positing the kind of paradise that may be possible. The novel ends on an optimistic note with the Convent women escaping the wrath of the men and carving out secure futures for themselves. And Billie Delia, who grew up as a pariah in Ruby itself as she was not an 8-rock, waits for them to return:

> When will they reappear, with blazing eyes, war paint and huge hands to rip up and stomp down this prison calling itself a town? . . . A backward noplace ruled by men whose power to control was out of control and who had the nerve to say who could live and who not and where; who had seen in lively, free, unarmed females the mutiny of the mares and so got rid of them. She hoped with all her heart that the women were out there . . . biding their time . . . but out there. Which is to say she hoped for a miracle. (308)

Perhaps Morrison is implying that only a miracle can save people and cleanse society of the spurious categories formed on the basis of gender, race and colour.

Notes

1. Toni Morrison, *Paradise (*New York: Alfred A. Knopf, 1998). All subsequent references to the novel will be incorporated in the text.
2. Gay Wachman, "Pride and Prejudice," *Women's Review of Books*, Vol. 15, No. 7, April 1998, 2.
3. Quoted in Paul Gray, "Paradise Found," *Time*, January 19, 1998, 67.
4. Gray, 67.
5. Quoted in David Hollinger, *Postethnic America* (New York: Basic Books, 1995), 19.
6. Hollinger, 8.
7. Otey M. Scruggs, "The Economic and Racial Components of Jim Crow" in Nathan Huggins et. al. Ed. *Key Issues In the Afro-American Experience (*New York: Harcourt Brace, 1971), 70.
8. Simone de Beauvoir, *The Second Sex (*Harmondsworth: Penguin), 138.
9. See Sandra Gilbert and Susan Gubar, *The Madwoman in the Attic: The Woman-Writer and the Nineteenth-Century Literary Imagination* (New Haven: Yale University Press, 1979), 34.

Voice-less Discourse:
Silence as Strategy in Toni Morrison's *Beloved*

MEENAKSHI PAUL
H.P. University, Shimla

Since sound first vibrated, its counterpart, silence, has been concurrently audible. Whether it be the progenetorial brooding before the 'word'; a tongue-less Philomela weaving her outrage; or the voiceless 'Scream' of Picasso's Guernica, the reverberating power of silence has been long acknowledged. Silence as narrative has been examined often and necessarily so. Yet, it lends itself more readily, either to romanticisation or to restriction as a 'weapon of the weak.' Further, its resonance being infinitely interpretative, silence becomes a goldfield for theoretical elitism and aesthetic fetishes. It remains to be seen whether silence is also strategy or a part of it, and if so, how effective it is.

Meaningful silence is a cauldron where resilience and rebellion often seethe. Perpetrators of gagging hegemonic structures repudiate this truth to their own peril. Here, it is essential to note that the indicators of silence as inferred in this study are not limited to the absence of words. They include non-verbal communication of gesture, totem, subtle social behaviour, encoded music and metaphor, as also verbal non-communication in which the unheard and unregistered are also effectively defined as silence, encrypted song and genealogy, cultural legend, and words not extended cognizance to, being instances of this articulate silence. This absence of voice, unsaid or unheard can become a potent means of alternative or alternate discourse. For, codified silence becomes a highly sophisticated and esoteric language engaged to exclude some 'other' from its expression.

The spectrum of silence spreads from meditative stillness to quiet resolve, as the protagonist of Margaret Atwood's *Surfacing* realises in her silence, "This above all, to refuse to be a victim."[1] Refusal to voice, then, is not essentially negation and can well be an expression of affirmation. Silent stemming from non-cognizance of the spoken has led to resistance movements around the world. The tribals in Central India, it has been observed, assiduously kept silence even when beaten. Their voicelessness was not due to an absence of words but because there were too many. They acknowledged the necessity and potency of articulation, but their collective unconscious avoided possible de-culturisation through direct expression. So, they sublimated or voiced their anger, despair, and their hope in encoded song and dance, thus generating silence of the unregistered and, hence, the 'unheard.' The averted eyes of black slaves, therefore, can also possibly be viewed as a deceptively submissive response to the master's presence. Perhaps, it was a willed refusal to make eye contact, and so reveal their feelings, as the force of history and culture behind them. Black music, from pulsating drums and field songs to gospel music and later the blues and jazz and manifests different aspects of slave experience. Ranging from intense, yet, harnessed passion of an individual to the interactive rhythm of the collective, blacks used music competently as an alternate text, of the unvoiced and unvoice-able, to the stated. This complementarity, direct or through inversion, of the said and the unsaid, of the said and the sung, underlines a very important component of the strategy of silence.

The metaphors of their hymns, such as 'Steal away, steal away to Jesus' and 'Swing low, sweet chariot' were employed by slaves to exchange meaningful discourse, whether it be stealthy flight or silent perseverance for the while. Through all this communication, whites were unaware of the superior encoding abilities of blacks and signified the silence of the unheard or the uncomprehended. The tables were turned somewhat on the oppressor, by blacks abetting this ignorance and closely guarding their skills in silence. Innumerable such manifestations of silence are evident as strategy to sustain survival, dignity, affirmation, and protest. Thus, abject and helpless silence has no role to play in strategy and passive, brutalised, and dumb silence is excluded from the ambit of voice-less discourse. Thoughtful and purposeful silence, on the other hand, is the turning point where the process of meaningfulness and proaction begins. It forms the interface between the heavy and mute silence of the marginalised and its articulation of protest. Thus, silence, words, and actions become strategic extensions and correlatives of each other. While focusing on the articulation, inaudible processes that made it possible, cannot but be considered.

Silence as a language of resistance has two operatives: those of psychology and of praxis. The former is limited to token protest as a feel-good exercise. Mimicry, behind the back spitefulness and disorderliness are some examples of silence that serve only to mitigate absolute helplessness. Strategic silence needs to be praxis-oriented. Often, the two intermingle as in this old, black folk-song:

> Got one mind for white folks to see,
> 'Nother for what I know is me;
> He don't know, he don't know my mind.[2]

The smugness of 'he don't know my mind' can effortlessly be undone by proposing that white folks do not want to know a slave's mind, even if they can bring themselves to admit his having one. Alternatively, the song could be the singer's fierce guarding of his identity, the refusal to be totally enslaved, a precondition to his protest. Roger D. Abrahams pertinently observes that certain black musical expressions represent their "hidden life and its accompanying hidden language . . . [and] is one of those features of the apartness of black-white existence which has proved convenient for blacks and which has therefore been capitalized upon and developed."[3]

Nowhere is the eloquence of such voice-less discourse more pregnant than, perhaps, in Toni Morrison in whose works these submerged voices of race and also of gender become almost deafening. She is acutely aware of evasion and silence through history in literary discourse. These are instrumental in engendering an *alternate* language which is encoded and, therefore, esoteric.[4] Morrison problematises the issue by speaking of words and of their absence in both the oppressed and the oppressors, and between them. Thus, muffled voices of the non-verbal and the uttered but unheard, half-heard, or mis-heard, acquire dimensions of the Tower of Babel, requiring careful unraveling. At the level of narrative, too, ironic inversion of the said reveals the pattern of the unsaid. The following analysis seeks to examine Toni Morrison's *Beloved* through this vital symbiosis of voicelessness and its discourse.

Beloved charts the movement of silences from the weak and the limited to the employment of silence for healing and regeneration. The novel opens with a pall of helpless numbness over house 124 because of the spite of a baby girl's ghost and its wordless, nevertheless, strong expression in overturned, broken and charred things. The family of the spirit, Beloved, can only muster willy-nilly coping tactics: of flight, by her brothers, Howard & Buglar; of fighting, "a perfunctory battle"[5] by her mother, Sethe, and sister, Denver; or of partial amnesia, by her grandmother, Baby Suggs, and Sethe. This helplessness and resignation gradually moves toward praxis where the entire community, in silent solidarity, decides that the phenomenon of Beloved must be "Disremembered and unaccounted for . . . [Since] It was not a story to pass on." (274-75) This resolution is not a relegating of the past to that silence which George Steiner rightly decries, "To unspeak the actual past, to eradicate the names, acts, thoughts of the unwanted dead, is a tyranny of peculiar horror. Pursued rigorously, it cuts off humanity, or certain societies, from the vital responsibilities of mourning and of justice. Man is set back in a landscape without echo."[6] For, in *Beloved*, the past is not eradicated but re-lived. Not only its words but its silences too are explored, claimed, and finally laid to rest. The mourning is just over and justice even now birthed. The clearest indication of this process is the protagonist being a visitor from a different time and place. Beloved is a complex and inexhaustible metaphor. She is the confluence of slavery, of being denied self-definition, of helplessness, and of despair turned on itself and therefore self-destructive. Yet, she is also the way out. Her tyrannical hold on Sethe exhibits control over feelings, familial ties, and the past; on Paul D over sexuality, dignity, and the present; on Denver over identity self-esteem and the future. So, it is imperative that Beloved be re-experienced to fill out the silent and the unsaid in her story and to rise beyond the death-in-life level of mere survival she forces her people to confront. The long-lasting effects of slavery are given shape by Beloved, thus, she must be 'disremembered' for free life to blossom. So, the community decides to bring forth a silence in which light, colour, water, and wind are not threatening anymore, for they finally are "Just Weather." (275) The novel completes the journey where the past is present in Beloved's footprints that "are so familiar. Should a child, an adult place his feet in them, they will fit" (275) but the brutality is past menacing and hardly dispiriting in the voice-less reminder. They have all walked that road, but the stage to alter course has been made possible, and here Beloved is a signpost that leads to the crossroads beyond which her people go.

The strategy thus effectuated is realised through a tactical pattern of alternate silence, and voice which it facilitates, throughout the novel. A perusal of the significant incidents in the narrative bears this out. The central image of the novel is that of Sethe standing with her baby she has just killed in her hand and surrounded by the babies she has tried to kill. The description is not verbal but strikingly visual in which Morrison focuses on the eyes of all present, living or dead, "Little nigger-boy eyes open in sawdust; little nigger-girl eyes staring between the wet fingers that held her face so her head wouldn't fall off. . . . But the worst ones were those of the nigger woman who looked like she didn't have any . . . she looked blind." (150) The contrast between the 'staring' eyes of the dead child and the unseeing eyes of her mother-murderer is built-up so, that it makes Beloved's return possible and evokes the inward-turning effects of dehumanisation. What follows is the chilling silence of the neighbourhood, "Sethe walked past them in their silence and hers." (152) It is the silence of mutual withdrawal based on incomprehension and seeming pride which takes a long time and Beloved's extended visit to overcome. So, the songs that would have reached out, "like arms to hold and steady her on the way" (152) are checked to mere, "Humming. No words at all." (152) This alienating and horrified silence draws into itself the dumbstruck response of animalised slavery. But, it also becomes the vortex where a design could be made toward assertion. In stark contrast to the frozen picture of Sethe and her children is the vacuity of the whites, stilled in a tableau of incomprehension. The blood of Beloved screams its answer to the 'skinless' nephew's uninformed, "What she go and do that for?" (150) It defies and reduces whatever the slavemaster had done or could do to utter insignificance and irrelevance. Nevertheless, Sethe's action is a silent scream of mutilated resistance and it draws the past and the future unto itself.

In the past is the slave farm of Kentucky, beautiful and lush, and deceptively named Sweet Home. The subterfuge of the place causes its slaves, Halle, the three Pauls, Sethe, and even Sixo— the relatively experienced, to be doubly victimised in their innocent acceptance of its promise followed by its ugly renegeur. It is only in hindsight that Sethe wonders, "if hell was a pretty place too." (6) Owned by Mr. Garner, whose attempts at 'civilized' slavery are not only ineffectual but dangerous in its contradictions, the Sweet Home 'men' and Sethe allow complacence to blunt their apprehension of the underlying menace. Garner's refusal to whip his slaves and to trust them with guns, does not make them less owned, as is amply proved in his bawdy jokes about his 'men' which highlight his manhood among other slavemasters. His wife, Lillian, who herself is a picture of the absolutely silenced in her tears and the lump in her throat which constricts her voice, is still capable of selling Paul F after Garner's death. Her calling for her brother-in-law Schoolteacher, to look after the estate in spite of her able and loyal slaves, breaks any illusions the slaves still had. From mild indicators of bondage, such as no wedding ceremony for Sethe and Halle; Baby Suggs being called by her tag name Jenny; and 'allowing' Halle to 'buy' his mother's freedom by renting himself out during

Garner's lifetime, the Sweet Home henceforth bonded, henceforth, feel the keen edge of slavery at the hands of Schoolteacher and the nephews. Being stripped of their guns effectively reduces them to hungry, pilfering boys. Locks and bars show them their place and being observed as guinea pigs disconcerts them. Schoolteacher's questioning and recording of their answers alienates and silences all of them, but it tears, "Sixo up . . . for all time" (37) and he gives up speaking English, for a while, as a language with no future in it and begins to use an alternative code. Sixo's refusal to use the oppressor's idiom, makes possible his conversation with the 'Redman's Presence' to seek permission for his rendezvous with the Thirty-Mile Woman, even though it comes to nought since the woman does not reach the appointed spot. Further, all his loquacity dissolves into raucous laughter and song when Paul D and he are caught trying to escape. The song convinces Schoolteacher of Sixo's unsuitability, and the breakdown of discourse between the two ends in Sixo being burnt at the stake. His ironic laughter and calling out, "Seven-O! Seven-O!" (226) before he is shot, "to shut him up" (226) are irrelevant to the whites as they themselves are to him. Only Paul D recognizes Sixo's marginal defiance in naming his unborn child as an extension of himself. Sixo's resistance is, thus, personal and his protest is proclaimed in death. However, it fails as a feasible stratagem for other slaves. Therefore, Paul D cannot join in his song, of loathing and defiance, perhaps of warning, because "the words put him off—he didn't understand the words. Although it shouldn't have mattered because he understood the sound." (227) It is this tone of hatred and Sixo's resounding laughter which urge a collared and shackled Paul D to try and kill Brandywine, his new master. The futile attempt sees him a prisoner at Alfred, Georgia. Feeling mocked at even by roosters, the seismic turbulence within him lies unseen, "the boiling blood was shaking him to and fro. But no one could tell" (107) till he is linked in more ways than one with forty-five other men. Far from the embrace of the tree "he called Brother" (21). Paul D joins the brotherhood of fellowmen and the trust common to both which was voiced to Brother is now signaled to the men.

Paul D's swerve away from Sixo's private protest to group dynamics begins at a place where all are imprisoned in individual cages but chained together when put to work. The efficiency of non-verbal language is explored fully by the convicts. Sustenance and support are quietly held out, although, "Not one spoke to the other. At least not with words. The eyes had to tell what there was to tell: 'Help me this mornin's bad' 'I'm a make it' 'New man' 'Steady now steady'." (107) The non-words called to begin or end work, 'Hiiii' and 'Hoooo,' become significant with the belief that Hi man "alone knew what was enough, what was too much, when things were over, when the time had come" (108). This trust in a fellow sufferer predicates the collective escape finally actualised. This confidence is further strengthened by their songs at work, encoded so only they understand the import of what they sing, "they sang it out and beat it up, garbling the words so they could not be understood; tricking the words so their syllables yielded up other meanings" (108). Their sledge hammers kept time in beating out all that reduced them to haplessness. United in anguish, Paul D's mouth is open in a scream whereas the sound may have come from "somebody else" (110), they are also banded together in overcoming it. The use of the very shackles that they seek to break away from, in their bid for freedom is the most ironic point in the narrative. The whole process demands transcribing at length: Convinced of certain death, Paul D intuitively throws himself in the envisaged but unvoiced plan of his confederates:

> It happened so quick he had no time to ponder. Somebody yanked the chain—once—He never figured out how he knew—how anybody did—but he did know—he did—and he took both hands and yanked the length of chain at his left, so the next man would know too . . . They waited—each and every one of the forty-six. Not screaming although some of them must have fought like the devil not to . . . . Then it came—another yank—from the left this time. . . . It started like the chain-up but the difference was the power of the chain. One by one, from Hi Man back on down the line, they dove. . . . Some lost direction and their neighbors, feeling the confused pull of the chain, snatched them around. For one lost, all lost. The

> chain that held them would save all or none, and Hi Man was the Delivery. They talked through that chain like Sam Morse and, Great God, they all came up . . . holding the chains in their hands, they trusted the rain and the dark, yes, but mostly Hi Man and each other. (110)

The escape postulates solidarity and implicit trust in the face of great risk as prerequisites in the silent conceptualisation of escape and its realisation. Still, Paul D lacks the tactically significant third dimension, that of mentally releasing the torture after its physical cessation, as also does Sethe. Paul D's heart closes shut like a rusted tobacco box just as Sethe clamps down on her reasons at being driven to slay her child.

The driving force is hidden in her flight from Sweet Home. Its first unstated existence is represented by Sethe's ritual of taking, "some pretty growing thing" with her to work in Mrs. Garner's kitchen, "to take the ugly out of it." (22) A more assertive avowal of her spirit than mere token aesthetic concessions to make life bearable is her response of quietly putting together a wedding dress after Mrs. Garner's non-response to her need for a wedding ceremony. Shocked by Schoolteacher's assignment to his nephews of listing her 'animal characteristics,' Sethe is plunged into bewildered agitation. So, Sethe falls into the plan for escape, brought by the Thirty-Mile Woman through Sixo to Sweet Home. Even as the men, taking her to be a soldier but not a strategist, silence her role in the devising of its details for all her early ignorance of even what a train is, it is only Sethe who successfully makes a getaway. Elaborately designed, the plot is hatched between Sweet Home and the Thirty-Mile Woman's place in conspiratorial whispers and initiated through codes. The time appointed was autumn when the almost ripe corn would harbour them in secret and the signal decided upon was a rattle's sound. When the time and sound arrive, Halle proclaims the action by beginning, "to sing to the others: 'Hush, hush. Somebody's calling my name. O my Lord, O my Lord, what shall I do?'" (224). Only Sethe, who is inside the house is removed from his song which is soon silenced and its message lost to her.

Nurtured long and hard, the Sweet Home men's bid to be free fails even though it has qualities of a fair game plan. Detailed planning, mutual trust, brotherhood, provisions, secrecy, and flexibility were all present, but the one thing they ignored was the contingency of failure. Speaking English again, Sixo has underestimated Schoolteacher. Once caught, none of them has a plan to fall back on, and fleeing like rabbits, are burnt, hanged or collared and sold. Presence of mind is Sethe's advantage in this exigency and she first sends her three children away to the train before returning in search for Halle in the barn. It is here that the seeds of what happened at the shed of Baby Suggs home are sown. Lactating and pregnant, Sethe suffers the worst a mother can. As she puts it, "those boys came in there and took my milk . . . Held me down and took it" (16). Her attempt to voice the violation to the almost muted, Mrs. Garner results in her back being opened by the boys' whiplash. What follow are two diverse aspects of silence, given in clear visual images. One, of Halle secreted in the loft seeing his wife being sported with and then sliding into the annihilating silence of the insane with butter smeared all over him. The second, of Sethe's dead back closing to form, "A chokecherry tree. Trunk, branches, and even leaves" (16). The pus blossoms and her torn feet notwithstanding, Sethe makes her way to Cincinnati and freedom. On the way she learns to count on the generosity and strength of total strangers. Significantly, the first person who props Sethe is a white girl who looks like, "The raggediest—looking trash you ever saw." (31-32) Marginalised herself, Amy Denver is the unlikeliest of all deliverers. Following her own dream of finding beautiful velvet, "Clean and new and so smooth" (33) Amy tarries to help bring just such a baby into the world. Years later, the child, named Denver after her, will unite the yearning for a dream of deliverance, with its fulfilment. Regardless of Amy operating within the language system where the word 'nigger' is available to her for self-definition, and despite Sethe's withholding her name and extending a fictitious one, the women establish a tenuous bond as seen in the one taking upon herself to massage the other's lacerated feet. Therefore, in the narrative's relative silence concerning the whites, where most are uni-dimensional and merely incidental to the stories of Beloved's kin, Amy Denver is the most visible. The points of reference in the novel are re-located from those visibly privileged to the seemingly superfluous. Accordingly, in order of their closeness to the blacks' life the whites are allocated prominence. Amy's foregrounding is underlined by the narrative providing space for her singing her mother's song. All other songs in the novel belong to the blacks who beside using them as signals as Halle did, employ the words and the rhythm for multitudinous expression. Songs are sung to express their suppression (221); to sing of their family—its uniqueness and its legacy (176); encoded expression of suffering for psychological survival (71); re-live the horrors of the past and keep the fire stoked (40); alienate oneself from the community (171); sustain life (89) and to as many more purposes.

After Amy's departure, Sethe relies on Stamp Paid's silent offering of food and covering for the infant. Trusting herself to him when, "Evening came and the man touched her shoulder," Sethe allows Stamp to ferry her across the Ohio, a taste of whose free waters he had already given her. Following an understood code, Stamp signals Sethe's arrival at the hideaway by leaving the sty gate open and tying a white rag to the post to announce Denver's presence. Sethe is soon taken quietly into the care of Ella who had perceived the signs. Ella provides for her and for her passage to Baby Suggs' home. Thus, strangers make it possible for Sethe to have twenty-eight days of freedom and family with her children and Halle's mother.

The astringent fruit of her tree, however, ripens with schoolteacher's arrival and her realisation that places in the memory never go away as she explains to Denver, "Because even though it's all over—over and done with—it's going to always be there waiting for you. That's how come I had to get all my children out. No matter what" (36). Schoolteacher's encroachment onto Baby Suggs' yard is thus countered with the blood of the children in her shed and Sethe's mystifying wordlessness. For "If they didn't get it right off—she could never explain. Because the truth was simple . . . She just flew. Collected every bit of life she had made . . . out, away, over there where no one could hurt them . . . outside this place, where they would be safe" (163). In her action and her refusal to explain its momentum Sethe defies definition.

The fixity of the dictum, "definitions belonged to the definers—not the defined" (190) is severed in the slit throat of Beloved. Notwithstanding the enormity of Sethe's action, it is an impelled reaction of a desperate victim, a gothic nightmare and, so, severely limiting. It is at once a frustration of schoolteacher's intentions but even more a mark of the extent of Sethe's brutalisation and its inward directed preoccupation.

The only two survivors of Halle's family from Sweet Home, beside Baby Suggs, further need to learn and discover affirmation beyond survival of using their past, silent except in 'rememory,' to live the present and devise a future—a lesson half-learned and half-taught by Baby Suggs in the Clearing. Her silent prayer and her Call to the gathering to laugh, dance, and cry evoked these responses without verbal signifiers dissolving in one message, of love, as a possible beacon in their lives. So, "In the silence that followed, Baby Suggs, holy, offered up to them her great big heart" (88). The Clearing assemblies, a celebration of the here and now, discounted both the terrible past as well as the nebulous promises of the Beatitudes. Outside the woods, however, the silence of the white world to her Call, the oblivion to and the disregard of "The word" (178) she offered, defeats Baby Suggs. She retreats to pondering colour, the harmlessness or perniciousness of pigmentation, and the only words left to her after the 'rout' are her quiet judgement on the whites that, "They don't know when to stop" (104).

The sum of all these silences, of defiance and of submission, of time and of place converges in the person of Denver. Born in untamed country, Denver steps "into the told story" (29) of her family. Yet, its telling and re-telling increases her silence and her withdrawal from the world outside the porch. Her only visits are to a womb-like enclosure of boxwood bushes in the wood behind the house. Armed with cologne, as incense to a shrine, Denver stood tall in its emerald light. The green of Denver's 'room' is in striking contrast to the 'red' light of Beloved's venom before it turns blue and harmless. Denver's loneliness at the leaving of her brothers and grandmother is increased by her awareness, "that her own father's absence was not hers" (13) and by her wariness of the killer mother's presence. Her longing for even the spite of Beloved underlines her silent retreat into the embracing bushes, "First a playroom (where the silence was softer), then a refuge (from her brothers' fright), soon the place became the point" (28). Enwrapped in a world where words fall soundlessly, Denver had shut her ears when a classmate, Nelson, had told her about Sethe and her baby sister. It will take the return of that sister for Denver to build power into her traumatised silence.

So, Denver, Sethe, Paul D, and Beloved congregate to play out their weakness and guilt, to re-define their words and to re-assign their silences. The battle begins with Paul D loudly and violently chasing Beloved's spirit from the house. A day of remission is spent by the three at the carnival. Sethe focuses on the significance of their shadows holding hands and the less abrasive resentment of Denver at Paul D's intrusion. The isolation clamped upon them by the haunting past seems to crumble a little with people acknowledging them while passing. Beloved's return, in person, sets the stage for their final confrontation with their own selves. Sethe becomes increasingly subservient to her. Her need to explain her 'too thick' love and have it accepted by Beloved gradually takes her away from Paul D, her work, Denver, and also from herself. The silence of the unvoiced 'Dearly' before beloved on the gravestone of her daughter breaks out resonantly at this juncture. Beloved is loved dearly but the price of that love is too dear both in the past and in the present. A chattel to Beloved, Sethe now realizes that, "Counting on the stillness of her own soul, she had forgotten the other one; the soul of her baby girl" (5).

Beloved's insistence that Paul D call her by her name and her seduction of him underscores his frigid impotence after the shattering of the Edenic illusion of Sweet Home. Yet, their turtle like coupling resuscitates his heart so he can feel again. Her moving him like a rag-doll breaks his judgemental attitude toward Sethe. The conviction and resolve he aspires for come to him with his acceptance of Sethe, her pain, and her "trying to outhurt the hurter." (234) The promise held out to Sethe when he gravitated to her house after eighteen years and "rubbed his cheek on her back and learned that way her sorrow, the roots of it" (17) is finally fulfilled. The pattern of alternate silence and the articulation it has now made possible is most clearly brought out here. By wanting "to put his story next to hers" (273) Paul D also acknowledges the silence which preserves the other's dignity and the quiet knowledge of having a friend of the mind. His assurance to Sethe "You your best thing" (273) after his prolonged silence would have meant nothing at all but for the silent expression of his touch, "He leans over and takes her hand. With the other he touches her face . . . His holding fingers are holding hers" (273). The entwined fingers speak of a tomorrow free; from flight, of possession, or possessing of claiming and owning, the runaway slaves can finally quit running.

The complex progression of Paul D and Sethe is more clearly visible in Denver's movement from mute silence to an articulate one and then on to visible expression. Part Three of the novel places Denver at the threshold of change with the words, "124 was quiet. Denver who thought she knew all about silence was surprised to learn hunger could do that . . ." (139). This quietness, coupled with the silence of being left out in the 'games' Sethe and Beloved play, since the last time all three skated as though in a ritual dance, and fell holding hands, is enervating and crushing. Denver is somewhat an outsider in the triad because of her non-experience of first-hand-slavery. It is this partial outside view which facilitates her arrival at a silent determination to protect Sethe from Beloved and "to look out for and preserve herself" (252). The resolve to, "go ask somebody for help" (243), thus, makes it possible for Denver to articulate her need and reach out across the alienating silences between her and the community. Beginning with a courteous greeting by two blackmen to which, "Denver believed her eyes spoke gratitude" (245) and a warm acceptance by Lady Jones, her childhood teacher, Denver is quickly embraced by the women of the neighbourhood. Food as metaphor has many aspects in *Beloved*: of a medium of forgetting for Sethe, a celebration of life for Stamp Paid, of generosity for Baby Suggs, of independence for Sixo. It now stands for breaking bread together, for unreserved acceptance. The women leave food quietly for Denver and two words of thanks suffice to complete the bond. The estrangement which had begun as resentment of Baby Suggs' bounty at the blackberry party and sealed by misunderstanding Sethe's silence as one of pride, is now overcome by Denver's proactive silence which made her words spoken and heard.

An ironic inversion of the central incident completes the reparation. Once more, a white man rides toward Sethe's yard but he is the man who had always helped her and even now is her landlord and Denver's employer. Once again, her offspring are out in the yard, and yet again Sethe feels, "Little hummingbirds sticks needle beaks right through her headcloth into her hair and beat their wings." (262) The difference now is that instead of taking the ice pick to Beloved, this time she flies at the intruder. More importantly, the sisterhood of a once indifferent community is present to wordlessly and efficiently help a quietly determined Denver hold Sethe from self-destruction. A final voiceless oneness, willing hands stretched out in solidarity, complete the strategy, "Leaving Beloved behind" (262) and with her, their helplessness and alienation too. George Steiner in his essay "The Distribution of Discourse" states:

> . . . there is a history, a morphology, a rhetoric of inner speech as there is of outer. The relationships of internal language to the environment are dialectical, precisely as are those of voiced utterance; they help to create the world of experience and, at the same time, reflect it.[7]

This premise of the unvoiced posits dynamics and change, and within the experience of Beloved, conceivable reparation and reclamation are brought about in its three prominent concluding images: that of Sethe and Denver joining a pile of people to make a hill, of Paul D's fingers holding Sethe's and of Beloved disremembered.

Silences, as discovered in *Beloved*, are more than private deviations which are of little significance in themselves. Rather they form a comprehensive system where a part contributes to the overall strategy for effecting a transformation. Thus, *Beloved* reveals layers of silence that accommodate: those words which are spoken, but lost due to mis-communication, or breakdown of communication; words that fail to bear the full weight of what is to be voiced; words and silence that alienate, and those that bond; the language of touch, of the eyes and the face, of gesture and the body; the silence of practised amnesia; the silence of encoded words; and the silence of the unspoken. Yet, it must be conceded that all strategies are finite and cannot exist always by themselves. The strategy of silence also needs to cultivate its familiars. Thus, silence which procreates and crystallises praxis-oriented thought and ultimately makes spaces for deep and forceful articulation is a powerful weapon of change. In tandem, silence, and its discourse—unvoiced before being voiced—provide for a highly complex but effective strategy.

Notes

1. Margaret Atwood, *Surfacing* (1972; Toronto: McClelland and Stewart, 1994), p. 191.
2. Qtd. Lawrence W. Levine, *Black Culture and Black Consciousness: Afro-American Folk Thought from Slavery to Freedom* (New York: OUP, 1977), p. xi.
3. Roger D. Abrahams, "Rapping and Capping: Black Talk as Art," *Black Americans*, ed. John F. Szwed (Washington D.C.: United States Information Agency, 1969), p. 144.
4. Toni Morrison, *Playing in the Dark* (1992; New York: Vintage, 1993).
5. Toni Morrison, *Beloved* (1987; London: Picador, 1988), p. 4.
6. George Steiner, *Extraterritorial: Papers on Literature and the Language Revolution* (1968; Harmondsworth: Penguin, 1975).
7. Toni Morrison, *On Difficulty and Other Essays* (1972; Oxford: OUP, 1978), p. 91.

From Neglect to Insanity: The Concept of Beauty in Toni Morrison's *The Bluest Eye*

RIJU GOPAL
M.S. University Vadodara

> A little black girl yearns for the blue eyes of a little white girl, and the horror at the heart of her yearning is exceeded only by the evil of fulfillment. . . . The damage done was total. (*The Bluest Eye* 204)

Every night before she slept, Pecola prayed to God for a pair of blue eyes. Maybe blue eyes would make her ugly face beautiful. Perhaps, then she would love herself and be loved by everyone around her. Toni Morrison's *The Bluest Eye* (1970) arouses great sympathy and wonder at the horrifying experience of a little black girl who yearns for a pair of blue eyes, and the tragedy that lies behind the fulfilment of her wish.

What made Pecola so desperate for a pair of blue eyes? Why did she loath herself? Why did she need blue eyes to be accepted and to be loved? What filled her with such a strong sense of worthlessness? Morrison raises these questions in *The Bluest Eye*. The novel tells the story of a young black girl, Pecola Breedlove and her family living in a society whose love for its fair skinned and blue eyed children can have devastating repercussions on the psyche of other neglected lot. The Breedlove family is representative of those African Americans who moved from the rural South to the urban North in search of economic prospects, but due to their desire to conform to white standards at various levels, they are completely displaced from their authenticity.

Morrison discusses the impact of white images of beauty and success upon how African Americans view themselves. They believe that white images of beauty correlate with success and happiness and that being white is prestigious. These white standards are instilled into them since early childhood. Pecola's desire for blue eyes is strongly driven by a sense of racial self-loathing and racial self-contempt. Blue eyes, blond hair and pink skin had become standards of beauty and anyone who possessed these was considered beautiful. Anyone who did not would weigh less on the beauty scale. The discussion that follows will focus on Toni Morrison's response to the reclamation of racial beauty in the sixties and her charged and painful recognition of a tragic fact that lies at the centre of *The Bluest Eye*.

From the very early stages of her childhood Pecola falls a victim to her black skin and ugly face. She is always condemned and hated by her own mother, Pauline, who perceives her as unfavourably ugly. At the same time Pauline loves and pampers another girl, almost of Pecola's age, in a white middle class house where she serves as a domestic. Pecola is a subject of hate and neglect even in school where everyone ridicules her for being ugly. Girls in white skin and neat dressing are always privileged over girls in black skin and Vaseline smudged faces. Even the teachers in school favoured fair skinned and blond haired girls like Maurean Peal. Boys always flocked around girls like Maurean Peal because they were smart and beautiful and they always harassed girls like Pecola because they were black and ugly.

The novel is narrated from the perspective of an adolescent child, Claudia Mc Teer, who is Pecola's friend. The privileges enjoyed by fair skinned girls in school and the pride of owning white features is reflected in Maurean Peal's comments on Pecola, Claudia Mc Teer and Frieda Mc Teer as she screams out to them, "I am cute! And you ugly! Black and ugly e mos I am cute!" (98). This remark from a fair skinned girl to Pecola and her friends is suggestive of the venomous and evil influences of racism and leaves the "ugly" listeners dumb and speechless. The realization they come to terms with and the maturity they gain is clearly evident in Claudia's words:

> if she was cute and if anything could be believed she was—then we were not? And what did that mean? We were lesser. Nicer, brighter but lesser. . . . What was their secret? What did we lack? . . . and all the time we knew that Maurean Peal was not the real enemy and not worthy of such intense hatred. The thing to fear was the thing that made her beautiful and not us. (62)

Pecola is hated and ignored by everyone around her. She is looked down upon and scorned by the very people that made her what she becomes. The final blow that drives Pecola into a state of madness is when she is raped by her own father, Cholly and she gives birth to his still born child. Driven from neglect into such a state of insanity, she searches for her child amongst garbage and assumes the fact that she has finally got blue eyes.

The Bluest Eye is Morrison's effort to decentralize and deconstruct this concept of racial beauty. In an interview with Milwaukee Journal staff writer, Fanny Leflore, Morrison has said that she "confronted and critiqued the devastation of racial images in *The Bluest Eye.*" For Morrison, "beauty was not simply something to behold; it was something one could do." (209) She very ably puts forth the main factor that makes significant that which is considered "beautiful." What is it that makes the beautiful "beautiful"? It is the absence of something that gives significance to that which is present? Pecola becomes all the waste and beauty in the world as Claudia says:

> all of our beauty, which was hers first and which she gave to us. All of us who knew her—felt so wholesome after we cleaned ourselves on her. We were so beautiful when we stood astride her ugliness. Her simplicity decorated us, her guilt sanctified us, her pain made us glow with health, her awkwardness made us think we had a sense of humor. Her inarticulateness made us believe we were eloquent? Her poverty kept us generous . . . we honed our egos on her, padded our characters with her frailty, and yawned in the fantasy of our strength. (205)

Morrison presents the difficulty of recognition of the beautiful. For most African Americans the degree of success they achieve and the extent to which they are accepted in society largely depends on how beautiful they are. White images of beauty are used as a yardstick to determine levels of interaction and social stratification. Pecola is a completely dehumanized and demonized member of such a society. Pauline, Pecola's mother, is so deeply influenced by white standards of beauty that she despises her own daughter for being ugly. Claudia is jealous of all the girls who are fair skinned, blond haired and therefore privileged over others like herself. This makes her destroy the yellow haired and blue eyed doll that is given to her as a Christmas gift. Why did all the dolls have to be yellow haired, blue eyed and fair skinned?

Despite her Italian white skin, Rosemary falls into the category of a minority. Yet she considers herself superior and more fortunate than African American girls because they are black and being black is viewed so negatively by the society. Geraldine prohibits her son, Louis, from interacting with black children because she believes that "niggers were always dirty and loud." (109) A close analysis of the above characters reveals how white standards of beauty and acceptance have instilled an inferiority complex in the minds of the blacks and other minority groups. They come to terms with the fact that white features correlate with beauty and start believing what the whites want them to believe—that they are black and therefore ugly.

Morrison here presents the problem faced by Africans Americans to establish self-worth and affirm themselves in a society that is both racist and classist. The characters in the novel are victims of subjugation at two levels: first, as blacks in a racialised world and secondly as women in a male dominated society. The novel also presents an understanding of the duality of black consciousness. The characters in the novel represent a view of how blacks perceive themselves in their own terms and how they see themselves through the eyes of others.

The Bluest Eye illustrates the tragic consequences of racism through the life of Cholly, Pauline and Pecola Breedlove. In fact the very name, Breedlove, is in itself ironical because they live in a society that does not "Breed love." Instead it breeds hatred of blackness, of ugliness and of the self. The scene of love making between Cholly and Darlene in the dark bushes being watched by white men in their torch lights; the hospital room where Pauline lay giving birth to Pecola and doctor's remark, "these here women you don't have trouble with. They deliver right away with no pain. Just like horses"; Geraldine, Junior's mother restricting him to play with black boys because "niggers were loud and dirty" (109); Pauline's dislike for Pecola because she is black and ugly, are all instances of the inhuman behaviour racism evokes. Geraldine and Pauline embody what the white culture wanted the minorities to believe—that they were inferior.

The most vulnerable and most deeply victimized character of the novel, however, is Pecola Breedlove—who without any doubt accepts the fact that white features correlate with beauty. Her unending and determined quest for blue eyes is symbolic of her quest for self-worth and self-esteem. Her quest ends with a total distortion and damage of her self and leaves her with nothing—taking away from her even the little that she possessed. With a pair of blue eyes that Soaphead Church gives to Pecola by means of a contrived miracle, Pecola is recreated. She is permanently blue eyed and insane. She is totally alienated and fragmented talking to an imaginary friend, i.e. her own self, about her newly acquired pair of blue eyes and how beautiful they made her look.

The novel journeys through all the four seasons and discusses Pecola's advancement from neglect and ignorance into insanity. She lives through adolescence, domestic violence, loneliness, sexuality, incest, childbirth, mental illness and finally becomes dismissed, trivialized and damaged completely—all this because of her being a female, a black and her desire for blue eyes.

Works Consulted

Bourn, B.D. "Portrait of a Victim: Toni Morrison's *The Bluest Eye.*" Internet. http://www.altavista.com.

Evans, Mari, (ed.). *Black Women Writers (1950-1980): A Critical Evaluation.* New York: Anchor/Doubleday, 1994.

Lott, N.G. "Ownership and loss of Communal Ties in Toni Morrison's *The Bluest Eye.*" Internet. "http://www.mcnair.berkeley.edu/96journal/lott.html."

Morrison, Toni. *The Bluest Eye*. New York: Penguin, 1994.

Showalter, Elaine et al. (eds). *Modern American Women Writers*. New York: Scribners, 1991.

Multiculturalism in Afro-American Poetry

MANOHAR SAMUEL
Madras Christian College

As the world enters the new millennium with its vistas of possibilities, the disturbing phenomena of increasing intolerance and racial/ethnic nationalism all over the world continue to plague us. This practice of ethnic hegemony has resulted in repression of ethnic minorities within the state/nation in the guise of ethnic purges. The images that sear our minds today are of the events in Kosovo, where ethnic Albanians were driven out and put to horrendous difficulties by the Serbs, or the East Timorese fleeing their state under attack by rampaging anti-independence militiamen, or the advance of Russian war machinery against Chechnya or the ethnic tensions in different parts of Africa, which in South Africa led to the slaying by Madubela, a black officer in the South African Defense Force, of fellow white officers and soldiers, or the war of attrition that has been going on for years between the Sinhalese and Tamils in Sri Lanka. All these incidents seem to point to the fragile nature of racial/ethnic harmony in our society and the harsh reality of racial/ethnic tensions all over the world. The emerging picture of the world that we inhabit is not of a global village but of one that is more and more a battleground with one ethnic group or the other striving for dominance and power, but at what cost? Race and ethnicity continue to be the defining and dividing elements in the world.

It is interesting to examine a report in *The Hindu* (October 18th, 1999), a leading Indian national newspaper, that the German authorities were offering an equivalent of Rs. 50,000 per person as "inducement money" to each of the over 3,50,000

Bosnian and Balkan refugees in Germany living as either "asylum seekers" or "displaced persons." It is also said that these people were reluctant to go back. This action by the German authorities is linked to racism along with xenophobia or dislike of foreign workers. History has shown us that racism in varying forms and degrees is prevalent in Europe and many other parts of the world. In Germany, Britain, France, Italy and Scandinavian countries illegal foreign workers are increasingly resented. And even legal immigrants are targets for racial hatred and frowned upon by indigenous workers. All the above mentioned happenings may not be recent phenomena, but, what is causing concern is that these seem to be on the increase and on a larger scale.

In recent times a wide range of views have been expressed on the nature of ethnic diversity and multiculturalism in America. It is interesting to study how these different ethnic groups relate with each other and how they coalesce into the larger American nation as a whole. The openness of American society, which has sometimes been called into question, gives respect to individual right and choice. In a divided world order, America, which is looked upon as the leading nation of the world, must lead by example to show that it is still possible for people of different ethnic backgrounds to live and share a common heritage. How has America resolved this issue of ethnic diversity and the growing influx of minority groups? My aim in this paper is to study how one ethnic group, the African American, uses a literary genre poetry to address ethnic issues. The skewed vision of Black experience in America makes it imperative for us to look at what the African American themselves have to say about their experience. That being Black or coloured in America has been a stigma is an irrefutable fact of history.

It must be mentioned here that the demography of America has been changing in the composition of its population growth. In recent decades there has been a spurt in the growth of ethnic minorities—African Americans have remained steady at 12 to 13 percent, but others such as the Hispanics and Asian Americans have gained significantly. What is the future scenario likely to be in a changing ethnic structure? According to projections made by

Current Population Survey, "by 2050 the U.S. population will be about 50 percent white (down from the current 73 percent), 24 percent Hispanic (more than double the current 11 percent (due to high birth-rate and immigration), 14 percent African American (slightly up from today's 12 percent), and 10 percent Asian American (more than double the present 4 percent)." (Takki 11). Native Americans constitute less than one percent of the total population. It is said that this demographic change will affect states like California and New Jersey in a few years so that minorities will outnumber the white population. This is already happening in a few cities across America.

In 1998, President Clinton's race advisory commission came under attack since it did not include Native Americans on its board. The Native Americans who protested against this denounced the President's "One America in the 21st Century" as a sham. This is not all. Hate crimes are on the rise in several regions of America. The early part of 1999 saw one of America's most gruesome hate crimes in Texas. John "Bill" King, a White Supremacist, dragged James Byrd, a Black, behind a pick-up truck till his whole body was lacerated, skin peeled off and limbs torn apart. This incident shocked America not only because of its racial motive but also because of its brutality. King is a member of the Confederate Knights of America White Supremacist Group. On August 13th, 1999, Buford Furrow, a member of the Aryan Nations White Supremacist Group, gave himself up to the FBI in Las Vegas after he had fired at least 70 sub-machine gun rounds at children in a Jewish Community Centre in Los Angeles. He was said to be an avowed racist. President Clinton's response to these hate crimes was to appeal for tighter laws against guns and hate crimes. Addressing the Congress, the President admitted: "It now appears they were motivated by racial and ethnic hatred." He appealed for racial reconciliation.

Today, as America is celebrating its achievements with its science and technology making rapid advances, the strongest challenge facing it is the problem of the colour line. If America can sink its differences and embrace what it has in common, there will be a perceptible change. On the positive side it must be recounted that in spite of prejudice, there is more integration than ever—shared neighborhoods, work, school, and social activities, religious activities, and marriage cutting across racial lines. There is a genuine effort to enjoy the distinctiveness of each other's culture. The race debates initiated by President Clinton in 1998, all over America, have helped in some degree to sensitize the citizens of America towards the need to share a common heritage.

The history of America informs us of the discrimination of Jews (anti-Jewish feeling); the cruel internment of Africans, their struggle for liberation and the subsequent segregation; the more recent resentment against Asians and Hispanics, just to name a few. As we enter the new millennium, we still see visible signs of tension between black and Hispanic customers, the Koreans and Arabs, the hostility to new immigrants from Asia, Latin American and the Caribbean. The dominance of one group, of West European origin, over others is inconsistent to the ideals of America in the treatment meted out to racial and ethnic minorities. The dreams and aspirations of great people like President Abraham Lincoln, who redefined equality as a right for every member of every race; President Franklin D. Roosevelt, who fought for the four freedoms; Martin Luther King's dream that one day this nation will rise up to see the American creed realized that all men are equal; have spurred the nation towards a more tolerant society. But equality as a fact is still a deferred dream for millions of Americans.

What is the main challenge facing the African American community today? The Civil Rights and Black Power Movements have helped the cause of the Black people to a certain extent. But there is a felt need that more has to be done. There are several hurdles before these problems can be fully addressed, one of these being the fear of minority nationalism. The dominant group, the White Anglo-Saxons, thus far, cannot and will not foresee a future in which power, in any form, should be shared. There are several other problems as well. The Neo-Marxist view has to be taken into consideration, that economic factors will decide ethnic/cultural relations. In this regard, it must be admitted that economic affluence, since the 1980s, has shaped and altered perceptions of a small minority of Blacks, who have risen up the social ladder. There is also another side to the problem, which is the nature of sexism within and without the group. By taking up a few African American poets, including women poets, I would like to examine how African American poets have imaginatively expressed their views in art form on racial/ethnic issues since the 1960s up to the present time. Through their poems, I intend to validate their attempt to express human values, including complex personal, social and political issues before them. Such a study affords a rich insight into the nature of American society and culture and some of the intricate problems that are inherent in it.

The earliest entry of Africans in America was in 1619, brought by a Dutch slave ship. The subsequent years saw masses of Africans being brought to the colonies to meet the labour needs of the tobacco plantations. History records the cruel internment of Africans as slaves, the fight for abolition of slavery as an institution, segregation and discrimination, the loss of human worth or dignity, the fight for racial tolerance and equity, and the gradual empowerment of the Black community.

During the 250 years of slavery, it was a crime for Blacks to read and write. In spite of the threat to their lives, they were resilient enough to speak out against oppression of all kinds and for liberation and equality. To a large extent, the social, political movements in the form of the Civil Rights Movement of the 1940s and 1950s, and the Black Power Movement of the 1960s, helped the black people to seek political and economic strength. While the Black Power Movement preached political nationalism, the Black Arts Movement of the 1960s and 1970s brought in Cultural Nationalism. Thus, emerged the Black Aesthetic Theory, one which is wholly indigenous to Black culture. Its emergence made a great change in Black literature and literary studies. Being denied human dignity and freedom, African American writers were forced to think of a separate identity, political and cultural. Thus, their writings reflect the struggle to maintain one's identity against a racist and sexist society, the silences that come out of repressed anger, and the need for a creative fulfilling life.

Let me examine two major African American male poets, Amiri Baraka (LeRoi Jones) and Haki R. Madhubuti, as to how they confronted racial/ethnic issues.

Amiri Baraka is one of the most gifted and brilliant poets of the post-sixties writers. D.H. Melhem praises Baraka as the figure to be reckoned with in Black political life and art. Baraka was the founder of the Black Arts Movement of the sixties and stands out in the creation of a black revolutionary tradition. He had a tremendous impact on American culture as a major poet, dramatist, essayist, screenplay writer, and music and literary critic. His career can be seen in three distinct stages: beatnik-bohemian (1957-1964), black nationalist revolutionary (1965-74) and Marxist revolutionary (1974 to the present).

Amiri Baraka (named Everett LeRoy Jones at birth) was born in Newark, New Jersey, on October 7, 1934. He came from a middle class background. From an early age he showed his intellectual promise by graduating with honors from Barringer High School in 1951. He went to Howard University in Washington D.C. and came under the powerful influence of Sterling A. Brown, Franklin Frazier, and Nathan A. Scott. He did not complete his senior year at Howard and joined the U.S. Air Force. In 1957 he moved to Greenwich Village in New York City, where he came under the influence of Allen Ginsberg, Frank O'Hara, and Charles Olsen. His first and experimental volume of poems came out as *Preface to a Twenty Volume Suicide Note* (1961). With increasing racial tensions Baraka moved to Harlem in 1965. With other black intellectuals, he advocated a cultural nationalist art and philosophy. It was during this period that he wrote politically charged poems, his collection *Black Magic Poetry* (1969) being an exemplum. In 1974 he rejected cultural nationalism and proclaimed his newfound faith in international socialism, the reason being that capitalism was more of an evil than white society for black people. Poems that come under this category are *In the Tradition* (1982), and *Wise, Why's Y's* (1995).

In Preface to a Twenty Volume Suicide Note Baraka notes dejectedly: "Nobody sings anymore." But the tone and vigour change dramatically in "Black Art," "Poems are bullshit unless they are/teeth or trees or lemons piled/on a step." He wants "poems that kill." "Assassin poems, Poems that shoot/guns." "Wise I" speaks of black people "lost and surrounded/by enemies/who won't let you, speak in your own language" and he feels it would "probably take . . . several hundred years/to get/out." In "Ka'Ba" he "looks down/on a dirty courtyard, and black people call across or scream across or walk across." He sees their "world is more lovely than anyone's/tho" they "suffer." "We are beautiful people," he states, "with African imaginations/full of masks and dances and swelling chants." "We have been captured,/brothers" and "We need magic/now we need the spells, to raise up/return, destroy, and create."

Ka Ba
A closed window looks down
on a dirty courtyard, and black people
call across or scream across or walk across
defying physics in the stream of their will

Our world is full of sound
Our world is more lovely than anyone's
tho we suffer, and kill each other and sometimes fail to walk the air

We are beautiful people
with african imaginations
full of masks and dances and swelling chants
with african eyes, and noses, and arms,
though we sprawl in grey chains in a place
full of winters, when what we want is sun.

We have been captured,
brothers. And we labor
to make our getaway, into
the ancient image, into a new
correspondence with ourselves
and our black family. We need magic
now we need the spells, to raise up
return, destroy, and create. What will be

the sacred words?

Haki Madhubuti, like Amiri Baraka, has been a powerful influence on black cultural nationalism. He has made immense contribution towards the development of black art, black consciousness, and black institutions. He was the co-founder of the Third World Press, one of the few black presses still in existence. In his book *Enemies: the Clashes of Races* (1978) he declared, "I use writing as a weapon, offensively and defensively, to help raise the consciousness of myself and my people." Through his poems he has encouraged black people to be what they are and not fit into the white people's image of what they should be.

Madhubuti (at birth named Don L. Lee) was born in Little Rock, Arkansas, on February 23, 1942 but grew up in Detroit. He had a traumatic childhood, with his father leaving him when he was a young boy and his mother, an alcoholic. He went to Dunbar Vocational High School and then to Wilson Junior College and Roosevelt University. He did a brief stint in the army and subsequently took up various odd jobs in Chicago. His first volume of poems, *Thing Black!* (1967) gives evidence of his black separatist philosophy. This was followed by *Black Pride* in 1968 and *Don't Cry, Scream* in 1969. The title poem remembers his mother's words: "nigger, if u is goin' ta open yr/mouth Don't Cry, Scream, which also means: Don't Beg, Take." In *Earthquakes* (1984), Madhubuti shows himself to be sensitive to the problems of black women. This volume and *Killing Memories, Seeking Ancestors* (1987) reveal that he has moved on to Pan-Africanism and highlights the sufferings of the Third World.

In "Two Poems" Madhubuti pictures the stark reality of the blacks, "I ain't seen no poems stop a .38,/I ain't seen no stanzas brake a honkie's head," and "until my similes can protect me from a night stick/I guess I'll keep my razor/& buy me some more bullets." "But He Was Cool or: he even stopped for green lights" describes a "super-cool/ultrablack" who was so cool that "he didn't know, . . . to be black/is/to be/very-hot." "My Brother" is a passionate utterance to black men telling them that

"Black women have not been/loved enough . . . we are at war & . . . Black men in america are/being removed from the earth/like loose sand in a wind storm. . . . I will make you aware of whose/ bellies/you dropped from." "Destiny" is another powerfully evocative poem:

> under volcanoes & timeless years within watch
> and low tones. Around corners, in deep caves among
> misunderstood and sometimes meaningless sounds.
> Cut beggars, outlaw pimps & whores. Resurrect work.
> Check your distance blue. Come earthrise men
> deepblack and ready, come sunbaked women rootculture on the move.
> Just do what you're supposed to do, what you say you gonta do
> not the impossible, not the unimaginative,
> not copy clothed as original and surely
> not bitter songs in european melodies. Take hold
> do the necessary, the possible, the correctly simple
> talk of mission and interpret destiny
> put land and selfhood on the minds of our people
> do the expected, do what all people do
> reverse destruction. Capture tomorrows

African-American women's poetry records the thoughts, words, feelings, and deeds of black women experiences that capture the realities of racial and gender differences. Insistently, they strike the note that being different does not mean being inferior. On the contrary, being different is good. The new African American literary tradition documents Black women as intellectuals, artists, and as symbol-makers. African American women's poetry has been in existence from the time they were brought to America 400 years ago in the form of slave songs and spirituals. The later half of twentieth century has seen a variety of African American women poets such as Margaret Walker, Gwendolyn Brooks, Maya Angelou, Nikki Giovani, June Jordan, Audre Lorde, Mari Evans, Sonia Sanchez, and Rita Dove to name some major poets. Let me examine two of these poets—Maya Angelou and Nikki Giovanni.

Maya Angelou is one of the major American writers of the late twentieth century. She has attracted the attention of readers from all backgrounds, including the President of the United States of America. She is a well-known activist in national and international Civil Rights movements. The autobiographical statement is used effectively and artistically in her writings. In her autobiographical writing, *Shades and Slashes of Light*, she states "We are a tongued folk. A race of singers. Our lips shape word and rhythms which elevate our spirits and quicken our blood. I have spent over fifty years listening to my people . . . I write for the Black voice and any ear which can hear it." (Evans 3)

Angelou was born Marguerite Johnson to Bailey and Vivian Baxter Johnson in St. Louis on April 4, 1928. She experienced a traumatic childhood—before she and her brother were old enough to start school, their parents were divorced and they were sent to Stamps, Arkansas, to live with their paternal grandmother; she was abused sexually in childhood. She attended schools in Arkansas and California and learnt music and dancing. A deep sense of inferiority took hold of her due to her ungainly height and her African American features. In an attempt to find love she was involved in a sexual relationship that resulted in her having a child (her son, Guy) out of wedlock in 1945. She then married an ex-sailor named Tosh Angelou and eventually got divorced. But she retained his name. Her life, as she herself describes it, was a "roller coaster one"—waitress, singer, actress, dancer, Black activist, editor, as well as mother (at sixteen).

She toured Europe and Africa in 1954. On her return she evinced interest in Civil Rights and decided to be a writer. She was influenced by the protest writer John Oliver Killens and later joined the Harlem Writers Guild, which had Paule Marshall and James Baldwin as members. In 1976 she was awarded the Woman of the Year Award in Communications by the Ladies Home Journal. She was appointed Reynold's Professor of American Studies, a life-time work which she accepted gratefully. Her recognition gained when she was asked to read her poetry at President Clinton's inauguration in 1993. She published several volumes of poems—*Oh Pray My Wings Are Gonna Fit Me Well* (1971), *Just Give Me a Cool Drink of Water Fore I Diiie* (1975), *And Still I Rise* (1978), *Shaker, Why Don't You Sing* (1983), and *Now Sheba Sings the Song* (1987).

In one of Angelou's most popular poems, "And Still I Rise," she speaks out for her race and, in particular, black women. The strength of her poetry lies in its intimate revelations about female emotions, loves, and aspirations. But she does not stop here. She has the larger concern of her people and the justice to be rendered to them. In "The Black Family Pledge," Angelou reminds her people "Because we have forgotten our ancestors our children no longer give us honor." They have left the path of their ancestors only to be lost in their way, they have abandoned the wisdom of the ancestors "of mothering and fathering" and have spawned "befuddled children" who "give birth to children/they neither want nor understand." In one of her most anthologized poems, "Still I Rise," Angelou loudly asserts though she may be written down in history with its "bitter, twisted lies," "But still, like dust, I'll rise." Her sassiness and her haughtiness, her laughter and springing steps may upset the dominant group, yet "still, like air, I'll rise." She proclaims herself as "the dream and the hope of the slave." Another popular poem of hers is "Phenomenal Woman," where she celebrates femininity. Phenomenal woman acts naturally, in her walk, gestures, "The swing in my waist,/And the joy in my feet." This leaves the men of this world bewildered because they have forgotten what a real woman is like, "They try so much/But they can't touch" her "inner mystery." A wonderful, short but powerful poem titled "Son to Mother" lays bare the hypocrisy of the white man's world, "I start no/wars, raining poison/on cathedrals, . . . I set no/store on the strange lands,/send no/missionaries beyond my/ borders, . . . They/say you took my manhood/Momma . . . tell me,/what do you want me to say/to them, just/before I annihilate/their ignorance." Let me quote in full "Equality," which seeks social and political equity.

Equality
You declare you see me dimly
through a glass which will not shine,
though I stand before you boldly,
trim in rank and making time.
You do own to hear me faintly as a whisper out of range,
while my drums beat out the message
and the rhythms never change.
Equality, and I will be free.
Equality, and I will be free.
You announce my ways are wanton,
that I fly from man to man,
But if I'm just a shadow to you,
could you ever understand?
We have lived a painful history,
we know the shameful past,
but I keep on marching forward,
and you keep on coming last.
Equality, and I will be free.
Equality, and I will be free.
Take the blinders from your vision,
take the padding from your ears,
and confess you've heard me crying,
and admit you've seen my tears.
Hear the tempo so compelling,
hear the blood throb through my veins.
Yes, my drums are beating nightly,
and the rhythms never change.
Equality, and I will be free.
Equality, and I will be free.

Nikki Giovani (b. 1943) shot into the limelight during the protest movements of the sixties and seventies. She became one of the popular poets of contemporary times, partly because, she infused her poems with idioms of the Black Aesthetic and because of her down-to-earth sensibility and empathy. Her poems record the racial issues and violence of the sixties. Since the seventies, she has focused more on personal and communal relationships. Though her poems are directed to African Americans, she touches a wider audience regardless of race. Giovanni represents a new sensibility, a new generation of black women poets writing of their pride in being black and a woman.

Giovanni was born in Knoxville, Tennessee, on June 7th, 1943 but grew up in Cincinnati, Ohio, where her family moved when she was small. Unlike many other black writers, she came from a middle class background. She studied history, literature, and fine arts at Fisk University, Nashville, Tennessee. She then moved on to the University of Pennsylvania and Columbia University at Fisk. She too, like Angelou, was influenced by the famed black poet John Oliver Killens. Her first volume of verse, *Black Feeling Black Talk (*1968), brought her great attention. Since then, she has published eight volumes of poetry, including *My House* (1972), *Ego Tripping and Other Poems* (1973), *Cotton Candy on a Rainy Day* (1978) and *Those Who Ride the Night Winds* (1983). Her most recent collection *Love Poems* is dedicated to the late rapper Tupac Shakur. She has won innumerable writing awards and honorary degrees. In an interview to *Publisher's Weekly*, she spoke of her responsibility to share a bit of the past with her audiences, "I have obligations. To history. To black Americans. I say this to the kids all time. You have to decide who you answer to, and unfortunately or fortunately I'm a poet so I don't answer to the bestseller Gods or to the big literary prize gods, but I answer to the ancestral Gods, and the people whose work means the most to me came in here in 1619." (June 28, 1999)

One of Giovanni's early poems "The True Import of Present Dialogue: Black vs. Negro," is a typical example of the sixties militancy, "Nigger Can You Kill" informs the central theme of the entire poem. It exhorts blacks to "kill the nigger" in them. "We kill in Vietnam for them/We kill for UN & NATO & SEATO & US/And everywhere for all alphabet but/BLACK/Can we learn to kill WHITE for BLACK." Another popular poem "For Saundra" provides her rationale for the emerging black consciousness. She realizes this is not the time to "write a beautiful green tree poem," or "a big blue sky poem." She concludes "maybe I shouldn't write/at all/but clean my gun and check my kerosene supply." In "Revolutionary Music" she clearly establishes the relationship between black militancy and black culture for she states, "we be digging all/our revolutionary music consciously or un/cause sam cooke said "a change is gonna come." In "Ego Tripping" connection is made between modern African American identity to its ethnic/cultural roots in ancient Africa till she becomes "so perfect so divine so ethereal so surreal . . . I mean . . . I can fly/like a bird in the sky."

> Poem for Flora
> when she was little
> and colored and ugly with short
> straightened hair
> and a very pretty smile
> she went to Sunday school to hear
> 'bout nebuchadnezzar the king
> of the jews
> and she would listen
> shadrach, meshach and abednego in the fire
> and she would learn
> how god was neither north
> nor south east or west with no color but all
> she remembered was that
> Sheba was Black and comely
> and she would think
> I want to be
> like that

One can conclude from the creative expressions of African American poets that they earnestly seek a just, equitable society. Will the new millennium see America light the globe, leading by example to show that race and ethnicity is not a barrier for people to live harmoniously. The images that we have of the future are not bleak. Concerted action is being taken for a better tomorrow and the day is not far when Martin Luther King's dream that people will be judged "not by the color of their skin, but by the content of their character" will be a fuller reality. The American experience should have relevance for other nations and peoples. As the nation wakes up into a new dawn, one hopes it will be a nation at peace with itself, with its shared values, dreams, opportunities, and respect for differences.

Works Consulted

Buenher, John, ed. *Multiculturalism in the United States*. New York: Greenwood Press.

Canady, T. Charles. "America's Struggle for Racial Equality." *Policy Review*. January/February, 1998.

Christian, Barbara. *Black Feminist Criticism: Perspectives on Black Women Writers*. Pergamon Press, 1985.

Evans, Mari, ed. *Black Women Writers (1950-1980): A Critical Evaluation*. Anchor Press/Doubleday, 1984.

Davis, Charles Tinetchell. *Black is the Color of the Cosmos: Essay on Afro-American Literature and Culture 1942-1981*. Howard Univ. Press, 1989.

Early, Gerald, ed. *Lure and Loathing: Essays on Race, Identity, and the Ambivalence of Assimilation*. New York: Penguin Press, 1993.

Funderburg, Lise. "Zeitgeist: Crossing the Demographic Divide." *American Demographics*. October 1998.

Johnson, Charles. *Being and Race: Black Writing Since 1970*. Bloomington: Indiana University Press, 1988.

Scott, Daryl Michael. "Postmodern Daze." *The Nation*. December,14, 1998.

Sitkoff, Harvard. *The Struggle for Black Equality 1954-1992*. New York: Hill and Wang, 1993.

Takki, Ronald. "Race in America: Perceptions and Parameters." *U.S. Society and Values*, September 1997.

West, Cornel. *Race Matters*. Boston: Beacon Press, 1993.

The Dialectic of History: Rudolfo Anaya's *Bless Me, Ultima*

KRISHNA SEN
University of Calcutta

It is by now a widely known theoretical position as regards both historiography and the literary projection of history in this postmodern and post-representational era that to assume a past to which one has unmediated access, is to be, in some sense, epistemologically naïve.[1] This is, of course, by no means an exclusively postmodern insight. Foucault[2] has drawn our attention to Nietzsche's *The Use and Abuse of History* in which history is said to be abusive when it confuses ontology with epistemology—that is, when it fails to distinguish between the past or event, and history or the mediated version of events—and thereby so overdetermines the present and the future as to render action impossible.[3] Again in *The Genealogy of Morals* Nietzsche read the history of morals, not as a collection of ethical absolutes, but as a man-made artifact deliberately crafted to serve the will to power.[4] But if the perception of history and culture as both relative and motivated is not an exclusively postmodern insight, it would surely be fair to characterize it as a major postmodern emphasis. Following Saussure and Lacan, Derrida, Barthes and Foucault have asserted the textuality of history; and building on this Hayden White, Dominick La Capra and others have described history as a construct comprising competing representations and meanings.

However, keeping in mind the ineluctable fact of situatedness, White et al's conception of competing histories has itself been challenged by subaltern voices for whom history is marked, not just by weighted (mis)representation, but more crucially by gaps, elisions and silences. Diana Fuss, for instance, has critiqued Hayden White's exhortation to 'get out of history' with the tart rejoinder that it is completely irrelevant for women, who have never been meaningfully included in history in the first place.[5] Stuart Hall shows how the retrieval of these "'hidden histories' [has] played a critical role in the emergence of the most important social movements of our time—feminist, anti-colonial and anti-racist."[6]

These revisionist histories not only defamiliarize but seek even to delete the old hegemonising narratives in order to clear for themselves a space on which to reinscribe identity. To quote Murugan from Amitav Ghosh's *The Calcutta Chromosome*, "knowledge couldn't begin without acknowledging the possibility of knowledge."[7] Writing here becomes a political act, subverting and modifying the accepted configurations of knowledge and perception.

My purpose in going over this well-trodden ground is to move on to the ways in which the problematized dialectic of history has been projected through literature. Foucault's vision of history as ruptured and discontinuous[8] is reflected, for instance, in *Midnight's Children* in the ruptured space of post-partition India which left Saleem Sinai with an "Indian childhood and Pakistani adolescence," provoking his outburst—"O eternal opposition of inside and outside," since "all kinds of everywhichthing are jumbled up inside," so that he is "one person one minute and another the next."[9] Saleem's predicament is that of the sophisticated, self-reflexive postmodern consciousness caught in the Foucauldian nightmare of "haphazard conflicts [and] the singular randomness of events."[10] Another model is the substitution of the orthodox narrative by a fully articulated alternate narrative, as in the case of much post-colonial and resurgent ethnic writing. In this kind of contested history in which alterity is power, the dominant strategy is not critical self-referentiality but validation through nostalgia. A third paradigm is Derrida's complex interweaving of repetition and change, iteration and alteration in the concept of the 'trace'—"a monumental, stratified, contradictory" history; a history that also implies a new logic of "*repetition* and the trace, for it is difficult to see how there could be history without it."[11] The dominant strategy here would appear to be negotiation.

The project of contesting received history and its epistemic violence opens up new discursive spaces in which to articulate marginalized subjectivities, oppositional agendas, and perhaps more crucially, redemptive strategies. It may be redemption through irony, as with Saleem Sinai; it may be redemption through rememorization, as when Carlos Fuentes says: "if I do not name, no one will; if I do not write, all shall be forgotten, and if all is forgotten, we shall cease to exist."[12] It may be redemption through oppositional articulation as with Maxine Hong Kingston in *The Woman Warrior*—"The reporting is the vengeance—not the beheading, not the gutting, but the words."[13] Or it may be through repositioning the data: thus Murugan in *The Calcutta Chromosome* says: "if you wanted to create a specific kind of change or mutation, one of the ways by which you could get there is by allowing certain things to be known."[14] Though Terry Eagleton has denoted "signifying practices of all kinds" as participating in "the maintenance or transformation of our existing systems of power,"[15] signifying practices are particularly potent symbolic forms as well as socially interventionist acts when they narrativize and thereby activate the 'political unconscious' (to use Fredric Jameson's phrase). Jameson, too, has likened the articulation of the 'political unconscious' to a signifying structure which absorbs and reconstitutes the signified within a potentially redemptive telos—"the vocation of this dialectic lies in the transcendence of this opposition toward some collective logic beyond good and evil."[16] My reading of the dialectic of history in Rudolfo Anaya's *Bless Me, Ultima* (1972) will be set against this conceptual frame, and will attempt to identify both the nature of its rereading of the received narrative and the kind of redemption it seeks.

Anaya is not a consistent theorist of the marginal position as is his compatriot, Chicano anthropologist Renato Rosaldo, nor is his vision of that deprived and mangled history as vertiginous and alienated as is Gloria Anzaldua's in her *Borderlands/La Frontera: The New Mestiza.* He appears to be rather more in the tradition of Tomas Rivera who said of his own seminal historical novel, *Y no se lo trago la tierra* (*And the earth did not part*), written just a year before *Bless me, Ultima* in 1971: "I began to see that my role would be to document that period of time, but giving it some kind of spiritual strength and spiritual history."[17] Though in the seventies, when *Bless Me, Ultima* was written, Anaya was reluctant to admit that his writing had political significance,[18] by the nineties he is convinced that "a writer has an obligation to become involved in political and social issues,"[19] and has gone so far as to term the Anglo occupation of Southwest United States after the Mexican-American War and the Treaty of Guadalupe-Hidalgo of 1848 as a form of "colonization" that destroyed "the roots that bind you to the authentic self."[20] Anaya shares the indignation felt by his compatriots at the forcible erasure of his community from the Anglo-American celebratory narrative of expansion and occupation. The specific strategy by which he seeks to relocate his community in history is by expanding the parameters of history to include cultural self-representation as well as political encounter, thereby opening up the field for literary "reaccentuation" (using the term in Bakhtin's sense).[21] This theoretical position to which Anaya worked his way through successive essays and interviews dating from 1976 (and which was perhaps intuitively implicated in *Bless Me, Ultima* written in 1972) is most succinctly expressed in his Foreword to the anthology entitled *Growing Up Chicana/o* (1993):

> Unfortunately, the history we read in school has often not portrayed the Chicano community of the southwest. . . . What is history? And why have we been left out of the history books? For me, history includes the daily life of people, and it is written in their stories, poems, songs and corrodes, and in their daily communication. Historians have often not looked at these sources. . . . Chicano writers and historians have set the record straight. We know who we are and we know our history, but belonging to an ethnic group within the confines of a wider society makes it necessary for us to constantly affirm this identity. . . . Language like history is at the heart of these stories. . . . If literature is a liberating experience,

> then the voice of the . . . writer in our culture is one of the most influential in helping to shape and change the cultural way.[22]

Gloria Anzaldua worked along similar premises in 1987 in *Borderlands/La Frontera.*

The historical dialectic in Anaya's work operates along a number of axes, superscribing history on to geography, or time on to space. Like Anzaldua later, he locates Chicano history as moving between two sets of compass points—East-West and North-South. Here is a conversation between Anaya and David Johnson in a 1979 interview:

> I'm very interested in the sense of direction in *Bless Me, Ultima* . . . it's obviously an archetype . . . The East-West axis is a Western axis, that is, it starts on the East Coast from a European source. . . . And the North-South axis is the other migration, the Asiatic migration through the Americas down south. But in terms of psychologies or world views . . . [the] North-South axis sees a polarity but it also sees a unity which the East-West axis doesn't provide us . . . it's the East for individuals, to save their own souls. You take up Zen, or whatever. And it's the North-South axis that is beginning to talk about the sense of the community being healed.[23]

The East-West axis represents the dominant site of conflict between the hegemonic Anglo discourse and its reverse, or the Chicano counter-discourse—"This push and pull between the world of our own culture and the larger Anglo-American world provides our literature with important subject matter."[24] The North-South axis represents the mestizo heritage of the Chicano, what Anaya describes as a "culture that has a 400 year history here in the Southwest, a culture that shares from the Spanish and Mexican and Native American traditions and religions and world views."[25]

This "unique mixture"[26] which Anzaldua also focuses in *Borderlands* leads Anaya (but not Anzaldua) to prioritize the term 'Chicano' as more descriptive of those historical specificities rather than the more general 'Latino' or 'la raza,' or the more limited 'tejano'[27]—an indicator of language constructing history. It is not Anaya's noting of this racial/historical dialectic but his approach to it which is of interest. Chicano critic Ramon Saldivar, for instance, has privileged (to borrow phrases from Renato Rosaldo) the "zones of consensus" rather than "the sites of struggle" within the Chicano psyche when he describes it as being marked by "historical differential unity"[28]; though Anzaldua's code-switching bi-lingualism troubles any possible claims about an unmixed cultural lineage, she can yet envisage a transcendent cultural homogeneity in which all differences will be subsumed—"I will no longer be made to feel ashamed of existing. I will have my voice: Indian, Spanish, white"[29]; even Rosaldo hypothesizes a unified Chicano self when he asks—"Can we be who we are and still belong as full members in a participatory democracy?"[30] But Anaya's claim that "we know who we are" is, on the evidence of *Bless Me, Ultima,* hedged about with contingencies that require to be addressed.

Chicano selfhood in *Bless Me, Ultima* is portrayed as a deeply fissured site of contending ethnicities, further complicated by Judaeo-Christian infiltration, and crucially inflected by the Anglo environment. This internal dialectic precludes on the one hand any simple hermeneutics of legitimation on the ground of nostalgia, and on the other any simple fiction of minority-majority or Chicano-Anglo dichotomy. History in *Bless Me, Ultima* is a many-layered palimpsest concealing contestation within contestation, violence within violence, silence within silence. Within this endlessly deferred dialectic no standpoint is either completely integrated or completely innocent.

Anaya plays out this dialogic interface between histories and cultures in a corner of the state of New Mexico which functions as a Bakhtinian chronotope, or what Bakhtin calls "a figural intersection of time and space around which the collective experience is organized."[31] Spatially it is bound by four points—the village or pueblo of El Puerto de los Lunas, the wide plains or llano of Las Pasturas, the town of Guadalupe (with its railroad, American school, bar and church), and Los Alamos, the testing site of the thermonuclear bomb. But these geographical points are emblematic of the pairs of binaries within which Chicano identity is suspended and problematized. The El Puerto/Las Pasturas or pueblo/llano binary is fleshed out through the characters of the young protagonist Antonio's parents. His mother belongs to the family of the Lunas whose settled pastoral lifestyle owes allegiance to the earth-centred American-Indian heritage, while his father belongs to the ranching family of the Marez whose restless nomadic lifestyle echoes the proud traditions of the Spanish conquistadors: their constant bickering over Antonio's future highlights the intra-cultural hybridity of the Chicano heritage. Guadalupe and Los Alamos represent the different ways in which Anglo intrusion has violated this (undoubtedly contested) Chicano heritage through commerce, Western education, religious conversion, urban evils like alcoholism, and the ultimate monstrous pollution of the sacred earth being defiled by the thermonuclear bomb. Characters in the novel like Chavez and the ill-fated Lupito represent the cultural evils of this heterogeneity. But the subterranean cross-linkages continue even here—Antonio's mother, despite her animistic American-Indian background, is a devout Christian who hopes that little Tony will some day become a priest, and this is a major bone of contention with his father.

Clearly, Anaya's projection of Chicano culture is not a nostalgic evocation of some hypothetical lost 'wholeness.' Seven-year old Antonio's spiritual journey represents a negotiation between these multipolar but interlinked hybridities. The ethnic or marginal *bildungsroman* (one thinks of Maxine Hong Kingston, Chinua Achebe and many others) is a classic example of the appropriation of a dominant metropolitan form for oppositional self-reproduction. Chicano literature has several other examples of counter-discursive *bildungsroman* such as Ernesto Galarza's *Barrio Boy: The Story of a Boy's Acculturation* (1971), Richard Rodriguez' *Hunger of Memory: The Education of Richard Rodriguez* (1982), and Anzaldua's *Borderlands* (1987). The ethnic *bildungsroman* also very often prioritizes the act of writing itself as an essential factor in the process of cultural self-definition. That *Bless Me, Ultima* is a portrait of the artist/writer as a young man is clear from the number of overt Joycean echoes in the text. Anzaldua's term 'autohistorias'[32] with its implied suggestion of a symbiotic connection between the self and history (that is to say, between culture and history) is far more illuminating than the more usual term 'autobiography' as regards the task performed by the ethnic *bildungsroman* for the ethnic group. *Writing the self* functions as a metaphor for the recuperation and reaccentuation of the marginal cultural matrix—reintegration of the fragmented self marks the possibility of salvation for the community. Anaya says—"Our growing up stories provide a history of our past, and in doing so they illuminate the present. . . . That is how I felt when I wrote my first novel, *Bless Me, Ultima*."[33]

Within the New Mexican chronotope Antonio's 'autohistorias' attempts to mediate between its disjunctive spatial polarities in terms of a concordance of temporal orders. The novel is set in 1945 and both the Second World War and the thermonuclear test explosions are emblematic of the violence wrought by man on nature and by man on man. Plotted against this historical specificity is an atemporal dimension of dream and myth. The point of mediation is little Antonio who quite credibly negotiates the multiple spheres of work, war and wonder with the ease that only a child can aspire to—that was "the summer I was almost seven. . . . The magical time of childhood stood still, and the pulse of the living earth pressed its mystery into my living blood."[34] Anaya has acknowledged his debt to Jung and the conception of the 'collective unconscious'.[35] Antonio is able to reach deep into himself and touch this collective unconscious because his childhood purity has still not been compromised by the fault lines of the adult Chicano self.[36]

One archetype of this Chicano collective unconscious is the shamanic Ultima with her familiar, the owl. Ultima is an aged *curandera* or tribal healer versed in Nature's primal lore who, unlike a modern physician, heals souls as well as bodies. The other archetype is the Manichean dyad of the Apollonian Fish-King, the Golden Carp, with its ominous Dionysian Other, the daemonic black bass. Most readings of *Bless me, Ultima* isolate the magic realism of Ultima and, since she is clearly a messianic figure, assess the novel as an Edenic fantasy operating "at the margin of history," to quote Roberto Cantu.[37] Both David Carrasco and Vernon E. Lattin have interpreted the novel as revisionary nature mysticism.[38] Ramon Saldivar follows Hector Calderon's portrayal of the novel as "wish-fulfilment fantasy"[39] and claims that its sphere of operation is "the consoling confines of romance beneath which the text of history may be subsumed."[40] But these ahistorical approaches misconstrue the dynamic of the novel and over-simplify its narrative strategies.

Ultima does indeed come across as a near-mythical figure but one must remember that, in this first person narrative, her persona is always filtered through the wondering gaze of a seven-year old acolyte for whom she is the ideal. That is to say, Ultima is always at one remove from the reader, and we in effect know her as Antonio perceives her—whereas to some of the adult characters in the novel she is only "La Grande" or respected old woman, while to the more sceptical or hostile she is just a meddlesome old crone or even a 'bruja' or witch. It is important to cut through the otherworldly aura with which Antonio invests her to see what exactly she stands for.

First, Ultima is no uncritical personification of some vaguely conceptualized Chicano soul. To Antonio her message of affiliation with the universe makes her more spiritually satisfying than either the Virgin of Guadalupe on the one hand, or La Llorona, the wailing woman of the waters of Aztec mythology on the other; and the wisdom she imparts about the goodness of earth and sky and the wickedness of alienated man is richer than the biased education at the American school, but richer also than the limited and self-contradictory worldviews of Antonio's father and mother. In other words, Chicano, no less than Anglo, values are critically sifted through Ultima. Secondly, Ultima's ancient herbal lore culled from "the Indians of the Rio del Norte . . . the Aztecas, Mayas and even those in the old, old country, the Moors," (39) affirms the values of alternate traditions (American Indian/African) within the primarily Hispanic/Mexican Chicano culture. Thirdly, it is Ultima who helps Antonio understand the endlessly deferred dialectic of history, that is, history is Janus-faced and no standpoint is absolute. For the grim irony is that what the Anglos had done to the Chicanos, the Chicanos had themselves done earlier to their predecessors in the American Southwest, the Comanche Indians. The political history articulated in the novel is thus a hall of mirrors. We have on the one hand the familiar anti-Anglo reverse discourse—"Then the railroad came . . . the meeting of the people from Texas with my forefathers was full of blood, murder and tragedy. The barbed wire came . . . the people were uprooted." (119) Set against this is another, even more concealed history of "blood, murder and tragedy"—"They [the mestizos] were the first cowboys in a wild and desolate land which they took from the Indians. . . . A long time ago the llano of the Agua Negra was the land of the Comanche Indians. Then the Comancheros came, then the Mexican with his flocks—many years ago three Comanche Indians raided the flocks of one man . . . and they hanged those three Indians. (119 and 216) In the context of this chain of violations, the chaotic tempest of rocks and stones caused by the thermonuclear explosion is, according to Ultima, yet another instance of man's diabolical quest for power. Ultima's wisdom is thus neither romance nor fantasy nor ethnic nostalgia nor revisionary nature mysticism deriving out of some Eliadean "in illo tempore," but a clear-sighted engagement with a dialectic of history in which there are no uncomplicated heroes, villains or victims.

Through the figure of Ultima, then, the novel explores the internal dialectic of alternate histories within a received 'History,' and then contrasts this endless succession with the absolute truth of Nature. Through the other archetype of the Golden Carp the novel addresses the external dialectic of linear and circular time, temporality and atemporality, or history and myth. It is important to remember that the novel nowhere suggests that the millennial empire of the Fish-King will ever be realized (Antonio specifically says that the Golden Carp will never be set free), but the point of imaginatively retrieving the old Aztec myth is to revivify the message of the Carp which is "Sin against no one." (111) Anaya has pertinently observed that myth and history are oppositional categories only within the dichotomic or binary conceptual framework of Western rationalism:

> Original man was in harmony with his metaphorical setup. . . . Now we call it mythical because we're so separated from it. It shouldn't be mythical. . . . And if I don't have the sense of harmony to understand myself in relationship to it, then I make it mythical and I separate myself from it.[41]

This harmony with the somewhat inadequately identified "metaphorical setup" obviously refers to the perception of inner and outer existence occupying a seamless continuum of being: Anzaldua calls this perception "la facultad" ("the faculty")[42] and describes it thus—"I look for omens everywhere, everywhere catch glimpses of the patterns and cycles of my life."[43] This weaving in of myth into the interstices of history is dismissed as superstition by Western empiricism that long ago rejected the interconnected or allegorical universe, but is understood very well in India, another culture of the global South.

Bless Me, Ultima, then, is no uncritical celebration of a vaguely utopian indigenous past. ('Ultima' means 'last,' something which is vanishing). This becomes clear if we compare this novel with two other novels by Anaya—the avowedly fabular *Heart of Aztlan* (1976), and the quasi-Biblical *Jalamanta, A Message from the Desert* (1996) with its *curandera* figure of Kindra.[44] While those novels inhabit mythical spaces, Antonio's experience is rooted in a specific time and place. Antonio is released from history not through some extra-sensory intuition from the fabular Golden Carp, but through the very humane wisdom communicated by Ultima—"And that is what Ultima tried to teach me, that the tragic consequences of life can be overcome by the magical strength that resides in the human heart." (237) Though the use of the narrative devices of dream and myth in *Bless Me, Ultima* have led critics to compare it to the visionary narratives of *Heart of Aztlan* and *Jalamanta,* the novel of Anaya which most significantly extends the concerns of *Bless Me, Ultima* would appear to be his urban novel *Albuquerque* (1992). Set against a totally contemporary cityscape (though the river and mountain and plains remain just beyond, impinging on the consciousness of the characters), *Albuquerque* traces the redemptive spiritual journeys of the half-Anglo half-mestizo Abran (a symbol of the Chicano predicament), and the writer Ben Chavez, an adult Antonio as it were, who hoped that his work "would help create a new consciousness for the people. A new identity for the downtrodden. . . . In the stories he wrote he would probe the dark center and attempt to bring a healing. Bring people together."

What then is the status of Anaya's recreation of Chicano identity in "Bless Me, Ultima"? The novel has argued that all historical insights are contingent and perspectival, and therefore limited. So here we cite the even more marginal voice of the Chicana, the Chicano woman, which has been inadequately represented in *Bless Me, Ultima* (Ultima herself being an exceptional figure).[45] One recalls Gloria Anzaldua's allegation against her fellow male Chicano writers and intellectuals of indulging in patriarchal discrimination in their (non)representation of the Chicana.[46] Anaya's occluding of gender[47] subsumes yet another 'hidden history' of the doubly deprived Chicana within the larger narrative of the marginalisation of the Chicano people. In other words, all narratives, even the counter-discursive narratives, remain perspectival.

It is important to appreciate the fact that all these fault lines in Anaya's narrative, whether consciously invoked (the hidden history of the Comanche) or unconsciously occluded (the hidden history of the Chicana), crucially inflect the Western postmodern metropolitan construction of the marginalized post-colonial self. In *A Critique of Postcolonial Reason* Gayatri Chakravorty Spivak has spoken of the way in which the Eurocentric gaze continues to displace the subject position of the native informant by consigning him to a perpetual oppositionality.[48] Since all cultural forms are dialogic in the truest sense, the project of reclamation of entitlement cannot be synonymous with a monologic oppositional ethnic self. In her perceptive essay, 'Resistance Theory/ Theorizing Resistance, or two cheers for nativism,' Benita Parry has argued convincingly against "the Eurocentric premises of a discursive apparatus which constructed the Third World not only for the West but also for the cultures so represented."[49] In reconstructing the Chicana self Anaya, too, is aware of the need to articulate new alignments rather than merely to retrieve a static image, either as constructed by the White imaginary or through an exercise in nativist archaeology. He has spoken of the kind of model of self and community that he aspires to, which is neither unidimensionally Anglo nor unidimensionally anti-Anglo. To R.S. Sharma of Osmania University, he said in 1992—"You said in your lecture last week that India is in many ways as an eclectic country. That it draws from many traditions and maybe that's its strength. I see myself as an eclectic person. I can draw from many traditions. If we are really to know ourselves, we have to rely on the vast storehouse of humanity, not just one narrow path."[50] In another interview with Laura Chavkin in 1995 he said—"it seems to me that a kind of shared value system, sharing back and forth, understanding back and forth, a kind of growth that is fluid and organic is much healthier in the long run than anything that tries to assimilate through repression."[51] That surely goes as much for uncomplicated colonial constructs of the native as for uncomplicated fundamentalist nativist constructs of some so-called essential ethnic self. In *Bless Me, Ultima* Antonio's father tells him—"Understanding comes with life . . . in the end understanding simply means having a sympathy for people. . . . And when we dream it is usually for a lost childhood, or trying to change someone, and that is not good. So in the end I accept reality." (237) History is a dialectical experience precisely because the past cannot be retrieved, and what we get is always the past in the present.

To go back to the original question—how does Anaya reinflect history, and what is the nature of the redemption he has posited? The conceptual model that we can apply would appear to be the Derridean 'trace' with its complex dialectic of statement and restatement. In *Of Grammatology* Derrida has given us the instance of the "mythogram" which bears quoting in this connection:

> And first of what Leroi-Gourhan calls the "mythogram," a writing that spells its symbols pluri-dimensionally; there the meaning is not subjected to successivity, to the order of a logical time, or to the irreversible temporality of sound. This pluri-dimensionality

> does not paralyze history within simultaneity, it corresponds to another level of historical experience . . . particularly the relationship between the ideogram and the pictogram. . . . Leroi-Gourhan recalls the unity, within the mythogram of all the elements of which linear writing marks the disruption: technics (particularly graphics), art, religion, economy. To recover the access to this unity, to this other structure of unity, we must de-sediment "four thousand years of linear writing."[52]

The mythogram, in other words, is pluri-dimensional because it transcends the spatio-temporal particularities that limit history—its simultaneity and its successivity. Perhaps this is what Anaya was tentatively moving towards when he spoke of attempting to represent "the continuing dialectic between us as Chicano, and the mainstream Anglo-American culture."[53] Through the character of Antonio, as he admits, Anaya sought to free himself of the many reifications imposed on the minority self (as marginal, as oppositional, as 'other'). "I was being led to believe I was too many other things by too many foreign outside influences that I didn't even know who I was"; and then again—"Looking back at *Bless Me, Ultima*, at least one way to describe Antonio is that Antonio is the beginning of my search for the New World person [who] incorporates . . . the old world and the new."[54]

Anaya's vision of the kind of "mythogram" that *Ultima* articulates is summed up in the 1979 interview with David Johnson and David Apodaca:

> the way in which you self-actualize is by discovering your total environment. Again, we very often talk in modern terms of being self-actualized with other people. . . . What I am talking about is that there are many more ways which complete the person. A person to me is the pole of a metaphor. Always searching for the other pole. Usually in tension with it. . . . You complete the metaphor by dissolving the tension with the other pole, social or communal, finding some kind of meeting ground. You also complete that by rediscovering the naturalness of the poles and the metaphor of man in his environment.[55]

This totality in perpetual tension is the dialectic of history envisioned in *Bless Me, Ultima*.

Notes

1. I am thinking especially of books like: Hayden White, *Metahistory: The Historical Imagination in Nineteenth Century Europe* (Baltimore: Johns Hopkins University Press, 1973) and *Tropics of Discourse: Essays in Cultural Criticism* (Baltimore: Johns Hopkins University Press, 1987); Dominick La Capra, *Rethinking Intellectual History: Texts, Contexts, Language* (Ithaca: Cornell University Press, 1983), and *History and Criticism* (Ithaca: Cornell University Press, 1986).
2 See Michael Foucault, "Nietzsche, Genealogy, History" in D.F. Bouchard and Sherry Simon, trans., *Language, Countermemory, Practice: Selected Essays and Interviews by Michael Foucault* (Oxford: Blackwell, 1977).
3 Friedrich Nietzsche, *The Use and Abuse of History* (1874), trans. Adrian Collins (rev. ed.; Indianapolis Liberal Arts, 1947), p. 19.
4 Friedrich Nietzsche, *The Genealogy of Morals* (1887), trans. Francis Golffing (N.Y.: Doubleday Anchor Books, 1956), pp. 220, 265.
5 Diana Fuss, "Getting into History," *Arizona Quarterly*, 45.4 (1989), pp. 95-108.
6 Stuart Hall, "Cultural Identity and Diaspora" in Jonathan Rutherford, ed., *Identity: Community, Culture and Difference* (London: Laurence and Wishart, 1990), p. 223.
7 Amitav Ghosh, *The Calcutta Chromosome, A Novel of Fevers, Delirium and Discovery* (New Delhi: Ravi Dayal, 1996), p. 88.
8 See e.g. Foucault, "Nietzsche, Genealogy, History," pp. 146-47; "Of Other Spaces," *Diacritics*, Spring 1986, p. 2.
9 Salman Rushdie, *Midnight's Children* (London: Picador, 1981), p. 236.
10 Foucault, *Language, Countermemory, Practice*, p. 154.
11 Jacques Derrida, *Positions*, trans. Alan Bass (Chicago: University of Chicago Press, 1981), p. 57.
12 Carlos Fuentes, "Latin America and the Universality of the Novel" in R.L. Williams, ed., *The Novel in the Americas* (Denver: University Press of Colorado, 1992), p. 1.
13 Maxine Hong Kingston, *The Woman Warrior: Memoirs of a Girlhood among Ghosts* (1975; N.Y.: Vintage, 1989), p. 53.
14 Amitav Ghosh, *The Calcutta Chromosome*, p. 179.
15 Terry Eagleton, *Literary Theory: An Introduction* (Oxford: Blackwell, 1983), p. 210.
16 Fredric Jameson, *The Political Unconscious: Narrative as a Socially Symbolic Act* (Ithaca, N.Y.: Cornell University Press, 1981), p. 286.

17 Quoted in Ramon Saldivar, *Chicano Narrative: The Dialectic of Difference* (Madison: University of Wisconsin Press, 1999), p. 77.
18 See Rudolfo Anaya's interview with Ishmael Reed (1976) in Bruce Dick and Silvo Sivias, ed., *Conversations with Rudolfo Anaya* (Jackson: Univ. Press of Mississippi, 1998), p. 8.
19 Anaya's interview with Laura Chavkin (1995), *ibid.*, p. 168.
20 Anaya's interview with Feroza Jussawalla (1992) and R.S. Sharma (1992), *ibid.*, pp. 134 and 143.
21 M.M. Bakhtin, *The Dialogic Imagination, Four Essays*, trans. Caryl Emerson and Michael Holquist (Austin: University of Texas Press, 1996), p. 421.
22 Tiffany Ana Lopez, ed., *Growing Up Chicana/o* (N.Y.: William Morrow, 1993), pp. 7, 8.
23 Anaya's interview with David Johnson and David Apodaca (1979) in *Conversations with Rudolfo Anaya*, p. 46.
24 Foreword to *Growing Up Chicana/o*, p. 8.
25 Anaya's interview with Paul Vassallo (1985) in *Conversations*, p. 99.
26 *Ibid.*
27 Anaya's preference for the term 'Chicano' is expressed in the interview with Vassalo, *ibid.*, p. 99. For Anzaldua's position see Gloria Anzaldua, *Borderlands/La Frontera, The New Mestiza* (1987; San Francisco: Aunt Lute Books, 1999), pp. 84-85.
28 Ramon Saldivar, *Chicano Narrative: The Dialectic of Difference*, p. 12.
29 Anzaldua, *Borderlands/La Frontera*, p. 81.
30 Renato Rosaldo, "Social Justice and the Crisis of National Communities" in Francis Baker, Peter Hulme and Margaret Iverson, eds., *Colonial Discourse/Post Colonial Theory* (Manchester: Manchester University Press, 1994), p. 242.
31 Bakhtin, *The Dialogic Imagination*, p. 81.
32 See Anzaldua, *Borderlands/La Frontera*, p. 13, n. 4.
33 *Growing Up Chicana/o*, p. 5.
34 Rudolfo Anaya, *Bless Me, Ultima* (TQS Publications, 1972), p. 1.
35 Anaya's interview with Cesar A. Gonzalez T (1985) in *Conversations,* p. 87.
36 See *Bless Me, Ultima*, p. 237.
37 Roberto Cantu, review of *Bless Me, Ultima*. Quoted in Saldivar, p. 106.
38 Saldivar, p. 107.
39 Saldivar, p. 107.
40 Saldivar, p. 121.
41 Anaya's interview with David Johnson and David Apodaca (1979) in *Conversations,* p. 35.

42 Anzaldua, *Borderlands/La Frontera*, p. 60.
43 *Borderlands/La Frontera.*, p. 58.
44 See Rudolfo Anaya, *Jalamanta, A Message from the Desert* (Rupa, 1996).
45 See Ramon Saldivar on patriarchal tendencies in *Bless Me, Ultima* in Saldivar, p. 122.
46 See Anzaldua, *Borderlands/La Frontera,* Chapter 7.
47 In his interview with Laura Chavkin (1955), Anaya, however, speaks of his awareness of neglected "gender communities." *Conversations,* p. 169.
48 Gayatri Chakravorty Spivak, *A Critique of Postcolonial Reason: Toward a History of the Vanishing Present* (Calcutta: Seagull, 1999), p. 170.
49 See Barker, Hulme and Iverson, ed., *Colonial Discourse/Postcolonial Theory*, p. 172.
50 *Conversations,* p. 143.
51 *Ibid.*, p. 169. See also p. 171, "the world is multicultural."
52 Jacques Derrida, *Of Grammatology* (1976), trans. Gayatri Chakravorty Spivak (Delhi: Motilal, 1994), pp. 85-86.
53 Anaya's interview with Ruben Martinez (1987), *Conversations,* p. 124.
54 Interview with Feroza Jussawalla (1992), *Conversations*, p. 133.

Forerunner of Revival: D'Arcy McNickle's *Runner in the Sun*

MAHESH M. NIVARGI
University of Bombay

D'Arcy McNickle (1904-77) is known for his contribution to the Native American community through his services as an official of the Bureau of Indian Affairs, as a founder of the National Congress for American Indians, and as an anthropologist and ethnohistorian. An author whose works are placed on the list of creditable Native American novels, McNickle is today considered as the grandfather of modern Native American Literature and Ethnohistory. *Runner in the Sun: A Story of Indian Maize* was published in 1954 as part of a series of juvenile historical novels. After a reading, the novel turns out to be something more than just a storybook for juvenile readers.

The novel was written and published during the Termination Era, a period which was particularly painful for the Native Americans. Between 1953 and 1958, the years called as Termination years, a severe anti-Native American policy was brought into effect by the government. The U.S. Congress resolved to end the special relationship with several of the tribes. The responsibility of the terminated tribes was transferred to the states. As a result, Federal programmes of education, health, welfare, housing assistance etc. were no longer available. Native Americans were burdened with state taxation from which they previously had enjoyed immunity. Tribal law and Federal law were no longer applicable because state judicial jurisdiction was imposed. Large areas of Native American lands were sold as the federal trusteeship over tribal and individual landholdings was ended. The relocation programmes by the Bureau of Indian Affairs encouraged the people to move to the urban areas. But those who shifted to towns were provided little help. As a result, those who had left the reservation found themselves in a much more deprived situation than before. Many returned to the reservation and turned to alcoholism in their frustration. By this time McNickle had worked with the BIA for more than a decade. When the policies of relocation and termination were being implemented, he felt that he could do nothing for his community by staying with the BIA. He took a leave of absence in 1952 and officially resigned from the Bureau in 1954.

As *Runner in the Sun* was written during such a period, one would expect the author to speak of the problems in contemporary Native American life, like McNickle had done earlier in his first novel *The Surrounded* (1936). But McNickle chooses to shift the focus to pre-Hispanic life of Pueblo or cliff dwellers in the Southwest. The place of action in the first half of the novel is the village of White Rock Place, whose people find themselves in a perilous situation. Their crops are growing badly because of the diminishing water supply. Then there is a power-thirsty person named Dark Dealer who has created a rift between his clan and other clans of the village. The protagonist of the novel, a newly initiated boy Salt, stands for the spirit of change. Independent, innovative, and intelligent, Salt tries to grow a new strain of corn on a piece of land, which is better irrigated, but away from the ancestral land; the tradition bound people are unwilling to accept this change. The situation worsens when Dark Dealer with his spider clan drives the other clans out of the village by trickery and captures the village. The people who were the earliest settlers of the village are now homeless. In the historical setting of the novel, we thus come across a situation that resembles the contemporary state of affairs.

To survive in this changed situation the people must find a new way of life. So the village chief sends Salt on a journey for acquiring a new way. The second half of the novel covers Salt's adventures and his journey. When Salt reaches his destination—the land of the Fables or Mexico, he tries to find out the secret of the power which has enabled the Aztecs to build such a magnificent civilization. But his host reveals that the civilization is now being destroyed by violent people-" we now have coming from all corners of the world, it seems, a race of men who have neither reason nor shame. . . . They think only in terms of size and number. . . . These later comers, . . . are devouring our people." (McNickle 204) Once again the novelist presents a picture which can easily find a place in the contemporary reality. Salt returns to his people, bringing a bride with him. It is the slave girl Quail whom Salt has rescued from the Aztecs. Quail gives the people a new stronger variety of corn which she has brought from Mexico. The novel ends when Salt, after becoming the chief, moves his village to a fertile land which he had discovered during his journey. McNickle calls *Runner in the Sun* 'A Story of Indian Maize.' The girl who marries Salt and gives the people the gift of corn is honoured with the name of Red Corn Woman. The significance of this can be understood by referring to the traditional story of the Origin of Corn. In the traditional story the Corn Woman goes to live with the people in the form of a beautiful maid when there is a famine. She marries a young man from the people and later gives them the gift of corn. McNickle thus portrays a figure representative of the Corn Woman who gives life to the people in times of adversity.

In its subject and technique *Runner in the Sun* stands apart from McNickle's other novels. *The Surrounded* speaks of a mixed-blood protagonist who finds it difficult to exist in a world where the communication between whites and Natives has become impossible. This problem of lack of understanding between two cultures is again presented in *Wind from an Enemy Sky*, which tells of a conflict with the whites over the issue of the construction of a dam. Both these novels are centered on the tragic situation arising out of the clash between two cultures. McNickle's concern seems to be to create an awareness of Native American culture and to point out the fallacies of the dominant society's attitude towards the Native Americans. Though the same concern can be seen in *Runner in the Sun*, the novel gives a distinctive message of hope and survival.

McNickle's regard for the Native American culture accounts for the accuracy and care with which the historical details of Native American life are presented in the novel. However, he was aware that venerating the past in itself would not solve the problems of the present. So the structure and content of traditional story telling is used by McNickle as a link between history and the present experience of life. In the Afterword to the novel, Alfonso Ortiz observes that "The form of *Runner in the Sun* is noteworthy. The book is more explicitly connected with the oral tradition than are the author's other two novels. Everything about *Runner* suggests that it is a story about Indians told in an Indian way, that is to say, it resembles a story that is told more than one that is written. Sentences are brief, coordination prevails over subordination, and nouns are repeated rather than represented by pronouns, to make the listener's task easier. The narrator is omniscient as well, as in traditional tale-telling." (McNickle 248)

In its technique and theme *Runner in the Sun* seems to be closer to the new Native American novel of the 1970s rather than to the novels of McNickle's predecessors and contemporaries. The tradition of the Native American novel had started exactly a hundred years before *Runner*, with the publication of John Rollin Ridge's novel *The Life and Adventures of Joaquin Murieta* which presented the story of California's legendary bandit Murieta. This was followed by Simon Pokagon's *Queen of the Woods* in 1899 and Mourning Dove's *Cogewea—The Half Blood* in 1927. John Milton Oskison's novels *Wild Harvest* (1925), *Black Jack Davy* (1926), and *Brothers Three* (1935) are about the adventures set in Native American territory, but the emphasis is on the portrayal of a developing frontier culture. However, John Joseph Mathew's *Sundown* (1934) seems significant as it presents for the first time, the Native American protagonist caught between his own world and the dominant white world. These early novelists wrote in a period, which was of humiliation and defeat for the Native Americans. This may account for their slightly pessimistic attitude which seemed to suggest that it was necessary to accept the dominant society's values for survival. With the arrival of McNickle and Momaday, a change in this attitude seems to have occurred. A need to move towards the Native American identify was felt. Later, in 1970s, the Native American novelists, being a product of new national awareness, consciously made efforts in this direction.

Most of the new Native American novelists have, in their own individual ways, used the form and content of traditional Native American story in their works. Like *Runner in the Sun*, Jamake Highwater's novel *Anpao* (1977) presents the saga of Native American life through hero adventure myth. *Anpao* consists of a chain of traditional stories woven in its plot. Another example of Native American boy hero can be found in Janet Campbell Hale's *The Owl's Song* (1974) whose protagonist succeeds in getting entry into adult life after a bitter struggle. Leslie Silko's employing of myth as a conscious literary device, Hemeyohsts Storm's use of myth as allegory, Gerald Vizenor's unique fusion of the postmodern tradition with the ancient oral tradition have become a characteristic feature of Native American novel today. In its creative use of Oral tradition both for form and content, *Runner in the Sun* seems to have indicated the direction and possibilities which the later day Native American novelists would be exploring. In this regard, *Runner in the Sun* can be looked at as the forerunner of the revival that was to follow in the later decades in the field of Native American literature.

Work Cited

McNickle, D'Arcy. *Runner in the Sun: A Story of Indian Maize*. Albuquerque: University of New Mexico Press, 1987.

Experiments in Cultural Politics in Thomas King's *Green Grass Running Water* and Paula Allen's *The Woman Who Owned the Shadows*

NILA DAS
University of Kalyani

In the last two decades the debates over culture have largely centered around culture as a crucial terrain of power and struggle. Some recent American intellectuals theorize culture in terms that differ from both the modernist macro-political and the post-modernist micro-political positions, the familiar combat zone. Staked out as a mode to meet the challenges of the rapidly expanding cultural industry of trans-national techno-capitalism, the standpoint demands attention.

A serious post-postmodernist reaction to totalitarian culture control is that it de-sensitizes the community towards history, heritage, and memory no less than towards the socio-economic-political imbalances within the status quo. In the process of massive subjective identification with the thought and behavior patterns codified and catered by the political-financial power centers, the thinking subjects are reduced to objective products of power.

In the early seventies, accentuating the necessity of a survival ideology, Herbert Marcuse wrote of opening to "the new dimensions in history." (71-72) A section of recent theorists of cultural politics lay stress on the socio-cultural paradigm shift, and the sequential systemic transformation of political power network. "It is culture that moulds the sensibilities and thus cultural politics attempts to undo the enculturation of the dominant culture by providing new ways of seeing, feeling, talking and being." (Kellner and Best 6) Some foundationalist futurists define the "new way of seeing" in terms of [re]emphasis on basic human values, the quality of life, the structural integrity of personality and relations, a cultural wholeness, without which, they postulate, no civilization can long endure. The trend of thought, evidently, expands cultural politics beyond the boundaries of exclusionary group, class, race, and gendered counter-culture collisions. In the context, contemporary Native American thoughts on cultural identity as a world view and basis of a broader political orientation, stand out heralding a therapeutic ideology, an integrating vision that in itself counter-balances if not de-centers politico-cultural imperialism.

Explicating the Native American worldview, Scott Momaday, the renowned Pueblo novelist, poet, and painter said in an interview, "the whole world view of the Indian is predicated upon a principle of harmony in the universe. You can't tinker much with that, it has the look of an absolute." (Bruchac 180) Peter Blue Cloud, the Iroquois poet, novelist and story writer speaks the similar way: "there is an essence in us, our own . . . mystery, which is power . . . and this is passed on to the other people." (Bruchac 210) Blue Cloud identifies the "power" with the Native American organic/circular perception of existence: "to live is to live in the past, in the present, and in the future. It is a continuous thing . . . going back to the circle." (Bruchac 39) To many contemporary Native American writers reverting to the "circle" is a matrix for creating collective consciousness against the "warp speeded" technocratic civilization given over to the "power of now."

Utilizing literature as a site for political socialization is not new. Development of a cultural paradigm and/or apparatus for socio-political analysis opens possibilities of going for new aesthetic forms. For the recent Native creative writers, restrained by historical contingencies and commercial vernacular as they are, it is a challenging venture to find a machinery of meaning that makes political sense, and can validate their socio-cultural paradigm as a viable if not vital part of the envisioned metamorphosis of the commodified civilization.

A number of recent Native American novels are experiments in living through the Native world view or ideology as an inroad to cultural politics. Mostly the novelists incorporate the view through history and lore. For this, they often revert to making wide use of culture specific images. Preservation and communication of knowledge, cultural history, value and belief systems through stereotypical images have been age-old devices in Native American oral literature. Especially folktales developed an entire technology of using images so that the community could memorize them, and retain the values through them.

Conscious, as they are, that the immediate identification of the culture specific images is no longer easy for the present readers or characters, contemporary novelists often develop the narratives over the initial distance, at times critical distance between the receiver and the received image or the concept evoked by it. In course of the novels, sometimes the received image is recognized as a cultural ideal, and the receiver resists counter-pressures to attune him/herself to it. Sometimes the distance between the image and the receiver widens, plunging the receiver into an irretrievable marginality. In some novels the distance initiates the character to a dialectical experience, with antithetical perspectives, value polarities, complex interacting relations finally shaping up a co-coordinated body of ideas about living in the society. In some novels the readers rather than the characters attain the dialectical perspective. Expectedly, the novels are resistant to conventional narrative patterns. Time jumps back and forth. Some novels are but a collage of memories, reflections, dreams, facts and fiction.

Let us read two Native American experimental novels and trace the pattern used to relate aesthetic forms to cultural-political implications. The random choice is self-explanatory.

We begin with Thomas King's *Green Grass Running Water* (1993). King, a Cherokee-German-Greek professor of American Studies chooses for the novel an intricately textured multi-perspective plot that blends cross-cultural mythology, oral history, literary allusion, symbolism, lived experience and fantasy. The novel, divided into four parts (four being a unifying number in the Native tradition} is woven in and out of several apparently disparate individual stories, that actually mirror a variety of socio-cultural-political attitudes. The attitudes predominate the novel. The short chapters frequently shift the point of view, diverting the reader's polemical participation.

The title of the novel refers to a standard phrase in nineteenth century land treaties protecting Indian rights in perpetuity. In the novel, the phrase also stands for the native perception of life as an originative fluidity, a resurging vitality that opens to unconstrained possibilities. The novel begins with the image of the water, the primeval life-source: "In the beginning there was nothing. Just the water." (1) Throughout the novel, the image is recurrently used as a cultural critical optic.

The story moves around the construction of a massive hydroelectric dam tied up in litigation suit over Indian treaty rights. The dam, erected over a sacred tribal river, betokens the hegemonic techno-capitalist version of reality, "Government built it to help Indians. . . . We are all supposed to be millionaires." (449) To Eli Stands Alone, the university professor who fights the suit, the actual combat is ideational: "It's the idea of the dam that's dangerous." (206) Eli's small ancestral property ("green grass") including a cabin, blocks the dam's spillway, keeping it from operating. In the context, the "green grass" counterbalances the adamantine scheme of things. Expectedly, doubts are raised over the outcome of Eli's anti-regime suit. "As long as the grass is green, and the waters run," replies Eli, himself all-too-aware that the phrase is but a metaphor. "Treaties were hardly sacred documents." In a novel of ideas, however, metaphor has its own strength.

Ideational and social resistance to hyper-culture's power and control is registered in the other stories too, although the cultural-political front line is not always sharply drawn for the Native characters themselves. The five Blackfoot Indians living on or near Blackfoot reserve, on whose life-narrative the novel develops, are adrift in time as barely observable parts of the overbearing hierarchical racist and resistant socio-political machinery. All have careers that range from T.V. salesman, tourist trap operator to lawyer and university professor. All find it hard to "accept the concept that lay at the heart of business and Western civilization" (330), yet none can do without it. In their own respective ways they search for a theme, a life-plot that truly includes them.

The immediate stories of the Blackfoot Indians are rotationally intersected by a surreal account of four aged Native shamans, the escapees from a mental institution or institutionalized power structure. Driven by a cosmic purpose, Lone Ranger, Hawkeye, Ishmael, Robinson Crusoe (names that make them a cross-cultural group) observe, comment on, and at times help determine earth bound action. In each part of the novel, one of the four takes turn as the narrator of a feminocentric Native myth of creation. Sometimes the storyteller de-/re-constructs the original tale, making it parallel to, or collide with and act as the catalyst of the stories of the present time. The legendary Coyote, the mischievous trickster of the Native lore, who sings and dances the world into existence, occasionally intervenes. His benign humor defuses the ideational collisions to gentle resistance and tolerant hope.

In Part I the Lone Ranger's tale of the First Woman who made the Garden and lived with Adam, cuts across the American frontier history as the mythical characters encounter "live rangers" pointing guns at both of them. The story trails off with the pair catching a train to Florida, with a bunch of Indians having chains in their legs. "Is this a puzzle?" asks Coyote. "We are going to set it right," says the storyteller. The de-/re-constructed myth can be read as a socio-political metaphor, if the reader is prepared to accept it.

In Ishmael's story of the Changing Woman, who falls down from the sky on the "white" canoe, the core character herself turns into a listener, and eventually into a participant in the Moby Dick adventure. "Why are you killing the whales?" she asks Ahab. "Oil, perfume too. . . . We kill things that are useful, or things we do not like," replies the captain, the mastermind of oppressive utilitarianism. The Changing Woman insists on identifying the whale as the black whale Moby Jane. The whale punches a large whole in Ahab's ship. "What happens to Ahab?" asks the Changing Woman. "He will be back. He always comes back," replies the whale. The recurrence, in the context, acts its own critique.

The novel ends with the Blackfoot Indians and the four Shamans preparing to gather for the Blackfoot Sun Dance ritual for the renewal of life. An earthquake breaks out. The dam gives way, so does Eli's cabin. The land rises around like waves, the water rolls on "as it had been for eternity." (455) The novel returns to the starting point with the image of water as the primeval life force. The aged four return to the asylum. "They always come back" comments an attending staff. "It is spring again. Everything is green. Everything alive" {461), says the relieved asylum in-charge. The images denoting apocalyptic reversal, renewal, continuity, and eternity hardly convince in the socio-political context. The imposed celebration invites more doubts than assurance. Throughout the novel the tolerant hope, the literary jugglery with mixed myths and metaphors fail to integrate the basically oppositional paradigms of Native and Euro-American cultures into a richer life-story for both.

Returning to myths necessitates re-entering another history of human spirit, another concept of the structure of human existence. The a-temporal transpersonal view of human situation in terms of renewal can counterbalance historical tensions and frame a healing ideology if the mind is oriented towards it. In *The Woman Who Owned the Shadows* (1982), Paula Allen, the Laguna-Lakota-Lebanese American novelist, poet, critic and cultural theoretician probes the issue through a close focus on the experience, thoughts, memory, imaginings and realizations of Ephanie Atencio, a mixed-blood middle-class Western educated Native American woman. Ephanie represents the Native generation caught between the none-too-acculturated Euro-American present, mostly in terms of mutual confrontation.

In her theories Allen prescribes a dialogue with the past as a way to reach beyond the limit situation of the present, and a better mode of coping with it: "the tribes seek through . . . sacred stories . . . to embody, circulate and share reality, to bring the isolated private self into harmony and balance with this reality." (Sacred Hoop 112-13) In *The Woman Who Owned the Shadows* she uses a large number of Native myths and legends, projecting every sacred myth as a symbolic process. The novel experiments whether a contemporary Native American woman (In Native myths woman is the harbinger and preserver of life, race and society) can own the multifarious socio-cultural-political "shadows" in her life and outlook, as she lives through contacts with the mainstream culture as well as with the other ethnic groups. In the context, absorbing the contraries synchronizes a larger ideological orientation.

Allen's novel too is frame worked in four parts, each part introduced with a feminocentric myth of creation and preservation. The myths mirror the organic wholeness of Native American life, sensibility, and culture. Ephanie's own life story sharply contrasts the mythical tales. The first part begins with Ephanie recovering from a severe psychic breakdown. She tries to sort the parts of her dislocated self through remembering her past, half hoping that memory would act the catalyst. The recollection of her childhood aspiration to be tall and serene (her name itself meant "someone tall and serene. Someone filled with grace"), and the reversed reality in course of her contact/confrontation with the dominant culture and its value systems, stimulates her to re-affirm herself through her Native cultural roots.

Back at her village, Ephanie meets her white American grandfather, who opted for the Native life way and shared joy, grief, life and death with the tribal community. The Native and the mainstream cultures did meet even if at the elemental level. "May be their bonds were more important. Who knows?" (4) Ephanie ponders. The basic human values, the integrity of relations need restitution as foundations of cultural-political ideology, say some recent theoreticians. Ephanie, however, cannot readily attune herself to this guiding principle.

The mythical story in the second part is on the rite of exorcism. In pursuit of psychic exorcism for herself, Ephanie makes for the Northwest urban life, imitates the money-status-success oriented white American life pattern. The Euro-American community does not own her: "she was not exotic." A collage read woman, who had involved herself in the struggle for civil rights, had smoked dope, worn mini skirts, Ephanie contradicted the stereotypical image of the Native female, created and fostered by the mainstream culture. Ephanie's second marriage to a Japanese American, who himself suffers from identity dislocation, presents another dimension of the socio-cultural-political situation. The marriage collapses as Ephanie refuses to seek any entry point to the Japanese American community and culture; nor does her husband to hers. The sickness remains in the Native woman's mind. The psychic exorcism is not performed. Incapable of owning or resisting the paradoxes in her life, the rebel-compromiser attempts to commit suicide, but stops at the last moment as she chance remembers her grandmother Shimanna, who had brought the "shadows" of two seemingly discreet cultures into accord in her own life. She had waited all her life, waiting being her way of coming to terms with her own self and the society. If waiting has been her motto, the granddaughter has evidently failed to inherit it. In Native belief, kinship bond ties succeeding generations to the core of cultural tradition. Ephanie knows it and accepts the responsibility of continuity. The unexpected decision makes one wonder if physical continuity guarantees the continuity of tribal spirit or vision.

In the last part of the novel, while on her visit to the grandmother who passes away, Ephanie realizes the value of coherence in life: "Indians lived in circles, did not care for lines, that broken went nowhere." (185) "Everything was related. . . . What had happened in time immemorial . . . happened now. Only the names were different." (191) The Native idea of eternal recurrence stirs Ephanie to re-view her own socio-cultural dislocations in terms of the old tale of the Sky Woman, "who from death made life. Who knew nothing was ever ended. Who just went on." (191) The "shadows" in Ephanie's life gradually assume the shape of women dancing in the ancient steps of the Spider, the creative and life restoring power, "in the careful balance of dignity, of harmony, of respect." (213) Ephanie's mind dances with the "shadow."

The novel ends on a poetic vision of the bigger balance or order, "the strong, viable, subtle, pervasive forces that operate behind each person's relationship with the world," to put it in the phrase of Mircea Eliade. The poet rescues the novelist. As it is, the Native woman's vision of harmony and wholeness comes too miraculously to be convincing. The conflicting forces of history, heritage and contemporaneity that wreck her psychic stability and her social life, remain as gnawing as at the beginning. Perhaps it is not for a poetic vision to framework an activating ideology.

For all the serious gaps in relating cultural-political implications to aesthetic forms, both the novels authenticate the necessity of [re]reading the history of human spirit, of having a wider scheme of ideas about human life, relationships, society and culture for an ideology of survival and renewal in the present socio-political-cultural context. Both the novels sensitize the readers towards issues related to the continuity/alteration of a system or life course, the worthwhile truth of a creed, the relevance of a worldview. It is said that aesthetic forms create culture in which their values are transmitted. The task is hard and prolonged. The uneven roads forged by the recent Native American novels are indicative of the miles still to go.

Works Cited

Allen Paula Gunn, "The Sacred Hoop: A Contemporary Indian Perspective on American Indian Literature." *Literature of the American Indians*, ed. Chapman Abraham. New American Lib., 1975.

______. *The Woman Who Owned the Shadows*. San Francisco: Spinsters/Aunt Lute, 1982.

Bertman, Stephen. "Hyper Culture." *The Futurist*. Dec. 18-23, 1998.

Bruchac, Joseph. *Survival this Way: Interview with American Indian Poets.* Tuscan: Univ. of Arizona Press, 1987.

Eliade, Mircea. *Myths, Dreams and Mysteries: The Encounter Between Contemporary Faiths and Archaic Realities*. Trans. Philip Mairet. New York: Harper Torch Books, 1960.

Kellner, Douglas and Best Steven. "Postmodern Politics and Battle for the Future." *Illuminations*. 1-13. c:/WIN.95/DESKTOP. 1999.

King Thomas. *Green Grass Running Water*. Boston: Houghton Mifflin Company, 1993.
Marcuse Herbert. *Counter Revolution and Revolt*. Boston: Beacon Press, 1972.

Metamorphosis and Assimilation in Sherman Alexie's "Integration" (*Indian Killer*)

P. RAJENDRA KARMARKAR
Andhra University Post Graduate Centre

Sherman Alexie's short story "Integration" portrays the situation of the Native Americans who subsist and bear the brunt as if their primogenitors had committed a tragic flaw against God and His people. They live in reservations which appear as bad as the dalit colonies constructed by the State Governments in India. Alexie sees the veiled apartheid existing in a country like America that preens itself as the most advanced and civilized nation. Being sensitive to the suffering of the hapless, he identifies himself with the people who are subjected to segregation and victimization by the dominant American white community. Alexie is celebrated for his detailed descriptions of the psychology and environment of the reservation. He presents 'humour and wit in the face of intense poverty and ravages of alcohol abuse that are part of reservation life.' (*CLC* 1)

Sherman Alexie was born in 1996 in Spokane/Coeur d'Alene Indian family in Spokane, Washington and graduated in American Studies from Washington State University. In an interview, Alexie said "I am a Spokane/Coeur d'Alene Indian from Wellpint, Washington, where I live on the Spokane Indian reservation. Everything I do now, writing and otherwise, has in that." (*CLC* 2) He has published seven collections of stories and poetry since 1992. Andrea Bess Baxter describes Alexie's work *The Business of Fancy Dancing* (1992) as "at once painful and compelling yet somehow balanced with humour and hope." (*CLC* 2) Alexie stated in his *The Lone Ranger and Tonto Fistfight in Heaven* (1993) that "Indians have a way of surviving. But, it's almost like Indians can easily survive the big stuff. Mass murder, loss of language and land rights. It's small things that hurt the most. The White waitress who wouldn't take an order, Tonto, the Washington Redskins." (*CLC* 1) "Alexie's first novel *Reservation Blues* (1995) centres on the American dream and the price of success. Young living in rural areas all over the world share similar dreams as their urban counterparts swayed by the images transmitted by the T.V. network and the lyrics of rock and roll music." (*CLC* 13) "Integration," an episode, is picked from his second novel Indian *Killer* (1996).

The story of "Integration" presents the grim reality of the American Indian life stamped out beneath the vistas of beautiful panorama of picturesque and voluptuous harmonies. The American Indians having a sense of loss of their homeland grapple with rootlessness, harbouring age-old grudge, an inherent antagonism explosively persisting in their hearts. Their actions are an expression of annoyance and anguish about their fate. American history narrates that Native Americans or Red Indians were the first inhabitants of the Northern America. They were believed to have settled in Alaska after they crossed the land bridge located on Bering Sea from the Siberian region. They lived uninterruptedly in the Northern part of America until the arrival of the Europeans especially of British descent. The White race in their advance took North America into its fold driving away the Native Indians, the less civilized race, to the Westward. They snatched their large tracts of lands and several years later created for them reservations signifying permanent imprisonment of *lettre de cachet*. In the course of time, no White Government tried seriously to safeguard the Indians' rights, culture and traditions. The treaties signed between the two were often dishonoured by the successive (White) governments. However, in the fight for supremacy of the Great Plains, 'the dynamic, more advanced, industrialized society was bound to conquer.' The statement made by the President Hayes in 1877 is a testimony to this: "The Indians were the original occupants of the lands we now possess. They have been driven from place to place. The purchase money paid to them in some cases for what they called their own has still left them poor. In many instances, when they had settled down lands assigned to them by compact and begun to support themselves by their own labour, they were rudely jostled off and thrust into the wilderness again. Many, if not most, of our Indian wars have had their origin in broken promises and acts of injustice on our part." (Dullies 41)

In the aftermath, Native Americans were fated to be involved in an unequal struggle which is in fact, a clash between two types of civilizations. During the last three centuries, their population was on the decrease because of millions of deaths owning to their contact with the Europeans who were initially responsible for spreading among the Indians diseases like smallpox, measles, diphtheria, influenza, malaria, yellow fever etc., against which they had no remedy. In the twentieth century, as result of the declining rate of infant mortality, the number of Native Americans began to increase not only in North America but in the American continent on the whole.

"Integration" deals with the disposition of a Native American Indian boy named John who was skyjacked in his infancy from an Indian reservation hospital. He was taken to Seattle where a childless White family adopted him. For many years, John suffered from self-inflicted psychological maladies emanating from the consciousness of his brown complexion, and his identity, which he finally beats back to lead a normal life.

The narrative of "Integration" begins in a hospital located in the Indian reservation in the 1960s. Alexie depicts the environment of the hospital marked by unhygienic conditions and squalid milieu. The predicament of the locale matches the palling plight persisting in the minds of the people. The scene is described as murky and dismal: "anonymous cries up and down the hallways. Linoleum floors swabbed with grey water. Mop smelling like old sex. Walls painted white a decade earlier." (16) The life of the Native Indians presages to be bleak and hazy and appears to be jolted by the imminent assault of existence. The driver who brings John's mother into the hospital, purports that he is mourning for the unknown fate. ". . . waiting room where a young Indian man sits on a couch and holds his head in his hands." (16) In the examination room, an Indian family of four is collectively coughing blood suggesting the dearth of medical facilities and the gravity of the situation as well as the callous attitude of the government. "In one of the exam rooms an Indian family of four, mother, father, son, daughter, all coughing blood quietly into handkerchiefs." (16) "Tap" "Tap" signifies lamentation for the loss of life line (umbilical cord) and placenta the remains (the evidence of injustice) which Native Indians are pressganged to live. "Tap, tap. The doctor cuts the umbilical cord quickly. A nurse cleans John, washes away the blood, the remains of the placenta, the evidence. His mother is crying." (17-18) The abduction of the child and strafing of the reservation area by the gunman from the helicopter testifies to the brutal force used against the Indians who resent it and attempt to resist. "The jumpsuit man holds John close to his chest as the helicopter rises suddenly as John imagines it, this is a war. The gunman locks and loads, strafes the reservation with explosive shells. Indians hit the ground, drive their cars off the roads, dive under flimsy kitchen tables." (18-19)

The new house of John is beautiful place surrounded by greenish meadows and gardens but he does not think that it is his. John, fed with a silver spoon, does not show the signs of royalty. In lieu, his personality is torn by anomie and alienation and carried in it his ancestral cry for justice and protests against the suffering and suffocating life led by his people. Being conscious of his identity through his brown complexion, he transforms himself into an inhibitive and introspective individual causing embarrassment to his fellow students. Sometimes, John attempts hard to overcome his difficulties. He is the only Native Indian in the school. He has friends, handsome white boys who headed off to college. John would never speak to any of them after graduation with the exception of one or two whom he comes across in the supermarket, movie theatre, restaurant, etc. "At first he listened to himself say the right things, respond in the right way. I'm good. Working Hard? Nah. Hardly working." (20) The more surprising trait in his personality is that he does not honour the greetings of his classmates and behaves as if he were not known to them. He cowers that his personality has come to their notice. When his girl friends conduct themselves in the most natural way and converse over various things in general, John feels insignificant and does not want to be in their company: "retreated into a small place inside of himself until the girls confused his painful silence with rapt interest." (21) He promises them that he will control his feelings and emotions that are near neurotic and will behave well in front of their fathers who feel that the boy is suffering from infra dig syndrome.

John, like any other underdog, is rebellious within himself and does not seek divine intervention and does not believe in prayer. He revolts against his condition and against the creation as a whole. He rather wages a metaphysical war against the conditions in which he is embroiled. For him, future is the only transcendence without God. His rebellion demands not life but unity and lucid awareness. His metaphysical revolt is aimed at realizing inner happiness in the face of an incomprehensible or malignant universe. Camus, the French existentialist writer, has defined the metaphysical rebellion of (an underdog) a rebel as "Metaphysical rebellion is the means by which a man protests against his condition and against the whole of creation. The metaphysical rebel declares that he is frustrated by the universe. In fact, in both cases we find an assessment of values in the name of which the rebel refuses to accept the condition in which he finds himself. An act of rebellion seems to him like a demand for clarity and unity. The most elementary rebellion, paradoxically, expresses an aspiration to order." (Camus 29)

John works out, and creates a design for applying it psychologically to strike equilibrium. He obtains a regular bathroom pass. In the bathroom, he fights against his anger, gnashing and biting his teeth and lips only to seek freedom from the surges of emotions and anger. After coming out, he does not manifest any of these psychomatic symptoms or 'any strange behaviour.' He forges this method into a regular process and baptizes himself as "an integrated one," a "trailblazer." His conditioned response to his prevailing mien is a quantum leap towards a resuscitation that enables him to progressively transmute into action orientated propria persona in time to come. His evasive action appears to be similar to what Camus has declared: "We all carry within us our places of exile, our crimes, and our ravages. But, our task is not to unleash them on the world; it is to fight them in ourselves and in others." (264)

Alexie suggests that many of the Native American Indians turn out increasingly desperate and lackadaisical and fall into dissipation and atheism owing to the loss of their homeland, and infringement of their values and customs and evanescence of their traditional pageantry by the intrusion of white man's modernity. John's teachers realized that his asymmetrical demeanour is phylogenetic: "If John happened to be a little frail, well, that was perfectly understandable, considering his people's history. All that alcoholism and poverty, the lack of God in their lives." (22)

Paradoxically, Native American Indians are abrasively insensate to the advancing enemy who has blended within himself the culture and civilization of Europe and is largely generous, healthy minded and pragmatic, refusing to accept the philosophy of despair and assuming the spirit of Prometheus, restless for the new, and waging an indefatigable warfare against the frustrating forces. Like an untouchable, Velutha in Arundhati Roy's *The God of Small Things* who emits 'a particular smell,' Native American Indian maintains 'silence' "which was older and better part of custom, still inarticulate." (Momaday 58) The protagonist, Abel, in Native American Indian novelist Momaday's *House Made of Dawn,* accuses his fellow Native Indians of ignoring the advancement and of their aversion to modernity. And they are lying low and revel in the cult of animism.

The people of the town have never changed their essential way of life. Their invaders were a long time in conquering them and now, after four centuries of Christianity, they still pray in Tanoan to the old duties of the earth and sky and make their living from the things that are and have always been within their reach; while in the discrimination of pride they acquire from their conquerors only the luxury of example." (58)

Under the given circumstances, what does the Native American do except join the mainstream? Many an Indian has met this contingency by settling in urban areas imbibing white man's education and culture simultaneously keeping Native American Indian's distinctiveness. It is significant what Momaday says: "It's a matter of identity. It's thinking about who I am. I grew upon Indian reservations, and then I went away from the Indian world and entered a different context. But I continue to think of myself as Indian. I write out of that conviction." (Momaday in Nabokov 438) But many of the Native American Indians show reluctance to merge with the Europeanized living style as they feel their ethnicity rather than modernity matters.

Works Cited

Alexie, Sherman. "Integration" from the *Best of Young American Novelists*, ed. Ian Jack. London: Granta, 1996.

Camus, Albert. *The Rebel (L'Homme Revolte)*. Harmondsworth: Penguin, 1971.

Contemporary Literary Criticism, Vol. 96 (Referred to as *CLC* in the text)

Dullies, Foster Rhea. *The United States Since 1865.* Delhi: Surjeet, 1985.

Momaday, Scott. N. *House Made of Dawn.* New York: Harper & Row, 1966.

Nabokov, Peter, ed. *Native American Testimony*. Harmondsworth: Penguin, 1991.

Wiget, Andrew. *Native American Literature*. Boston: Twayne, 1985.

Is Charlie Chan Really Dead? The Evolution of Asian American Characters and Images in American Mainstream Media

SOMDATTA MANDAL
Calcutta

Let me begin with some interesting quotations describing the first and most popular stereotypical figure in Asian American fiction—Detective Sergeant Charlie Chan of the Honolulu Police: "A modest detective" (9); "He's not very impressive to look at, but . . ." (8); "He flies so low that he skims the daisies" (8); "He has the patience of the East, you know" (8); "an unimpressive little man with a bulging waistband and a very earnest expression on his chubby face" (13); a disciple of the famous philosopher—Old Man in China who said, "The fool questions others, the wise man questions himself"; he sat "huddled up on his chair like some fat, oblivious Buddha." (240) When it comes to the display of wit and intelligence, this apparently shy detective becomes rather street-savvy and even preaches a lot of his own home grown philosophy. He remains in San Francisco because he wants to "add [his] minute brain power to [Scotland Yard's] famous capacity in the same line" (75); "Coarse food to eat, water to drink, the bended arm for a pillow—that is an old definition of happiness in my own country" (18); "Chinese funny people. They say no, no is what they mean. They say yes and they are glued to the same." (26); "Maybe I am stupid Chinese from tiny island. I know nothing. But if this was my case." (57) "Surprise is not in the lexicon of the race" (105); "My race has old saying, Captain. Muddy water, unwisely stirred grows darker still. Left alone, it clears itself." (97-98); "You land people—I observe what home is to you. An unprivate apartment, a pigeonhole to dive into when the dance, the automobile ride is ended. We Chinese are different. Love, marriage, home, still we cling to unfashionable things like that. Home is a sanctuary into which we retire, father is high priest, the altar fire burns bright. (90); "That you once listened to a Chinaman is, after all, no lasting disgrace." (252)

These random quotes are all taken from a single book entitled *Behind That Curtain,* by Earl Derr Biggers published in New York in 1928 by the Reader's League of America. What is more significant is the fact that the author was not a Chinaman, but a male WASP (White Anglo Saxon Protestant) and interestingly, the title page also states that "This Special Edition is Published Especially for The American Red Cross." So, exotic locations with exotic Asian characters were created by Biggers with the primary aim of providing some kind of relaxation to the Red Cross Volunteers at the end of a long and tiresome day's work. His Charlie Chan bequeathed great influential images of 'bad' and 'good' Chinese along with Sax Rohmer's Fu Manchu. A brief survey of American literature, both serious and popular, for the last century and half, shows that 'Orientals' or 'Asian Americans' were mostly characterized in broad stereotypes as alien 'Others,' either as sinister villains, dragon ladies, brute hoardes, helpless heathens, comical servants, loyal sidekicks, coolies, cooks, launderers, Suzy Wongs, Charlie Chans, or wily asexual detectives. The myth of the 'erotic Oriental' and her objectification as sexual mannequin continued to haunt the portrayal of Asian women—from Ah Choi ["the girl in the green silk pantaloons"] to Suzie Wong to sultry Indian princesses of the kind depicted in the movie *Far Pavilions*. With the proliferation of a significant amount of Asian American writing in the last three decades, this world view has undergone a considerable change. Social historians and literary critics alike have emphasised how with the emergence of cultural pluralism in America and the production of literature by hyphenated ethnic groups, Asian Americans have come a long way from being depicted as "model minorities." They propose that with Charlie Chan, Fu Manchu and Suzie Wong dead, characterization in literature no longer caters to the age old stereotypes which primarily represented the white man's point of view. "The question need no longer be 'either/or,'" says Elaine Kim in her introduction to an anthology of contemporary Asian American fiction, entitled *Charlie Chan is Dead*, and she goes on to explain the change in perspective thus:

> Instead of "model minorities," we find human beings with rich and complex pasts and brave often flamboyant dreams of the future. There are dysfunctional families that bear no resemblance to the Charlie Chan version of "Chinese family values," tragic stories of suicide, incest, child abuse, as well as bittersweet songs about ageing, love and death. (xiii)

Kim also aptly explains the reason for this shift in the art of characterization:

> Charlie Chan is indeed dead, never to be revived. Gone for good his yellow-face asexual bulk, his fortune-cookie English, his stereotypical Orientalist version of "the (Confucian) Chinese family," challenged by an array of characters, some hip and articulate, some brooding and sexy, some insolent and others innocent, but all as unexpected as a Korean American who writes in French, a Chinese-Panamanian-German who longs too late to know her father, a mean Japanese-American grandmother, a Chinese-American flame-diver, or a teenaged Filipino American male prostitute. (xiii)

Thus most critics agree that the "fresh-off-the-boat" image of Asian Americans has been successfully done away with in literature and the fresh ethnic voices are clearly being heard above the noisy din.

While this new perspective rejoices the reader, writer and critic of Asian American literature alike, a survey of American mainstream media shows that this is not always true. Right from the beginning of Hollywood cinema where, like the Blacks, Asian Americans were always depicted in stereotypical roles, to the present day when three major film festivals are held in the United States each year, the scenario has not changed radically. This paper therefore proposes to examine whether the stereotypes of the Chink, the coolies, cooks, launderers—all alien 'Others'—still exist in American mainstream media or whether they have been done away with after the emergence of a whole new brand of Asian American directors who could successfully do away with the myth of the Asian stereotypes.

"He's handsome. He's tough. He's worth millions. He's Asian American (Learn his secrets inside.)" Thus begins a mailer advertising *Transpacific Magazine*, directed at a young and supposedly very mobile new class of Asian Americans. Next to these words, Russell Wong appears, elegantly dressed in a tuxedo. He is meant to represent the minority that made it big, who has arrived as a powerful force in American and global life. Yet the secrets that lie behind Russell Wong are not his alone. If he represents the success of Asian men in becoming mainstream in America, he also represents their failures and their history. The history of Asian American men in mainstream media is largely found in the visual medium of the motion picture. Asian Americans can be found in the very first black and while silent shorts of the late nineteenth century and in films of every successive decade. Sometimes these characters were more popular, sometimes less. Sometimes they had large roles, sometimes the most minute. Sometimes they were played by actual Asians and sometimes by Whites in yellowface. But whatever the means, Hollywood has consistently produced some version of Asian and Asian American men to present to the American public.

Hollywood however, has often failed to make a distinction between Asian Americans and Asians. Therefore, attitudes towards Asian American men have been heavily influenced by portrayals of Asian men. As Eugene Franklin Wong puts it, "the hand-me-down potential of stereotypes, especially negative ones, can be activated by the presentation of motion pictures that were made years earlier." (ii) Though several critics have also noted two distinct types of representations of Asian men in American movies, iconized by the fictional characters of Fu Manchu and Charlie Chan, only a few of them have attempted to differentiate between portrayals of Asian Americans and Asians. This is because the films rarely differentiate. The fact is that Charlie Chan may have been the very first well-known Asian American man. This is not how the movies present him, however. According to the films, he is a "Chinese detective" who happens to speak perfect English, dresses in suits, lives in Hawaii and has Americanized children. These things merely make him an acceptable hero, but do not make him into an American or even a "Chinese American detective." Over twenty-five Charlie Chan movies were made during the 1930s and 40s creating a genre all their own. Chan is the most famous of the Asian male detective, yet he is practically sexless. An intellectual man, he never shows an emotion, let alone lust. Fu Manchu, on the other hand, epitomized the threatening foreigner. Although very different, these two characters have been the archetypes for representations of both Asian and Asian American men.

The first Asians to come to the US in significant numbers were Chinese labourers. Correspondingly, the first images of Asians to appear in the mainstream media were of those men. "When Asian immigrants appeared in newspapers and magazines in the 1900s, they were depicted with slanted eyes, buck teeth and yellow skin." (Choy 23) Perhaps these were also the first images of Asian American men. The emphasis at the time was clearly what was foreign about them, however, and not on what they may have assimilated. The anti-Asian sentiment, fuelled by several immigration exclusion acts, probably influenced these portrayals. "Culturally biased perceptions of the Chinese as uniquely non-western in dress, language, religion, customs, and eating habits determined that the Chinese were inferior." (Wong vi)

The early presence and size of the Chinese population has been reflected in the fact that of Asian countries, China has been shown in feature films by far the most frequently, with Japan rapidly catching up. To the extent that representations of Asians were representations of Chinese, supposedly general characteristics of Asians drew upon stereotypes of the Chinese. And Anti-Chinese bias translated into anti-Asian bias. Rather than acknowledging the differences between Asian cultures, American versions of Asians often borrowed haphazardly from all cultures, so much so that all of the dozens of Asian and Pacific Island cultures got lumped together into one common homogeneous identity. One early example can be cited from D.W. Griffith's 1919 film *Broken Blossoms* where the Chinese character commits *hara-kiri* and Buddhism is randomly associated with all Asians. Boris Karloff, in the title role of Fu Manchu in *The Mask of Fu Manchu* (1932) offers Karen Morley as a blood sacrifice. In the end, the image of both the Chinese and Japanese in the media depended more on political factors among the dominant Caucasian population of the United States than upon the characteristic behaviour or attitudes of either immigrant group.

The early Chinese labourers entered American mainstream media as coolies. They could be easily recognized in magazines and newspapers of the day by their queues, coolie caps, slippers, and jackets, often with braiding or buttons. Long after the coolie disappeared in reality, these exotic items implied a connection to the stereotype that Asian men are economically inferior, strange eunuchs who speak with an accent and although outwardly submissive, may not be trustworthy. Usually small in stature, the coolie was early on given the particular tasks of cooking and cleaning too. To a large extent, Asians found themselves in these positions because these were the ones allowed them. Trapped in real life, men of Asian origin also became trapped in the fantasy world of Tinseltown. One of the first attempts at film comedy went by two names, "Robetta and Doreto" or "Chinese Laundry Scene" (1894). This short film stars the Chinaman Hop Lee who employs tremendous ingenuity and dexterity to elude the Irish policeman who chases him. In this and other films of the first few decades of movie making, the Chinese were presented mainly to provide comic relief and to establish local colour. Around the 1930s, in movies like *Song of Kong* (1933), *San Francisco* (1936) and *The Painted Veil* (1934), another version of the coolie appeared. From laundry man to domestic, the Asian man became more specifically a manservant, tending to the personal services of a White man. What interests us is the fact that while these three films are set in places as far apart as China, America and the make-believe Skull Island, the Asian character in them does not change.

The coolie laundry man stereotype of the Asian domestic servant seen right from the beginning of cinematographic history and continuing in several variations down the decades can be found on television as late as the 1970s. He is Hop Sing from *Bonanza*—the Western series that dominated the Sunday-night ratings for over a decade. As Hop Sing, Victor Sen Yung wears coolie attire and speaks in a high-pitched voice with an accent. Like a harried housewife, he literally runs and hops around, cooking, cleaning, and completing all domestic errands. More than just a good servant, Hop Sing's Asian eccentricities serve to amuse the Cartwrights, their guests and supposedly the audience. His complaints cannot be taken seriously because he is not taken seriously, proving the fact that these characters were not presented as Asian Americans—at best they were seen as resident aliens. However, there is a second type of coolie in *Bonanza.* Those who speak more English seem to have a more 'American' attitude, speaking casually to their bosses. There seems to be some recognition that Asians were assimilating, although they were still relegated to being servants.

In the few films of the first half of this century in which there was an Asian lead, it usually went to a White actor. This was especially true if the character was sympathetic, such as in *Broken Blossoms* and *The Bitter Tea of General Yen* (1933). It is seen that major roles or characters have been reserved for the whites and minor roles or characters were often open to, but not necessarily reserved for the Asian actors. (Wong 12) The practice of Yellowface continued for several decades, including *Breakfast at Tiffany's* with Mickey Rooney and *A Majority of One* with Alec Guinness in the yellowface roles as late as 1961. Films with Chinese characters played by Whites allowed audiences to experience exotic locales and vicarious thrills while minimizing the threats involved. Yellowface is an example of "Hollywood orientalism [which] could bring once-forbidden pleasures to the mass movie audience as long as actual Asians were kept out." (Rogin 1050) Sometimes, the Asian man also took the Madame Butterfly role of self-sacrifice and paid the penalty for inter-racial love. Wong associates the assignation of suicide to Asians as "a racist justification for white devaluation of Asian life." (29)

It must be mentioned at this juncture that by the 1930s, the Asian manservant of the movies had begun to change his Eastern clothing for the Western. Based on a derogatory term for Japanese houseboys, this version of domestic servant was known as Charlie. Historically, the second wave of Asian immigrants to America was indeed largely young Japanese men who did domestic work while furthering their education. Both the coolie and the Charlie versions of the servant continued to make their appearances. American attitudes were reflected in the 1942 flick, *Across the Pacific*, in which Humphrey Bogart comments that the "Japanese make great servants." That little has been written about the Charlie character in movies can be ascribed to the fact that by the simple act of donning a suit, the Asian man may as well have assumed a cloak of invisibility. At least as a coolie, his character had some notability, if only for comic or exotic purposes. The Western suit implies that he has been assimilated as a servant, perhaps domesticated. In the MGM musical *Easter Parade* (1948), Fred Astaire has an Asian manservant in full formal attire. He also has the accent, small stature and submissive cheeriness we have come to recognize in Asian man servants. He changes Mr. Hughes's [Astaire's] coat and answers the door to receive guests. In *Torch Song* (1953), which has an infamous performance by Joan Crawford in blackface, we have a character called Tai. This houseboy is short, balding, wears a white coat and says "I'm sorry" with an accent so many times that his boss tells him to stop. In response to that order, he apologizes again, of course and quotes Confucius. The fact that these portrayals are so easily forgettable is of great importance. Charlie is a great servant, assimilated just enough to wear Western clothes and speak English. He is probably an Asian American. However his character provides little or no basis for a lead character or a romantic one. Wong blames the lack of Asian lead roles on a "racialist belief that Asians (especially Asian males) lack desirable human qualities, which are viewed as marketable commodities by white executives." (256)

The Charlie stereotype complements the better known geisha stereotype created for Asian women. Regarding the geisha, Renee Tajima writes, "these Oriental flowers are utterly feminine, delicate and welcome respites from their often loud, independent American counterparts." (26) Together the geisha and Charlie create a feminized, domestic Asia that cares for and soothes the White man. They are fantasies of submission, passivity and loyalty. With their Oriental affectations, which make them distant and exotic, the Asian face has rarely been free of associations with strange affections and this allows the individuality of these characters to be largely disregarded. They become more an appendage to Whiteness than people in their own right. In the film *My Geisha* (1962), an American man praises Japanese women because instead of suing for alimony like American women, they commit suicide by "jump[ing] into volcanoes." It is interesting to note here that unlike Charlie, the geisha is often glorified and often held up as an example which white women should follow. This is because she is endowed with acceptable sexuality and therefore one can have them in romantic lead roles. According to Gina Marchetti, the geisha became such a popular character that "it appeared as if the geisha was Hollywood's chief emblem of post-war reconciliation." (178) Several examples of films which star geishas include various versions of the Madame Butterfly story—*My Geisha* with Yoko Tani, *Sayonara* (1957) with Miiko Tara and *Teahouse of the August Moon* (1956). Together they create a genre of films in which the submissive Asian woman plays a prominent part. Many specifically compare Asian and White women, only to find the White women lacking. *Sayonara* for example holds Katsumi up as a paragon of female virtue. Later, she is shown performing her domestic tasks, cooking, serving guests, bathing her husband, cheerfully and quietly.

As a direct descendant of the geisha, the submissive Asian woman thus became an icon. Recent films like Oliver Stone's *Heaven and Earth* (1993) both contain and deny the misconceptions about Asian women. On the one hand, the American GI says things like "my first wife taught me a real lesson" and "I need a good Oriental woman," implying that Asian women are somehow more desirable than white women. But if he had in mind a submissive wife in his Vietnamese bride, he turns out to be mistaken as she Americanizes in the States. Ultimately, she does sue for alimony instead of committing suicide the way the American man fantasized in *My Geisha*. The stereotypes do not disappear as the foundation of representations, but they do become ironized and played upon. Rarely can they be taken at face value anymore. Unlike the Charlie character, the geisha in all her variations was seen by the white man to be a role model for White women and thus were happy to either glorify or exploit her image.

The other reigning stereotype of the Asian woman is the dragon lady. Anna Mary Wong gave her version in several films including *A Study in Scarlet* (1933). This popular stereotype continues to affect portrayals of Asian American women. An episode of *Saturday Night Live* (1995) had a sketch based on Connie Chung which showed Chung purposefully tricking Newt Gingrich's mother, putting words into her mouth, misquoting her and finally forcing her to lie at gunpoint. "Connie Chung is evil," Newt tells his mother. The dragon lady stereotype has specific consequences for Asian men as well. It helps emasculate them. In several films, the Asian woman is presented as the ringleader, usually of a criminal group. In addition to *The Black Widow* (1947 serial), these include Luana Walters as Sonya Rokoff in *Shadow of Chinatown* (1936), Carmel Myers as Madame Ying Su in *Chinatown after Dark* (1931), and Beatrice Lille as white slaver Mrs. Meers in *Thoroughly Modern Millie*. Interestingly, all these films also have Asian men play coolie characters subordinate to these women. However, the ladies are usually the stars and visual centres, not thc men who are alluded to but may never appear at all. Like the submissive geisha, the dragon lady also has a penchant for White men. Usually dressed in tight silk dresses, bodies on display, she is terribly sexy but can also be sly, cruel and continually popular. In James Bond films, "Oriental women, always potentially treacherous, must be watched with especial care." The question therefore remains whether there is an invisible equation that subtracts power from Asian men to the extent that Asian women are shown in positions of authority.

Another area where the Asians were stereotyped was in the concept of Americanized Asians. Several films from the 1960s were particularly explicit in portraying a young generation of Asians both in America and the East whose main interests are the same as any American teenager. In the Rodgers and Hammerstein musical *Flower Drum Song* (1961), almost the entire cast is Asian but there is at the same time no evidence that the Chinese people and the White people live and work together. The movie also calls upon the stereotype of illegal immigrants and makes the point that there are Asians who are more American than Chinese. Another aspect of the yellow peril is that overwhelming masses of yellow people are either coming into America, or are already there, or are ready to attack the Americans in Asia. Movies which present hordes of Asians vary from fantasies like *Lost Horizon* (1937) to war films like *The Killing Fields* to the James Bond genre in *You Only Live Twice* to the "memorable Asian masses" in *Apocalypse Now* (1979). The endless list also includes *Shanghai Express* (1932), *The Bitter Tea of General Yen, The Thief of Baghdad, The Painted Veil* and *The World of Suzie Wong* (1960). In fact, most films which highlight Asia at all will have at least one scene which pans a sea of Asian faces. Sometimes it is a sea of peasants and sometimes a sea of soldiers, but the message is clear—there is a lot of them. The numbers also mean that probably life is cheap.

With World War II, America found in the Japanese a way to combine their largely irrational fear of people of colour with a military fear. Pearl Harbour enabled Hollywood to revive all the old 'Yellow peril' characteristics. Caricatures of the Japanese can even be found in cartoons of the day. Warner Brothers' *Looney Tunes* created a duck version of the Jap who has glasses, buck teeth and cries 'oh sorry, sorry, sorry" (with slurred 'r's). They also created *Tokio Jokio* and *Bugs Bunny Nips the Nips*. In fact, the bucktoothed Japanese became a standard cartoon figure. Max Fleisher created a Popeye the Sailor cartoon entitled *You're a Sap, Mr. Jap* which is a song Popeye sings over and over. This cartoon shows the Japanese deceiving our hero causing Popeye to cry out righteously "double-crossing Japanese." Even the Chinese got their chance to be ridiculed. This is reflected in the continuing popularity of Chinatown as a setting for crime and Chinese mafia as villains. Chinatown is also caught in two worlds, created by its conflicting themes. "Chinatown fulfils a commercial hunger for a domesticated otherness that can represent both the fulfilment of the American myth of the melting pot and play with the dangers of the exotic." (Marchetti 204)

Before concluding this random survey, I would also like to emphasise the point I made at the beginning that unlike in literature, American mainstream media has not been able to do away with its stereotypical images of Asians and Asian Americans even today. Thus, the 'typical' Asian workers portrayed as coolies at the turn of the century are in today's media mirrored in one-dimensional Chinese laundry men, Japanese gardeners and Filipino houseboys. Asian men still appear as grocers and restaurant workers, with heavy accents. Of course, in addition to these continuing domestic stereotypes, *Kinjite: Forbidden Subjects* and other films exploit a new popular stereotype, that of the Japanese businessman. Yet, they are largely portrayed as using their financial superiority to maintain their tradition and foreign culture. For example, the 1985 film *Gung Ho* attempts to both reflect and deny these stereotypes especially when Gette Watanabe's exaggerated politeness, awkwardness and appearance are the basis for most of the humour in the film.

Martial arts also brings us full circle from Peter Lorre in 1939 to Russell Wong today. Wong is one of the few, if not the only, Asian American heroes in American mainstream media today. His television show, *Vanishing Son*, is syndicated, but has never appeared on one of the major networks. Though Wong is treated as a sex symbol, *Vanishing Son* still builds upon stereotypes we have seen before. Each episode opens with the words, "running from oppression, searching for freedom, he came to America" while we see Wong doing martial arts. The secret behind the handsome, tough, worth millions Asian American Russell Wong may be that in fact he is half-White. Thus he represents only limited possibilities for other Asian American men to be seen as sex symbols and heroes. And even though he is half-White and probably third generation, he must still play a Chinese illegal immigrant whose specialty is martial arts. Though he is a desirable star among Asian Americans, *Vanishing Son* also shows that representations of Asian American men have a long way to go before they shake off one hundred years of Fu Manchu and Charlie Chan characterizations. Perhaps the opening line of the serial should really be "running from stereotypes, searching for freedom."

Works Cited

Biggers, Earl Derr. *Behind That Curtain.* New York: Reader's League of America, 1928

Choy, Christine. "Cinema as a Tool of Assimilation: Asian Americans, Women and Hollywood," in *Color: 60 Years of Images of Minority Women in Film: 1921-1981, A Project of the Exhibition Program of 3rd World Newsreel.* University of California Santa Cruz Library, 1993.

Kim, Elaine H. Introduction. *Charlie Chan is Dead: An Anthology of Contemporary Asian American Fiction.* Ed. Jessica Hagedorn. New York: Penguin, 1993.

Marchetti, Gina. *Romance and the "Yellow Peril": Race, Sex and Discursive Strategies in Hollywood Fiction.* Berkeley: University of California Press, 1993.

Rogin, Michael. "Making America Home: Racial Masquerade and Ethnic Assimilation in the Transition to Talking Pictures." *The Journal of American History*, Vol. 79, No. 3 (1992).

Tajima, Renee. "Asian Women's Images in Film: The Past Sixty Years." *Color: 60 Years of Images of Minority Women in Film: 1921-1981, A Project of the Exhibition Program of 3rd World Newsreel.* University of California Santa Cruz Library, 1993.

Wong, Eugenie Franklin. "On Visual Media Racism: Asians in American Motion Pictures." Dissertation, University of Denver, 1978.

Zero IQ to Straight A: Maxine Hong Kingston's Journey from Enforced Silence to Articulation in *The Woman Warrior*

SHUKLA SAHA
Agartala

Maxine Hong Kingston's *The Woman Warrior* is a succession of highly dramatized narratives building on each other as they portray an intense struggle between two divergent cultures—Chinese and American—and a final resolution of that struggle in the author's life. From the first episode "No Name Woman" to the last episode "A Song for a Barbarian Reed Pipe," Kingston elaborates on the theme of articulation. Kingston does not attempt to make the Chinese culture more American nor the American culture more Chinese. She tries not to harmonize one to another or to make one subservient to another, but to give equal validity to both cultures through articulation.

The Woman Warrior begins with the protagonist's mother's caveat against utterance. Her mother warns her "You must not tell anyone . . . what I am about to tell you." (3) Despite this injunction, she goes on to lay bare everything in writing. Her need for self-expression is evident; she shields herself with words; realizes her latency and makes herself heard through articulation. Maxine has to tide over prohibitive sexual, racial and linguistic barriers in order to convert her socio-cultural incapability to felicity. Her attitude towards her culture is one of attraction and repulsion. The reason for this is both social and psychological. Her ancestral culture, besides providing her personal identity, also provides a scope for resisting the mainstream culture that dehumanizes people. But the myth that gives sustenance to the imagination and the spirit also consigns women to an inferior position; and the society, instead of suffusing them with warmth, confines them to a role of serving men and obstructs their growth. "Living among one's own emigrant villagers can give a good Chinese far from China glory and a place. . . . But I am useless, one more girl who couldn't be sold." (52) As an immigrant woman in America, Maxine realizes that she has no place between the two cultures. She works her way from silence to eloquence not just by covering the historical stage feminist writers have traversed—from enduring patriarchy, to revolting against its conventions, to creating her own ethos—but also by evolving a style that develops from her culture. In the course of her quest, the subversive weapon of culture is turned into a creative tool, and speech impediment becomes a blessing in disguise.

The text begins with a woman—Maxine's unnamed paternal aunt. As she is castigated for adultery, she is not permitted to speak with others. She is treated as taboo. Hence, no one is expected to speak about her. Ironically, the male culprit is not only unpunished, he also joins the mob that attacks her house for this "unnatural" crime. His identity is not disclosed by her because he had warned her not to do so. Silence entombs her and she commits suicide after giving birth to an illegitimate child. Her own family expunges her even after her death.

Maxine also has a maternal aunt, Moon Orchid, who has come from China in search of her husband only to find that he has taken a new wife. When she finally meets him, she is silenced by his angry stare and consequently loses her sanity. Her niece later on draws a link between muteness and insanity: "I thought talking and not talking made the difference between sanity and insanity. Insane people were the ones who couldn't explain themselves." (186) Reacting to Moon Orchid's total silence concerning her husband's bigamy and abandonment, Maxine remarks: "I would've told. If I were his wife, I would've told." (150) "'Telling' thus becomes a significant metaphor in her search for a viable female identity," notes Wen-ching Ho "for only through 'telling' can she expect to achieve sexual equality." (26) Maxine experiences the spell of verbal power at an early age, but it takes time for her to learn to fight and create with words. As a child she had a hard time talking. She surmises that her difficulty may have resulted from her mother's cutting the frenum of her tongue despite the latter's proclamation to the contrary. However, she remained silent for the first three years in school. The difficulty of speaking is compounded for Maxine by a second language. Her voice vacillates initially when she has to learn English and she is considered retarded by her American school teachers. Unable to communicate in class, in speech or in paper, she "flunked kindergarten and in the first grade had no IQ—A zero IQ." (183) She recounts:

> My silence was thickest—total—during the three years that I covered my school paintings with black paint. I painted layers of black over houses and flowers and suns, and when I drew on the blackboard, I put a layer of chalk on top. I was making a stage curtain, and it was the moment before the curtain parted or rose—I spread the pictures out (so black and full of possibilities) and pretended the curtains were swinging open, flying up, one after another, sunlight underneath, mighty operas. (165)

Maxine is fully conscious of the inconsistency between her external silence and her inner speech. She does not just paint layers of black; she paints them "over houses and flowers and suns." To call the layer of chalk "a stage curtain" suggests that it will rise someday. But then Maxine alone knows what is behind the curtain. The intensity of the passage lies not so much in the fact of silence as in the tension between layers of black and the veiled sunlight, between the stage curtain and the reverberating operas. The sense of imagination being inhumed alive—concealed in black—is stifling.

While attending both Chinese and American schools simultaneously, Maxine finds herself perplexed by "I" and "here" in the American language, which are so different from the corresponding Chinese ideographs. This suggests that since childhood she has been trying to grapple with the problem of self and place, identity and home. Then one day in the secluded girl's lavatory, Maxine in her sixth grade attempts in vain to make a mute Chinese-American girl speak. She pulls her hair, squeezes her face and tells her: "If you don't talk, you can't have a personality . . . you've got to let people know you have a personality and a brain." (180) In tormenting the quiet girl, who is "her anti-self, an alter ego" (Kim 153), Maxine has symbolically renounced that part of herself which is Chinese feminine. Behind the gender bias in the conventional Chinese society lies the deep-rooted concept that "when you raise girls you are raising children for strangers." (54) Hence when Maxine excels in studies after her initial setback and tells her mother that she got straight A's, the latter infers "[she] was getting straight A's for the good of [her] future husband's family, not [her] own." (47) The traditional idea that a woman, once married becomes a member of her husband's family, has aggravated the anti-female bias as reflected in common sayings like "Girls are maggots in the rice," "It is more profitable to raise geese than daughters" (43) and "Feeding girls is feeding cowbirds." (46) In equating girls with maggots that eat up rice or cowbirds that build no nests but lay their eggs in the nests of other birds, the Chinese community has negated their humanity on the one hand and dispossessed them of their self-worth on the other. Such sexist attitudes produce in Maxine a mixed feeling of indignation and unalterable fear. At times she curses herself for being so debased. Therefore, when she hears any of the sexist gibes, she thrashes on the floor and screams very hard; thereby provoking her mother to call her "bad girl." (46) But her protests go unheeded, for her ancestral culture does not sanction free speech, especially to women: "The Chinese say 'a ready tongue is an evil'." (164). The Chinese language too propagates sexism: "There is a Chinese word for the female I—which is 'slave.' Break the women with their own tongues." (47)

Maxine tends to register her anger against sexism either by refusing to do what a traditional Chinese girl is expected to do—household chores—or by spoiling it purposely. While strongly refuting that she is a bad girl, young Maxine also harbors unpleasant feelings, which arise from her fear that her parents might sell her when they return to China. This fear springs from the messages conveyed through some of her mother's talk stories, which have inscribed in her mind a realistic picture of China where women were afflicted. For example, in one of her talk story sessions, while relating about her life in China, Brave Orchid told Maxine how, after graduating from To Keung School of Midwifery, she bought a slave girl from the market and trained her to be her nurse. At this point, Maxine connects the story of girls as saleable items with the probability of her going to China and suffers from a sense of insecurity. She observes: "Whenever my parents said 'home,' they suspended America. They suspended enjoyment, but I did not want to go to China. In China my parents would sell my sisters and me." (99) Maxine's fear is intensified further when Brave Orchid tells her of the brutal practice of killing girl babies at the birth beds: "The midwife or a relative would take the back of a girl baby's head in her hand and turn her face into the ashes." (86) On another occasion, Maxine was aghast to see her parents' "Ink drawing of poor people snagging their neighbor's flotage with long flood hooks and pushing the girl babies on down the river." (52) Not only sexist but racial discrimination also muffles Maxine. It thickens the silence in Maxine's family whose predisposition to secrecy is reinforced by anti-Asian immigration policies. "There were secrets never to be said. . . . Immigration secrets whose telling could get us sent back to China." "Don't tell" (183), the parents time and again caution Maxine and her siblings for fear of deportation. Maxine observes, "We couldn't tell if we wanted to because we didn't know." (183) Muffled at home, Maxine also fails to raise her voice at work. When her boss at an art supply store devises the phrase "nigger yellow" (48) to describe a paint color, she tries to protest, but is unable to make herself heard: "I don't like that word, I had to say in my bad, small-person's voice that makes no impact." (48) When an employer at a land developers' association decides to host a company banquet in a restaurant picketed by CORE and NAACP, Maxine again lodges a weak protest: "I refuse to type these invitations, I whispered voice unreliable." (49) Her "small person's voice" (48) is ignored and then she is ousted from her job. The unsaid testimonies become powerful accusations on the page as the racist bosses are caught red-handed in the text. She expresses her grievances in pen and paper and thereby seeks redress. Constantly confused, Maxine takes recourse to writing as a way to escape mental distortions and to lessen her loneliness and agony. The more she is asked to keep quiet, the more unrestrained is her impulse to cry out, if only on paper. To smoothen the agonizing process of breaking silence, Maxine communes with an imaginary being—the legendary warrior, Fa Mu Lan. For some one beleaguered by silence, self-expression is a valiant act. In her imagination she coalesces with the warrior, who must undergo rigorous training and sustain harsh discipline before wielding a sword in the battle. In her real life she has to take speech therapy and work through "layers of black" before she can regulate the voice and the pen that are her arm. Her probation as a writer is arduous, but her accomplishment is noteworthy. Her status progress from a "Zero IQ" pupil to a "straight " student and finally to a writer.

Maxine overcomes her initial dependence on the imaginary being, comes to command full articulation and attain positive identity as woman through the influence of actual female figures: the no-name aunt and her mother Brave Orchid. In "naming the unspeakable" at the outset of the first chapter, Maxine at once ratifies the no-name woman's aberration and declares her own ambition. When Kingston breaks her mother's injunction to silence, ending twenty years of complicity in her family's unrelenting punishment of the wayward aunt, her telling of the story "No Name Woman" becomes an act of defiance both of her mother and of the communal values the mother seeks to transmit. Her mother Brave Orchid, who initially seems to be an abettor in enforcing female silence, is a "champion talker." Her behavior is often contradictory. She forbids Maxine from speaking about her aunt but she herself disobeys her husband by relating the story to her daughter. She teaches Maxine the songs of the woman warrior but predicts that Maxine will grow up to be a slave and a wife. Hers is the feminine presence, which represents a contradictory blend of wordlessness and talking story which sends a confusing message of misogyny mixed with feminine self-determination that baffles her daughter. Brave Orchid had herself refuted Chinese tradition by becoming a medical practitioner at her village in China—a profession unimagined for Chinese women at that time. As a child Maxine deplores her mother's ambiguity—her blending of fact and fantasy. But as she grows up she is inspired to adopt this fusion as a narrative technique. Fa Mu Lan, Brave Orchid and the no name aunt are feminist models who dare to affirm their independence, challenge patriarchy, and cast off feminine dependency. These women teach Maxine how to speak and write. Inspired by females, Maxine metamorphoses from victim to victor by vociferously accusing her oppressor. As Maxine begins to comprehend the importance of self-articulation in the dominant white society, she finds to her displeasure that the wealthiest villager wife names her as a "pressed-duck" voice. (223) Moreover, branded as physically unattractive by her mother, Maxine finds to her disgust that her parents try to marry her off, first to one of the FOBs and then to a rich but mentally retarded boy. She discourages the FOB from courting her by purposely affecting a limp, dropping dishes, spilling soup on him, and sweeping under his chair—an act which would bring him bad luck. The mentally retarded boy pursues Maxine at the Chinese school. Later on, he comes to sit on the crates of the laundry with his boxes of pornographic pictures—a gesture symbolic of sexual oppression. Just as the sitting ghost at To Keung School of Midwifery haunted her mother, so does the hunching sitter haunt Maxine. Like Brave Orchid, who chanted and shouted to drive out the sitting ghost, Maxine finally finds her voice to talk out the hunching sitter, thereby establishing herself as a new exorcist:

> One night my throat burst open. I stood up, talking and burbling. I looked directly at my mother and my father and screamed, 'I want to tell that hulk, that gorilla—ape, to go away. . . . I know what you're up to. You're thinking he's rich and we're poor. . . . You think you can give us away to freaks. You better not do that. Mother I don't want to see him or his dirty boxes here tomorrow. If I see him one more time, I'm going away. . . . I am not going to be a slave or a wife. (201)

Thereafter the huncher disappears. This act of bursting out speaks of Maxine's affinity to her mother. By lashing out at her mother, she also expresses her desire for selfhood and independence. Maxine has finally mapped out a paradigm of her selfhood—to be a woman warrior in America—as manifested in her decision to go away from home.

Maxine's mother's talk stories have enriched her imagination and enabled her to master the art of story-telling. While trying to reshape these talk-stories which have played a crucial part in shaping her girlhood experience, Maxine discovers that writing provides the very medium to realize her aspirations toward woman as a warrior. She redefines heroism and unlike the mythical warrior woman, she avenges herself by twirling words. Her liabilities are turned into assets. Her mother tongue, that has hindered her communication in English, now rejuvenates the language she has embraced with new idioms, fresh metaphors and unique images. In Maxine's imagination, the blade that is used by her parents to carve words on the warrior's back is both hurting and authorizing. The carvings of her back reflect the misogynist sayings that have marked her growing up. In her fancied battle with the wicked baron, she transfers the sexist remarks into his mouth and beheads him. By doing so she not only gets rid of the lump in her throat but also absolves her parents who have afflicted her girlhood. She goes on to acknowledge the source of pain as the source of strength; the parents who have belittled her have also emboldened her. Maxine says, "the ideograph for revenge are 'report a crime' and 'report to five families'" and adds "the reporting is the vengeance—not the beheading, not the gutting, but the words." (53) Hence, by penning "the words at our backs," she has avenged the honor of her family, thereby showing herself as a filial daughter like the mythical Fa Mu Lan. She states: "May my people understand the resemblance soon so that I can return to them." (53)

As she gains confidence in her female identity, Maxine finds new voices and new prototypes, and shifts her loyalty from an awe-inspiring authority to a friendly muse, a second century Chinese poetess Ts'ai Yen. Captured by a chieftain of a barbarian tribe, Ts'ai Yen was presented to another chieftain as a gift. She bore two sons who spoke a barbarian tongue. To continue the family line of her father, whose only daughter she was, Ts'ai Yen was then sent back to China. While returning from the alien land she brought back her "Eighteen stanzas for a barbarian Reed Pipe," which moved the foreigners and Chinese alike. Ts'ai Yen bears resemblance to the influential female figures in Maxine's life, but she outstrips them. She fights in a battle as a captive soldier and also takes up writing—not in disguise—thereby showing that authorship and wielding the sword are not men's prerogative. Like the no-name aunt, Ts'ai Yen is raped, conceives and gives birth on sand. But instead of being abominated and banished, she achieves immortal glory by singing about her exile. Like Brave Orchid, she speaks to her savage children in Chinese but gradually learns to value the barbarian music. Maxine's life parallels that of Ts'ai Yen, as the former too strides two cultures. Moreover just as Ts'ai Yen's song exposes her painful experience as a slave and a wife, Kingston's text reveals her torturous experience in the face of sexism and racism. "The refrain of this final section is reconciliation," as King Kok Cheung points out, "between parents and children, between men and women, and between cultures." (171) The admonition to silence provokes expression as the mitigation sought by those thwarted by silence can come only through articulation.

Maxine's voice has carried her beyond her expectation—from enduring to protest, to recognizing herself as a storyteller. Instead of the confusion and humiliation about her Chinese roots that she felt as a child, she now finds, in the legends and customs that differentiated her from her Caucasian classmates, her heritage and treasure, her strength and identity. Kingston has allowed her protagonist to break through coercion to create opportunities. As she writes about the speechlessness peculiar to minority women, she pays tributes to the female bearers of culture. Her way out of imposed silence is not by melting into the mainstream but by rendering her discrete voice.

Works Cited

Cheung, King-Kok. "Don't Tell: Imposed Silences in *The Color Purple* and *The Woman Warrior*." *PMLA*, 103:1,1987. 162-74.

Chin, Frank et al. eds. *Aiiieeeee An Anthology of Asian- American Writers*. Washington: Howard University Press, 1974.

Kim, Elaine H. "Visions and Fierce—Dreams: A Commentary on the Works of Maxine Hong Kingston." *Amerasia.* 8 (2), 1982. 145-61.

Kingston, Maxine Hong. *The Woman Warrior: Memoirs of Girlhood among Ghost*. New York: Alfred A. Knopf, 1977.

Ling, Amy. 1990a. "*Chinese American Women Writers: The Tradition behind Maxine Hong Kingston.*" in *Redefining American Literary History*. Ed. A. LaVonne Brown Ruoff and Jerry W. Ward. Jr. The Modern Language Association of America, 1990. 219-36.

Robin, Leslie W. "No Lost Paradise": Social Gender and Symbolic Gender in the Writings of Maxine Hong Kingston." *Signs: Journal of Women in Culture and Society*: 12, 1987. 471-92.

Sau-ling, Cynthia Wong. *Maxine Hong Kingston's The Woman Warrior: A Casebook*. Oxford: Oxford University Press, 1977.

Wen-Ching, Ho. "In Search of a Female Self: Toni Morison's *The Bluest Eye* and Maxine Hong Kingston's *The Woman Warrior*." *American Studies*, XVII, No. 3, 1987. 1-44.

On Their Immigrant Mothers' Trails: Chinese American Daughters' Search for Identity in Amy Tan and Maxine Hong Kingston

HIMADRI LAHIRI
K.K. Das College, Kolkata

Critical studies on matrilineage in the works of women of colour began to proliferate mainly since mid-1980s. Social constructions of motherhood and of daughter's filial duties have come in for strong critical reviews, particularly by feminist writers. A daughter's struggle for selfhood by working through the mother-daughter dyad in a diasporic community is also being studied with increasing interest as it is found to be more problematic in view of transcultural perspectives. The diasporic community with a strong mother culture pull finds itself displaced from its natal cultural space and is in confrontation with the hegemonic culture that considers the diasporics as 'others.' Women supposed to be bearers of mother cultural norms in such a community try to inculcate their beliefs and worldview in their daughters who, however, have a strong affiliation to the American mainstream culture. Mothers who mark their daughters' growing up with stories loaded with cultural morals face protests from their daughters who find in their mothers' way attempts to stifle their voices. In spite of cultural and generational differences that generate tension and crisis between them, they show a strong sense of bonding. Elizabeth Brown-Guillory, while surveying mother daughter relationship in the works of women of colour, comments that this mother-daughter dyad experiences a love/hate relationship, often because the mother tries painstakingly "to convey knowledge about how to survive in a racist, sexist, classist world while the daughter rejects her mother's experiences as invalid in changing social times. . . . Sometimes the daughter rejects her mother's values as inappropriate to her reality. . . . It is the friction, inextricably linked to fear and frustration, which challenges both mothers and daughters to create a space in which the experiences of both members of the dyad can be valorized." (2)

Critics like Orville Schell and Walter Shear link Amy Tan's novel *The Joy Luck Club* (1989) to the Chinese diaspora of World War II and the fighting from which the Communists emerged triumphant. All the mother characters arrived around 1949. Brave Orchid, the emigrant mother in Maxine Hong Kingston's *The Woman Warrior* (1976), left China in the winter of 1939 and arrived in New York Harbour in January 1940. These characters, like millions of other Chinese, were subsequently cut off from the mainland China. They could renew their touch only after liberalisation process started in China. Jing-mei Wong, a daughter in *Joy Luck Club* visited China in 1987 and, seeing the luxurious hotel and the capitalist boom in the market, wondered whether it was really the communist China. Walter Shear notes that the novel's structure manifests "not only the individual psychic tragedies of those caught up in this history, but the enormous agony of a culture enmeshed in a transforming crisis." (193) In such a diasporic cultural context, women characters in the two Chinese American women writers' works I propose to discuss here—Maxine Hong Kingston's *The Women Warrior* and Amy Tan's *The Joy Luck Club*—fiercely contest for self-realisation. In both these works China remains a constant reference point. Old China, through its ideology, controls the behaviour and imaginings of the diasporic mothers who, in their turn, try to pass the cultural norms to their daughters.

Despite having gender affinity and the same ethnic descent, mothers and daughters approach the question of selfhood with different worldviews. Generational differences and exposure to the hegemonic mainstream culture in the diaspora are important determinants in the formation of female subjecthood. Mothers are deeply entrenched in ethnic sub-society, which is again immersed in old-world ideology of the country they come from.

The daughters, on the contrary, belong to the new 'American' generation. The two sets of women, therefore, perceive the question of female subordination and resistance to it with different perspectives. In the books the mother texts and the daughter texts offer two opposite versions. In the mothers' texts, however, 'silent' stories are embedded, stories which the daughters try to decode as these come their ways.

It needs to be noted that a sense of history informs both the works we are going to discuss. The Chinese immigrant characters are sometimes found to be very secretive about their past. The mothers' narratives are full of gaps and silences, disjunctions and, as the daughter in Kingston's book asserts, 'lies.' War and famines, feudal oppressions and sexual exploitations have muffled articulation. Amy Tan's novel recounts tales of horror in the lives of mothers which remained buried for a long time. Kingston's work is also set against the background of prejudicial immigration acts. The Immigration Act of 1924 was a major legislation designed to stop the Japanese immigration but also stopped Chinese wives from joining their husbands in the USA. (Mylan 145) Chinese wives trying to enter the country were detained at the Angel Island immigration Station. Maxine, the daughter in Kingston's novel says: "The Chinese I know . . . guard their real names with silence." (5) Maxine was often confused by the mysteries surrounding her mother's life. But Sheryl A. Mylan rightly says, "Although the worst of the deportation fear was over by the 1950s when Maxine was a girl, the fearful memories from earlier years surely must have remained strong in the tightly knit Chinese communities." (145)

Maxine Hong Kingston's *The Woman Warrior* tells a matrilineal story. At the centre of the narratives is the commanding figure of Brave Orchid, mother of the autobiographer Maxine. The "great power" of her voice tries to subjugate her daughter into filial submissions through a succession of talk-stories, maxims and legends. Her daughter, in "solid" American landscape, participates and suffers in her mother's stories, extends and renarrativises them according to her own worldview, thus really critiquing them.

In an interview Kingston wonders whether the dominating mother was very much usual in Chinese families:

> My father was a poet, and my aunts and mother could read, that was unusual, okay? You know, people ask me is brave Orchid truly that large in real life, or is that my poetic license. But in truth I calmed her down for the book. She is even larger than that. Sometimes I wonder, do I come from a normal family or do I come from a family that is *very irrational*? (Brownmiller 176; emphasis original)

Although the mother is foregrounded in the text and there is obvious evidence of her attempts to realize some kind of selfhood, she works within the larger patriarchal structure. Her concept of selfhood, as we shall see, is compromised with the greater need of community and must be in consonance with patriarchy. She enforces the legitimacy of the old culture and ultimately works towards erasure of female selfhood when it is in conflict with patriarchy. She is an accomplice in her husband's deliberate erasure of the memory of his sister—Maxine's No Name aunt—whose deviant behaviour challenged the normative concept of patrilineal descent. The daughter's narrative shows that she is strong only on her own turf—the old China—and her notions are so outdated and irrelevant in the diasporic space that her image of the woman warrior takes a beating. This is sufficiently evidenced in the story of her own sister Moon Orchid described in "At the Western Palace." Deserted by her husband, and prodded by Brave Orchid, Moon Orchid comes to the USA from China on a husband-reclaiming mission. Totally ignorant of the US laws, Brave Orchid advises Moon Orchid to claim certain privileges that first wives in China are entitled to. The actual meeting with the husband is disastrous as he refuses to have any relation with her and pushes her to the brink of erasure: "You became people in book I have read a long time ago." (154) Unable to cope with the stress and the shock, Moon Orchid went insane.

Maxine, with her life dotted with mother's talk-stories[1] which reiterate the discourse of the community and oblivion of the female subjectivity, struggles to find a voice of her own. Mary Field Belensky, in *Women's Way of Knowing*, reiterates that voice is "more than an academic shorthand for a person's point of view . . . it is a metaphor that can apply to many aspects of women's experience and development. . . . Women repeatedly used the metaphor of voice to depict their intellectual and ethical development . . . the developments of a sense of voice, mind, and self were intricately intertwined." (qtd. M. Marie Booth Foster 208) One of the central notions that obsesses Maxine is the struggle for voice as against silence which gains momentum in the last narrative "A Song for a Barbarian Reed Pipe" where she objects to her mother's act of cutting her frenum during her childhood—an act which literally muffles possibilities of speech and thus voice. She subconsciously associates this mutilation, this 'tampering with speech' (165) with the Chinese custom of footbinding which restricts movement. The mother's act thus assumes greater gender connotations. Maxine further connects the cutting of her tongue with ethnic reality in the USA, the mutilation affecting her performance. This is further associated with her lack of English proficiency. She accuses her mother for not teaching her English, the consequence of which stretches beyond the classroom:

> When I went to kindergarten and had to speak English for the first time, I became silent. A dumbness—a shame—still cracks my voice in two, even when I want to say "hello" casually, or ask an easy question in front of the check-out counter, or ask directions of a bus driver. (165)

Her silence was the 'thickest' during the first three years at the American school which worried her teachers. However, she discovered that other Chinese girls who were noisy at the Chinese school did not talk either, which made her come to the decision that "the silence had to do with being a Chinese girl" (166), thus connecting the silence ultimately to the Chinese cultural norms.

The struggle to fill silence with voice is seen not only in her personal life, in the context of her dialogic relationship with her mother, but also in the family history where silence often dominates. This is eloquently evident in the first narrative of the book where Maxine re-imagines her deviant aunt's story. The aunt was a 'gold mountain wife' whose husband left for America ('gold mountain') soon after their marriage, leaving her in a lonely, uncertain life. She conceived a child out of an extra-marital relationship. She did not name the father of the child. The villagers who were watching punished her and her family by invading their house at night, destroying their property and live-stock, and assaulting the aunt. This is a cautionary story to 'grow up on,' the aunt being a negative model for growing girls. She ends the story with a moral: "Now that you have started to menstruate, what happened to her could happen to you. Don't humiliate us. You wouldn't like to be forgotten as if you have never been born. The villagers are watchful." (5)

Adultery is a crime that disturbs the smooth partrilineal descent. In contrast to the American reality where Maxine was being brought up, such transgression of social norms was severely dealt with. As demanded by the Chinese community: "a family must be whole, faithfully keeping the descent line by having sons to feed the old and the dead, who in turn look after the family." (13) The aunt disturbed this law by conceiving an illegitimate child. Nobody sought to detect the male accomplice or punish him. But the female body on which the female deviance was inscribed must endure the social reprimand, and had ultimately to be destroyed. The aunt was forced by circumstances to commit suicide.

Maxine, as a Chinese American girl who wants to be 'American feminine' tries to figure out how "the invisible world the emigrants built around our childhoods fits in solid America." (5) As one belonging to a different time and space, as one struggling to emerge out of ghost ridden[2] ancestral history where female sexuality and selfhood was a taboo, she reads a new meaning into her aunt's life. In her aunt's deviance, she finds the relevance of her own struggle: "Unless I see her life branching into mine, she gives me no ancestral help." (8) Maxine considers the aunt as her 'forerunner,' as one, who left alone, "crossed boundaries not delineated in space." (8) Maxine perceives her to be "a lone romantic" who, caught in a slow life, "let dreams grow and fade." (8) "Fear at the enormities of the forbidden kept her desires delicate, wire and bone." (80) She is imagined to be appreciative of her own beauty and that of her lover. "For warm eyes or a soft voice or a slow walk—that's all—a few hairs, a line, a brightness, a sound, a pace, she gave up family." (8) She then shifts the possibility to her being raped by one in her village and threatened not to disclose his name. "Women in the old china did not choose. Some men had commanded her to lie with him and be his secret evil." (6) The aunt herself was silent. By imagining her story, Maxine tries to give her a voice. The act of devoting pages of paper to her is an act of writerly rehabilitation of the aunt which is relevant to her own struggle. Sidonie Smith in her article "Filiality and Woman's Autobiographical Storytelling" considers Maxine's "appropriation of the pen, that surrogate sword" to be an act of reporting of a crime. She asserts that Maxine publicly inscribes, not the story of the aunt only but of those she heard or experienced in the entire range of "her own childhood among ghosts." It becomes the reporting of the crime of a culture that would make nothing of her by colonizing her and, in so doing, steal her authority and her autobiography from her as her mother's legend would do." (68)

Brave Orchid, in the conventional sense, is a courageous woman, who resists the erasure of her own desire. She becomes a midwife after being trained at To Keung School of Midwifery. Sidonie Smith observes that in her daughter's text, Brave Orchid becomes a kind of "woman warrior": "both women leave the circle of the family to be educated for their mission and both return to serve their community, freeing it through many adventures from those forces that would destroy it. Both are fearless, successful, admired." (68)

The mother's story of confrontation with the Sitting Ghost at the school hostel is however, otherworldly, and runs counter to the western notion of medical science, as does her adventures as a doctor. Her narrative, full of irrational details, sets the westernised daughter quite apart. Maxine also questions her mother's professional skill and mentions that the degree she obtained in China is useless in the USA.

Although there is a simmering tension between the mother and the daughter, the daughter sometimes perceives flashes of affection from beneath the hard veneer. She does not agree with Maxine who wants to leave California to pursue her own interest but she nevertheless gives her permission. Her use of "Little Dog," a term of endearment not used for a long time, lifted a weight from her. A similar phrase of endearment "Meimei" (200) was used by Waverly Jong's mother Lindo Jong in Amy Tan's *The Joy Luck Club*, a term that considerably eased the mutual misunderstanding between the mother and daughter, a misunderstanding relating basically to the right cultural code. Waverly comments: "It seemed like the first time we had an almost normal conversation." (202) At the end of the meeting Waverly has a soft reconciliatory tone: "in the brief instant that I had peered over the barriers I could finally see what was really there: an old woman, a wok for her armor, a knitting needle for her sword, getting a little crabby as she waited patiently for her daughter to invite her in." (204) In Waverly's language, Lindo, a sort of woman warrior who weathered so many obstacles in China and America is now tamed, much domesticated, one who now is ready to listen to the daughter's voice. In Maxine's case too the mother is ready to give in to the daughter's point of view: "I've found some places in this country that are ghost-free. And I think I belong there. . . . Here I'm sick so often, I can barely work. I can't help it, Mama." (108) The mother responds, "Of course, you must go, Little Dog." (108)

The Joy Luck Club (1989) is Amy Tan's first novel. Like Kingston's book, it is also based on family narratives. "Four immigrant mothers, from mainland China, bewildered at the mainstream American culture, attempt to bring up their daughters according to their own ideology. Possessive love and fierce misunderstanding characterise their relationship. The novel constitutes sixteen interlocking stories told by seven of the eight women characters—four daughters and three mothers. The mother-daughter pairs are: Suyuan and Jing-mei Woo, An-mei Hsu and Rose Hsu Jordon, Lindo and Waverly Jong, and Ying-ying and Lena St. Clair.

The stories move back and forth between the USA and China. Marina Heung observes that the stories move both synchronically and diachronically, defeating "any effort to read it according to linear chronology alone." (612) Dispersed throughout the novel is a consciousness of disruptions that socio-historically affected the mothers. Fragments of the bizarre tales are revealed either through mother's recapitulations or through daughters' narratives.

In China An-mei's mother was a 'ghost'—unmentionable—to her family, as she became a rich merchant's concubine. An-mei was brought up by her grandmother Poppo. Her mother returned to Poppo's deathbed and she took her daughter back with her to Shanghai. An-mei was adopted in the family. She learnt there that her mother was raped and forced into concubinage. Ying-ying, another mother, had a very unhappy marriage. When she conceived, her husband left her for another woman. She decided to undergo an abortion. Lindo Jong accepted an unhappy marriage only because she could not refuse to obey her filial duty. Her husband was discovered to be frigid. Later, however, she came out of the marriage using a ruse which allowed her not to be disobedient either to her own parents or her mother-in-law. The fourth mother Suyuan Woo was a war victim. She had to flee Kweilin to escape Japanese invasion of the town. On her way she became seriously ill and had to abandon her two baby girls on the road. Even after her emigration to the USA, she continued to search for her lost babies through correspondence with her friends.

All of them escaped the war-ravaged, overtly patriarchal China. They left their other lives in China traces of which, however, they have to carry in their immigrant lives. Their daughters, born and brought up in America, look at distant lives of their mothers as exotic, fairytale-like. But on closer analysis, they come nearer to understanding their mothers and their country of origin.

In "Lost Lives of Women" Amy Tan speaks of a family photograph that inspires her to write of her 'foremothers':

> When I first saw this photo as a child, I thought it was exotic and remote, of a far-away time and place, with people who had no connection to my American life. Look at their bound feet! Look at that funny lady with plucked forehead. The solemn little girl was in fact, my mother. And leaning against the rock is my grandmother, Jing-mei. . . . This is also a picture I see when I write. These are the secrets I was supposed to keep. These are the women who never let me forget why stories need to be told. (qtd. Foster 209)

The 'secret' lives of the mother characters in *The Joy Luck Club* bear significance to Tan's concern expressed in the extract. Theirs are the stories of war, disaster, exploitation—stories lying buried in memories characterised by pain and suffering. This the daughters only partially understand in the beginning but later realise more properly.

Mothers never really understand their "American" daughters. This is mainly because they cannot decode the American cultural norms, or even if they understand, they cannot appreciate these. Lindo Jong remarks that she wanted her children "to have the best combination: American circumstances and the Chinese character. How could I know these things do not mix?" (289) This is said in the context of her daughter Waverly's habit of "talking back" which however is not to accept anything blindly. In Lindo's worldview, daughters are to be obedient and should not argue. She herself obeyed her parents when married off to a frigid boy. As one of the mothers significantly points out, a girl even though she springs from her mother like a 'slippery fish,' swims away from her ever since. Waverly is visualised by her mother as essentially American: "Only her skin and hair are Chinese. Inside—she is all American-made."

Lindo, as an immigrant, has learnt the use of two faces—'Chinese face' and 'American face'—and she alternates between these two cultural appearances superficially to subvert any attempt to befool her. She realises that immigration has changed her culturally. From her recent Chinese trip, she understood that she was not "hundred percent Chinese" to the Chinese of China. Obviously, she is not hundred percent 'American' as is evident in her cultural behaviour pattern.

The daughters' responses to their mothers' behaviour range from simple boredom to indignation. They resent their mothers' attempt to control their lives. Waverly Jong reacts angrily to her mother's attempt to appropriate the fame she wins as a young chess player. Jing-mei is deeply disturbed when her mother experiments to make her a child prodigy. Mothers and daughters often do not understand each other. Jing-mei, for instance, does not understand her mother's explanation of the difference between the Chinese mah jong game and the Jewish one. She says: "These kinds of explanations made me feel my mother and I spoke two different languages which we did. I talked to her in English, she answered back in Chinese." (23) When Jing-mei is not sure what and how to tell her half-sisters in China about her mother, Auntie An-mei is scandalised, and says: "Your mother is in your bones." (31) Jing-mei's explanation is worth noting:

> They are frightened. In me they see their own daughters, just as ignorant, just as unmindful of all the truths and hopes they have brought to America. They see daughters who grow impatient when their mothers talk in Chinese, who think they are stupid when they explain things in fractured English. . . . They see daughters who will bear grandchildren born without any connecting hope passed from generation to generation. (31)

Despite this insight into the mother's psychology, she had earlier fiercely resisted her mother's attempt to transform her: I won't be what I'm not," (144) and more severely: "I wasn't her slave. This wasn't China." (152) But when she referred to her two half-sisters abandoned in China "I wish I were dead! Like them," the mother was stunned. She was like "a small brown leaf, thin, brittle, lifeless." (153)

The crisis was resolved later because of the mother's gesture. On her thirtieth birthday she was offered the piano she used to play in her childhood. It was considered by the daughter a sign of forgiveness. She was relieved of a tremendous burden. Later on, her mother presented her a jade pendant with the words that convey her long-cherished desire for a connection: "For a long time, I wanted to give you the necklace. See, I wore this on my skin, so when you put it on your skin, then you know my meaning. This is your life's importance." (235)

The desire for 'connection' is perhaps best conveyed by Jing-mei's visit to China in 1987 to meet her mother's abandoned daughters who were saved by a poor couple during the war. In Kingston's *The Woman Warrior* Maxine was not initially very willing to visit China, but later expressed her desire to go there to discover for herself the reality. Jing-mei's actual visit to the Communist China, however, suggests the possibility of a connection that transcends geographical boundary and generational gap. When she met her twin sisters, all of them were overwhelmed with joy. Standing on her ancestral soil and meeting the 'traces' of her mother's past, she realises how true her mother, now dead, was when she had said, "You don't even know little percent of me!" (15) The snapshot of the polaroid camera showed: "Together we look like our mother. Her same eyes, her same mouth, open in surprise to see, at last her long cherished wish." (332) Ultimately she was able to realise her connection with her mother and the country of her descent: "And now I also see what part of me is Chinese. . . . It is my family. It is in our blood." (331)

Both Kingston and Tan, as our discussion of *The Woman Warrior* and *The Joy Luck Club* shows, explore matrilineage in the Chinese immigrant society in the USA. Working with an acute sense of patriarchal dominance in old China and its remnants in the diaspora, both the authors have explored the problematics of transcultural and inter-generational dynamics. The mother-daughter dyad provides very complex perspectives of the ethnic community in the diasporic space. Walter Shear observes, "the ability of both Kingston and Tan to render the experience of a culture through vividly dramatic individual narratives provides a sound basis for what seems to be a developing tradition of Chinese-American women's writing." (199)

Notes

1. Susan Brownmiller, after a talk with Kingston, informs us that "talk-story" is actually a Hawaiian pidgin phrase. The phrase de-

scribes "the passing down of tales from the old generation to the young" (Brownmiller 178). In Chinese American women writers, 'talk-stories' were a source of empowerment for them.

2. The word 'ghost' recurs in both Kingston and Tan. It may literally refer to dead persons, but both the writers, particularly Kingston, have used the word ambivalently. According to a character (An-mei Hsu) in *The Joy Luck Club*, it "was anything we were forbidden to talk about." (33) Brave Orchid, the mother character in *The Woman Warrior*, refers to non-Chinese people as 'ghosts.' Susan Brownmiller observes that Kingston uses the English word "to represent both the spirit demons that haunt her Chinese ancestors and the paleface Americans that her uprooted family must cope with in California." (177-78) Sheril A. Mylan asserts that for Maxine in *The Woman Warrior* "the real ghosts are Chinese, those shadowy, inexplicable presences that haunt her life." (146) Used from Chinese American perspectives, the word is thus invested with several meanings.

Works Cited

Brown-Guillory, Elizabeth, ed. *Women of Color: Mother Daughter Relationships in 20th-Century Literature*. Austin: University of Texas Press, 1996.

Brownmiller, Susan. "Susan Brownmiller Talks with Maxine Hong Kingston, Author of *The Woman Warrior*." Ed. Sau-ling Cynthia Wong. *The Woman Warrior: A Casebook*. New York: OUP, 1999. 73-179.

Foster, M. Marie Booth. "Voice, Mind, Self: Mother-Daughter Relationships in Amy Tan's *The Joy Luck Club* and *The Kitchen God's Wife*. Included in Brown-Guillory. 208-27.

Heung, Marina. "Daughter-text/Mother-text: Matrilineage in Amy Tan's *Joy Luck Club*." *Feminist Studies*. 19.3. Fall 1993. 597-616.

Kingston, Maxine Hong. *The Woman Warrior*. New York: Random House, 1989.

Mylan, Sheryl A. "The Mother as Other: Orientation in Maxine Hong Kingston's *The Woman Warrior*." In Brown-Guillory. 132-52.

Schell, Orville. Rev. of *The Joy Luck Club* by Amy Tan. *New York Times*, 19 March, 1989: VII, 3: 1, 28.

Shear, Walter "Generational Differences and the Diaspora in *The Joy Luck Club*." *Critique*. XXXIV.3 (Spring) 1993, 193-99.

Smith, Sidonie. "Filiality and Women's Autobiographical Story telling." Ed. Sau-ling Cynthia Wong. *The Woman Warrior: A Case Book*. New York: OUP, 1999. 57-83.

Tan, Amy . *The Joy Luck Club*. New York: Ivy Books, 1989.

Women of the South Asian Diaspora: Chitra Banerjee Divakaruni's *Arranged Marriage* and Ginu Kamani's *Junglee Girl*

REBECCA HAQUE
University of Dhaka, Bangladesh

The worldwide dispersion of South Asian peoples from countries such as India, Sri Lanka, Nepal, Pakistan, and Bangladesh is now a sociologically acknowledged phenomenon known as the South Asian Diaspora. Multiple migrations—from South Asia to Europe, and from Africa to Europe and the United States—and multiculturalism are essential facts of dispersion of such magnitude and dimension.

Voices of the women of the South Asian Diaspora, hitherto silenced by the reconfiguration of patriarchal systems in the new land, are heard loud and clear in the 1990s. Two such voices are those of Chitra Banerjee Divakaruni and Ginu Kamani. Their collection of short stories *Arranged Marriage* (1995) and *Junglee Girl* (1995) provide a platform not only for students of literature, but also for anthropologists and ethnographers who can use the narratives and the narrative voice as the basis for the study of life as it really exists. All the stories are vividly narrated and palpitate with the rhythm of fresh lived experience.

Young, avant-garde, provocative, and born in India, both Divakaruni and Kamani live in the United States and use English as their first language. This paper will focus on the way each writer develops brief succinct images of women caught between the old world and the new world values, how women cope with cross-cultural sexual relationships, and how women ultimately try to achieve self-esteem and autonomy denied to them within their own somewhat insular and bigoted community. The attempt to find and fuse a viable self-image within the mainstream United States culture is a crucial factor in the short stories.

Arranged Marriage contains eleven stories out of which I am selecting five which deal with women who have traveled to the United States either to live as the spouses of men already living there or as students flying off from India to study in the various American colleges and universities. Most of these stories are first-person narratives and this is what gives them the quality of immediacy and interaction with the reader; we are bound to become involved in the lives of these women. The prose in Divakaruni's prize-winning volume is lucid and penetrating and it takes us effortlessly into the heart of the matter.

"Clothes" is the story of one arranged marriage, between Mita and Somesh Sen who live in California and owns a 7-Eleven stores there. It opens on a magical note: "The water of the women's lake laps against my breasts, cool, calming. I can feel it beginning to wash the hot nervousness away from my body. . . . I close my eyes and smell the sweet brown odor of the *ritha* pulp my friends Deepali and Radha are working into my hair so it will glisten with little lights this evening. They scrub with more vigor than usual and wash it out more carefully, because today is a special day. It is the day of my bride-viewing." (17) Mita dreams of a handsome prince who will take her to his kingdom beyond the seven seas, and her father shows her on the globe where California is situated exactly. Back in the States, living in one cramped apartment with her in-laws, Somesh and Mita secretly dream of living the American dream once Somesh has made enough money to finish paying the loan on his shop and strike out on his own and be totally independent. In the meantime, Mita maintains the status quo and remains the meek, submissive daughter-in-law. But

> Late at night I stand in front of our bedroom mirror trying on the clothes Somesh has bought for me and smuggled in past his parents. I model each one for him . . . just like the models on TV, while he whispers applause. I am breathless with suppressed laughter (Father and mother Sen must not hear) and my cheeks are hot with the delicious excitement of conspiracy. . . . I'm wearing a

> pair of jeans now, marvelling at the curves of my hips and thighs, which have always been hidden under the flowing lines of my saris. I love the color, the same pale blue as the *nayantara* flowers that grow in my parents' garden. The solid comforting weight. The jeans come with a close-fitting T-shirt which outlines my breasts. . . . The T-shirt is sunrise-orange—the color, I decide, of joy, of my new American life. (24-25)

Mita's joy and her honeymoon come to an abrupt end, however, when one night Somesh is killed at his store by a gunman in an act of robbery and random violence. We then see the other Asian women dress Mita all in white and hear the sound of glass bangles shattering as Mita is quietly and absolutely transformed from a glowing bride into a mourning widow, now forever the property of her in-laws who will now go back to India. But Somesh had wanted Mita to go to college, choose a career and this makes Mita rebel against tradition and make her own choice as to her future path in life; she takes her fate into her own hands:

> I know I cannot go back. I don't know yet how I'll manage, here in this new, dangerous land. I only know I must. Because all over India, at this very moment, widows in white saris are bowing their veiled heads, serving tea to in-laws. Doves with cut-off wings. . . . I straighten my shoulders and stand taller, take a deep breath. . . . I tilt my chin, readying myself for the arguments of the coming weeks, the remonstrations. In the mirror a woman holds my gaze, her eyes apprehensive yet steady. She wears a blouse and skirt the color of almonds. (33)

The conclusion of "The Ultrasound" is not as definitive or as positive as the conclusion of "Clothes." Although it defies closure, it leaves us nevertheless with a sense of unease as to the ultimate fate of Arundhati. The story is narrated by Anju and she traces the different routes that her and Runu's life take as they grow up together in Calcutta. Both without fathers, but with hard-working, struggling mothers, their lives take different courses because Anju's father had left his wife money and property in the form of a bookstore in a prime College Street location, whereas Runu's father, dying after a long illness had left only debts and

> Protima-auntie, like most genteel Bengali widows, was always struggling to make ends meet. Runu never had new dresses and shoes like me, or large plush teddy bears or wind-up dolls from America that could dance and say hello. Or, later, silk saris or gold earrings with matching bracelets for the birthdays. But she wouldn't let me give her any of my things. . . . Somehow she never did as well academically either, though I believed she was quite as intelligent as I was. Encouraged by my mother to be competitive, I went on to win spelling bees and debate contests, and later in college to grapple with Chaucer and Thomas Hardy and W.B. Yeats in my English Honors classes. I browsed through our bookstore and the USIS library, reading Hemingway and Kerouac and Willa Cather and longing to visit the places they wrote of. Runu took up Home Science, which everyone admitted was the major that the dullest girls chose. She seemed to enjoy it, though. . . . So maybe it's fitting that Prajapati, the winged and capricious god of marriage, set us down in such different places—me here in San Jose with Sunil, and her in provincial Burdwan, the eldest daughter-in-law of a large, traditional brahmin family. (206-7)

Anju keeps up with Runu through long-distance phone calls to her own mother and sometimes to Runu herself at her place in Burdwan, and it seems like an act of mercy and an act of god certainly when both become pregnant at the same time. They eagerly await the results of their respective amniocentesis tests, but when it is revealed that Runu's fetus is female her husband and her in-laws want her to go for an abortion and try later for a male child. Naturally, Runu runs away from home, and Anju, aghast at the criminal form of pre-natal female infanticide being perpetrated on innocent victims vows to try to bring Runu to America at all costs. She ends: "Tomorrow I'll ask Sunil about sponsoring Runu, maybe getting her a student visa. I know he'll fight it at first, give me a hundred reasons why we can't do it. Why we shouldn't. But I'll fight back. Already I am learning how. I'll use what I have to—my pregnancy, even. It's worth it—for Runu and, yes, myself. I'll get my way. I know I will, I say to myself, and smiling, I drift into sleep." (230) The reader, however cannot retreat safely or securely into this somnolent daze with Anju, because we know, as Divakaruni knows, that visas and immigration take time and money and patience and Runu back in Calcutta has none of these things at her disposal. Who will take care of her in the meantime? What will become of her? Will Anju be able to save her? We can only hope and pray.

The protagonist-narrator of "The Word Love" has her own deep problems with her widowed mother back in Calcutta. The nameless protagonist, a Ph.D. student at Berkeley, has fallen in love with an American and is living with him, but she loves her mother fiercely too and is terrified of her finding out that she is living in sin and living for love, for her mother would never understand, would never forgive. To forestall any event of her mother ever finding out she has given strict injunctions to her lover never to answer the phone.

> 'It isn't you,' you'd said, gathering up the books guiltily, smoothing the covers. Holding them tight against you. 'I'd have the same problems no matter who it was.' You tried to tell him about your mother, how she'd seen her husband's face for the first time at her wedding. How, when he died (you were two years old then), she had taken off her jewelry and put on widow's white and dedicated the rest of her life to the business of bringing you up. We only have each other, she often told you. 'She lives in a different world. Can't you see that? She's never traveled more than a hundred miles from the village where she was born; she's never touched cigarettes or alcohol; even though she lives in Calcutta, she's never watched a movie. . . . I love her, Rex.' (58)

The inevitable happens nevertheless, the phone is one day answered by Rex—and the relationship between mother and daughter is torn asunder. The mother wilfully changes her phone number and moves to a new location, and all of the daughter's letters are returned to her unopened, address unknown. The mother is righteous in her anger and cruelly disowns the daughter for her act of sacrifice. The daughter, on the other hand, cannot accept this separation, this yawning gulf, this denunciation and her guilt in turn destroys her relationship with Rex. But she does not give up altogether. She vows to make a new life for herself and to make it on her own: "you will pack your belongings. A few clothes, some music, a favorite book, . . . And a word comes to you out of the opening sky. The word love. You see that you had never understood it before. It is like rain, and when you lift your face to it, like rain it washes away inessentials, leaving you hollow, clean, ready to begin." (71)

Divakaruni makes us realize that all human relationships are in fact a gamble, a throw of the dice, a matter of chance and destiny. Arranged marriages are no more or less so than the ones made out of love and choice. All marriages, it is said, are made in heaven, but we cannot begin to realize what powerful urges and inchoate emotions makes the wife in "The Disappearance" turn her back upon her own arranged marriage and quietly disappear in the urban jungles of the cities of America into a self-made exile. She even leaves her son behind and takes only her wedding jewelry, only the pieces given to her by her own parents. It is a complete renunciation of her alliance with her husband and total disavowal of her parenthood. Was she so unhappy, trapped in a loveless marriage? or was she mentally unstable? We never find out, for she is never found, even though her husband puts up a reward of $100,000 for any information leading to her whereabouts. The man's widowed mother shuts up her small flat back in India and is delighted to come and keep house for her son and grandson in the new country:

> As the year went on, the husband stopped thinking as much about the wife. It wasn't that he loved her any less, or that the shock of her disappearance was less acute. It was just that it wasn't on his mind all the time. There would be stretches of time—when he was on the phone with an important client, or when he was watching after-dinner TV or driving his son to kiddie gym class—when he would forget that his wife was gone, that he had had a wife at all. And even when he remembered that he had forgotten, he would experience only a slight twinge, similar to what he felt in his teeth when he drank something too cold too fast. The boy, too, didn't ask as often about his mother. He was sleeping through the nights again, he had put on a few pounds (because he was finally being fed right, said the grandmother), and he had started calling her 'Ma,' just like his father did. (175)

A marriage can fall apart for many reasons, tangible like marital infidelity or intangible like the oft-quoted "irreconcilable differences" of American divorce cases. Divakaruni presents us with one case where the cause of the break-up is a visitor from India. In "Doors," Preeti, living in the United States since the age of twelve marries Deepak, a man straight out of India, and receives a giant culture shock when his friend Raj comes to Berkeley to stay with them while he does his Master's there. The men carry the buddy-buddy thing too far and encroach upon Preeti's privacy. Raj especially is a lout and a boor as well as a bore, but Deepak is delighted to have him in the house and relive their schooldays and look at endless videos of Kishore Kumar songs. Much to Preeti's chagrin, her private space is violated one day when her bedroom door is thrown open by Raj who walks in to share a piece of good news. Like Deepak, Raj too is from the old country where there is little use for closed doors and privacy in a large traditional family. Raj is simply bewildered by Preeti's extreme reaction and decides to leave her house. Simultaneously, Preeti, too decides to leave her marriage:

> Preeti would shut the study door before settling down with her Ph.D. dissertation. When in the garden, she would make sure the gate was securely fastened as she weeded. If there had been a door to the kitchen, she would have closed it as she cooked. Deepak was puzzled by all this door shutting. He had grown up in a large family, and although they had been affluent enough to possess three bedrooms . . . they had never observed boundaries. They had constantly spilled into each other's rooms, doors always left open for chance remarks and jokes. He asked Preeti about it one night just before bed. . . . She wasn't able to give him an answer, 'I don't know,' she said, her brow wrinkled. . . . 'I guess I am just a private person. It's not like I am shutting you out. 'I've just always done it this way. Maybe it has something to do with being an only child.' Her eyes searched his face unhappily. 'I know it's not what you are used to. Does it bother you?' She seemed so troubled that Deepak felt a pang of guilt 'No, no, I don't care, not at all,' he rushed to say. . . . And really, he didn't mind, even though he didn't quite understand. People were different. He knew that. And he was more than ready to accept the unique needs of this exotic creature—In-

> dian and yet not Indian—who had by some mysterious fortune become his wife. So things went on smoothly—until Raj descended on them. (188-89)

Ginu Kamani's prose is no less trenchant and penetrating than Divakaruni's. In *Junglee Girl*, Kamani has two stories, one at the beginning and one at the end, which are about women of the South Asian Diaspora. The word "junglee" in Kamani's title refers to the sense of wildness that comes with freedom, sexual as well as social. The protagonists of Kamani's stories are young, good-looking, well-educated second-generation Indians living in the West. They are confident about themselves, their position, their identity and their sexuality. The stories are optimistic and buoyant and Kamani's prose vividly renders this buoyancy transferable to the reader as well.

"Ciphers" is the enigmatic title of the first story. It refers to the identity of the protagonist herself which is an enigma to the Gujarati woman with whom she happens to be sharing a berth on a train while travelling in India. With her hair cut short, and in a knee-length dress, but with her dark complexion, the Gujarati woman finds it very difficult to place the protagonist. The story slowly weaves back and forth between the attempts of the Gujarati woman to pin the protagonist down as an identifiable ethnic entity—Bengali, Maharashtrian, Punjabi, Moslem from Delhi, or a Christian from Goa—and the protagonist's own definition of herself as "other, oblique" in this society where being just Indian had no meaning. Definition meant belonging to a certain class or ethnic group within the melting pot of races and she wonders if she would have been more recognizable and definable in a sari or a *shalwar kameez*? In the United States she is no more definable and her Indianness disappears in her chameleon like ability to be taken for any race, from Brazilian to Mexican. Towards the end of the story, the protagonist asserts that what matters is not where she comes from but the fact that she is different because she has sexual power and she is definitely a sexual being in opposition to the Gujarati woman who is just a mother with her *palloo* over her head. At this point in the story the true meaning of the title is forced into our awareness as we realize that the Gujarati woman is as much a "Cipher" to the protagonist as she is to her, for here in a sudden move the Gujarati woman removes her *palloo* and uncoils her dark coiling hair and the protagonist is shocked at the truly strikingly sensual and sexual beauty of the woman. In a lyrical conclusion the protagonist achieves a kind of epiphany as she feels a oneness with all Indian women and literally feels a tingling in her groin and at the roots of her hair as in her imagination she sees herself being transformed with long hair which so bewitchingly frames and captures the essence of the Indian woman.

The penultimate story in Kamani's collection is a sharp diatribe against the Indian expatriate community where the elders take it upon themselves to make the lives of their Americanized daughters miserable by trying to trap them into arranged marriages with whosoever is considered suitable and is available. In "Just Between Indians," eighteen-year old Daya has her vacation spoiled as her parents and friends zoom in on her as the target for a favorable match between Ranjan, the older brother of Sahil. But Daya rebels against any such occurrence not only verbally but also insidiously by undermining the rules of her patriarchal upbringing—she quietly and secretly has sex with Sahil one night before she leaves the house. The conclusion of the story is a glorious celebration of Daya's freedom and her ability to metamorphose into a beautiful woman for any man who looks at her. This ability comes, as Kamani points out, from her Indian, South Asian origins, where so many races and bloodlines mingle and blend to give her a unique quality of indefinable mystery.

Works Cited

Divakaruni, Chitra Banerjee. *Arranged Marriage: Stories*. New York: Anchor Books, 1995.

Kamani, Ginu. *Junglee Girl*. San Francisco: aunt lute books, 1995.

A Comparative Study of the *Black Boy* and *AthavaninchePakshi*

R.G. KULKARNI
Sangli

In "Hymn to Liberty" Shelley describes how exploitation, injustice, and oppression have been universal phenomena through all times. The tyrants, the religious authorities, the kings, the rich have exploited and oppressed the people from time to time. In other words, exploitation of the people in one form or another has occurred throughout the history of mankind. The same phenomenon has recurred in the form of colour distinction in America, namely of the blacks by the whites and of the untouchables by the upper classes in India. It is with this viewpoint I propose to undertake a comparative study of Richard Wright's autobiography, *Black Boy* and Marathi Dalit writer Pralhad Sonkamble's autobiography, *Athavaninche Pakshi.* I would like to undertake the proposed study in the perspective of the thematics of social awareness, class consciousness, racial prejudices, and caste discrimination.

Black Boy treats the issue of apartheid and arouses not only pity for the boy but also horror and admiration for his courageous and unyielding spirit. It is the plight of a boy who has undergone humiliation, horror and mental tortures at their worst. It is a presentation of facts. It is an attempt to communicate to the white world, what whites have done to the Negroes. It is a mirror of white deeds.

Wright did not get sufficient meals to feed himself. He says, "I had to work because I had to eat." (213) His primary object was to claim two meals a day. He spends all his energy towards this end. He accepts petty small jobs at several places. We see him as a washer of eyeglasses in the optical company, as a dishwasher in a hotel, as an errand boy, and as a helper in a drug-store. Everywhere he experiences humiliation because he is a brand Negro in his place. The whites restrict his freedom, his ambition and treat him as a subordinate.

Athavaninche Pakshi is a story of a boy from mahar caste who is an orphan from his early childhood, uprooted on both levels, the familial and the social. The boy's life drifts without promise and direction. The journey of his life-time from primary education to college is neither comfortable nor smooth. It is full of hardships and bitter experiences. Sonkamble tells us about his humiliating experiences while he is unable to satisfy the basic needs for drinking water and food. Being a social outcast he has to drink water at a place which is meant for cattle only. The food that he gets is nothing but stale and unhygienic pieces of bread. In order to meet the expenses and satisfy his hunger he has to engage himself in a number of lowest types of manual labour from selling cattle bones to collecting firewood and cattle dung. All this is done by this poor and miserable boy without any grudge and complaint. However, Sonkamble's monotonous and laborious days are made somewhat hopeful and comfortable by the encouragement he receives from sympathetic teachers like Vinu Guruji and Dr. Wankhede. But nobody sympathises with Wright whole-heartedly. "There is not a single broad minded, open-hearted white person in [*Black Boy*]." (Buttler 68) Thus both the writers begin with the search for identity, for the painful torturous experience during the process. Both record the moment of final fulfilment, one becomes a writer (Wright) and the other becomes a lecturer (Sonkamble).

After going through the brief resume of development of their personalities, we are bound to discover some points of similarities and differences between the two autobiographies. The experience of Richard Wright and Pralhad Sonkamble are the representations of the downtrodden community. Both share the experiences of exploitation and humiliation. The Negroes and the Dalits are the sufferers. In India, the uppercastes have been responsible for the miserable and wretched condition of the Dalits. Similarly the whites have been responsible for the harassment and torture of the Negroes. The colour of the skin is a deciding factor in their subjugation. Wright walks day in and day out in search of a job and everywhere he is unwanted. The whites are not prepared to welcome him, because they do not like the 'look' in his eyes. In a house he milks a cow, he feeds chickens, he gathers vegetables, he serves breakfast, but the white man gets angry with him . At the breakfast table he shouts, "What in hell are you glaring at me for, you Niger bastard?" (164) Consequently he has to lose the job. In another incident he refers to his experience in the cloth shop. Wright watches the brutality with growing hate. The boss looks at him and tries to avoid his eye. The son of the boss corners him and says, "I don't like your looks, nigger. Now, get!" (201) He remains an unwanted and unloved member of the society. According to Wright, there is a plot, a conspiracy against the Negroes. It has been worked out with utmost skill. The Negro workers are denied the opportunities of training and promotions. Their services are not counted. Not only that but the Negroes are not even considered as human beings. When Wright looks at a white naked prostitute, he says, "It was presumed that the black boy took their nakedness for granted that it startled us no more than a blue vase or a red rug. Our presence awoke in them no sense of shame whatever, for we blacks were not considered human anyway." (221) Ignorance is thrust upon them and therefore *Black Boy* is an outcry of the entire Negro community.

In respect of Sonkamble, the inhuman treatment reaches its climax when we read about the account of his laborious and extremely tiresome jobs such as looking after the cattle, collecting their dung, and fetching the rough grass from far away places for them. The most repulsive part of it is that he is given only the left over crumbs of food, which he has to swallow at a place where children defecate. Not only that but he has to accept another such job which is to collect human excrement in his own hands. Although he felt extremely depressed, he could do nothing but clean his hands by rubbing them against the soil. The next incident shows how the very sight of an untouchable is supposed to be ominous. He is reproached harshly when he comes face to face with the upper caste girl who is to set off for the first time from her home to her husband's home. He is strictly ordered not to show his face on such sacred occasions. On another occasion he is asked to drag the dead body of a dog, but is denied in return the scanty piece of bread promised to him by the householder. On the other hand, he is taken to task for demanding something more than his yearly allotted share for the duty. All these events and incidents indicate the shameful burden of inhuman torture and humiliation from which the writer suffered.

Both Wright and Sonkamble are the victims of the privileged societies. The problem of hunger is common to both. Both are denied adequate food to live on. But they quench their hunger through water. A reader of world literatures can find this experience as the universal problem of hunger associating with the remedy of drinking water. As in *Black Boy*, Wright says "I learned a method of drinking water that made me feel full temporarily whether I had desire for water or not, I put my mouth under a faucet and turn the water on full force and let the stream cascade into my stomach until it was tight. Sometimes my stomach ached, but I felt full for a moment." (114) The same experience we find with Sonkamble in *Athavaninche Pakshi*, when he says, "As I went to well near the house of Deshmukh, I observed a few women drawing up water from the well. I appealed to them for water and one of them who took pity on me, poured it in my hands. I drank the water with hollowing my palms. Thus it was with water and not with bread that I filled my stomach to the full." (66-67)

Black Boy is a portrait of hunger and starvation. Each night Wright sees hunger standing at his bedside, staring at him. Later at the foster home, when he has to cut the lawn by pulling up the grass in his hands, he is too weak to pull the grass. Uncle Hoskin is his only support during the miserable days. But he is killed by the whites and the ordeal of hunger remains a big question mark before him. Then they go to Granny's house. She cannot afford the sumptuous breakfast. They rarely have meat. He does not look for delicious meals. What he is used to get at breakfast is only mush and gravy made from flour and lard and for hours afterwards he belches it up into his mouth. He cannot think of preferences referring to meals, but the poverty makes him greedy and so the desire to eat more is dominant in him. He has compared himself to an average size dog. This is an eye opening account for the readers. A feel of self-esteem, however, is never sacrificed in both writers. For example, in the playground the playmates ask Wright whether he would share the food with them. His response to them is politely negative, even though he is starving. Like Wright, Sonkamble rejects the food served to him in the plate of a leper, though he is on the point of starvation. He shows signs of morality imbibed in him.

Sonkamble has to face the problem of survival in the form of hunger. He narrates an incident how he sees a dog carrying a piece of meat in his mouth and how he tries hard to snatch that piece of meat. In his efforts to snatch it away he gets wounded severely after the dog bites him with his sharp teeth. What can be more ironical and agonizing than the fact that a human being has to snatch a piece of meat from an animal to satisfy his hunger?

The problem of hunger faced by Wright and Sonkamble indicates how the downtrodden were no better off than animals. Both the autobiographies reveal how the basic need of human beings is on the level of the beast or animal who has to search for food. Both these writers have to give up human emotions and feelings of self-respect and shame. They have to wander like homeless animals to get their food.

While there are some common points in the lives of Wright and Sonkamble, the mental makeup and consequently their attitudes are radically different. While Sonkamble has gone through the beastly and inhuman treatment with the attitude of compromise and resignation, Wright is an angry young man. He is rebellious against the whites as well as his own community. Brignano observes, "*Black Boy* reveals Wright's ambivalence towards Negroes in general, perhaps partially because of their passivity. With obvious hatred he condemns poor Negroes." (11) His autobiography has an additional dimension namely his defiant attitude towards religion. To him, "The Bible stories seemed slow and meaningless when compared to the bloody thunder of pulp narrative." (171) Although Sonkamble cannot be described as a wholehearted theist, he possesses a religious bent of mind. Silent and passive suffering is the keynote of Sonkamble's autobiography and indignant outburst of passion is the keynote of Wright's autobiography. In other words the attitude of philosophic resignation characterises *Athavaninche Pakshi* while the language of protest, confrontation and rebellion characterises *Black Boy*. As a result, there is a defiant and challenging tone in Wright's autobiography while that of Sonkamble is mild and restrained.

Both the autobiographies have echoed the sensitive picture of the suffering of the oppressed. However, both the writers seem to be self-complacent because neither of them has taken any concrete steps to improve the lot of their own communities. Within their limitations they have succeeded in projecting the suffering on the subjective level as well as at the level of community. Irrespective of similarities and variations, both the writers have focused the extreme anguish through which the oppressed classes have emerged. Both the writers depict pain, pangs, ridicule, criticism, and conflict in their personal life.

The two autobiographies represent different cultures. Poverty is the main drive behind their hidden impulses. Exploitation of the weaker is always the policy of the haves. Both the writers belong to have-nots. They try their best to overcome the cycle of exploitation and within their limits they try to rebel against their establishments. Have they succeeded? The answer to this question will always be with the readers.

Works Cited

Brignano, R.C. *Richard Wright.* University of Pittsburg, 1970.

Buttler, Robert J., ed. *Critical Responses to Richard Wright.* Connecticut: Greenwood Press, 1995.

Sonkamble, P.I. *Athavaninche Pakshi.* Aurangabad: Chetna, 1983.

Wright, Richard. *Black Boy, A Record of Childhood and Youth.* New York: Harper and Row, 1945.

Race and Gender in the Works of Claude McKay and Bharathidasan

S.S. KUMAR
Presidency College, Chennai

The twilight of the twentieth century threw more light on the centenary celebrations of Claude McKay (1891-1964), the Jamaican troubadour wanderer of the Harlem Renaissance and Bharathidasan (1891-1964), the revolutionary poet of the Tamil Renaissance. This paper aims at comparing a few general trends in gender representation in the Harlem and the Tamil Renaissances focusing more on remedies than illustrations from the individual poets.

Harlem, a congested section of New York, became the queen of black belts in America when World War I brought great waves of Southern blacks to industrial centres. Black writers, singers, and artists also gathered there and generated a significant resurgence in the 1920s known as the Harlem Renaissance. McKay is a major poet of Harlem since he fits well into Arthur P. Davis's definition of a major black writer: "One whose work deals largely with black experience, measures upto appropriate aesthetic standards and influences to some extent his contemporaries and/or those who come after him." (xiv)

In Tamilnadu, India, the founding of the Madurai Tamil Sangam (Academy) by Pandit Durai Thevar in 1901 may be taken as the beginning of the Tamil Renaissance. Bharathiyar and his disciple Bharathidasan are taken here as the representatives of revival in the field of Tamil poetry. Bharathidasan who fits well into the definition of a major black poet if "Tamil" is substituted for "black," is a pole star in the Tamil firmament.

Bharathidasan's Puducheri (Pondicherry) and McKay's Jamaica were the colonies of France and England respectively.

Kailasapathi observes that "a general pattern exists wherever European culture came to dominate through conquest and colonial rule some less 'advanced society'." (10-11)

The two-race theory in America and the Varnasrama concept in India have certain common elements: servility, segregation in public places, and untouchability. Shaped by similar sociocultural global events, McKay and Bharathidasan emerged as the leading poets of the respective Renaissances in their native lands. In the Tamil resurgence, Tamil evolved as a symbol of ethnic and cultural identity, whereas in Harlem, more importance was given to racial identity.

The feminist struggle in the societies under study may be summarized under the following categories: liberal feminism in which women demand equality, radical feminism in which women reject the male symbolic order, and rejection of dichotomy in which the dichotomy between the masculine and the feminine is rejected which challenges the very notion of identity. (Moi 12) Second generation feminism "challenges the gender bias in language, law and philosophy" and argues that women "should not just aim to be like men . . . but should aim to develop a new specifically feminine language, law and mythology." (Lechte 158)

Representation of middle class values and aspirations as a means of combating racism (Davis 107) and casteism is another general trend in the cultures under study. The female subaltern, to borrow a phrase from Spivak, is portrayed as doubly marginalized by virtue of relative economic disadvantage of gender subordination. (Moore 80)

Both McKay and Bharathidasan have painted images of ordinary, middle class women in their works. The black lass in the "Harlem Shadows" is a street walker pushed into that life by poverty, dishonour, and disgrace. Some withered women, dancers in night clubs, country girls who lose their innocence in towns, and midnight girls portray lives of black women in Jamaica and Harlem. Bita Plant, the female protagonist in *Banana Bottom*, is a skillfully drawn character who returns to her roots in

Jamaica after receiving English education from white missionaries.

Most of the women in Bharathidasan's works are taken from the lower rungs of society: a huntress, a servant, a cart man's love, a factory worker's wife, tribal women, weavers etc. Even a princess becomes an ordinary woman when she is disinherited by the king for falling in love with a Tamil poet. But she raises her voice of protest against the dictator, wins popular support, saves her lover, leads a revolt, and finally establishes a republic. Bharathidasan has re-created two women characters from Tamil epics in his ideological moulds: Kannagi and Manimegalai.

McKay's women also raise their voices of protest. An apple woman's complaint and a midnight woman's protest against the police are noteworthy. From these instances it can be inferred that the reformist zeal and protest are more pronounced in Bharathidasan than in McKay.

McKay and Bharathidasan who wanted to prepare their respective races for transition to the modern age propagated the importance of education in their works. In that attempt the latter depicted the better side of the Tamils, while the former painted the other side also of the blacks. The whites, as expected, opposed attempts to educate the blacks for "the fear of black rule and the defence of white women from rape by blacks." (McKay *Negroes in America* 81)

In ancient India, the Gurukulas, residential schools in which students lived with their teachers, were meant for upper caste men only and education was linked with religion in the Indian tradition. When V.V.S. Aiyar revived that system at Seranmadevi, Bharathidasan opposed the segregation of castes there. Once he was asked to compose a song in praise of Jules Fery, a French President who had delinked education from religion. He condemned the priests who denied education to the poor in France. Although the priests in the audience were shocked to hear this direct onslaught, the chairman—a Frenchman, encouraged the poet to complete the song. Bharathidasan sang: The priests prevented the fragrance of education from reaching the poor. That evil vanished when slashed. The stream of education flowed all over the land. (qtd Mannar Mannan 47)

In another poem, he goes to the extent of demanding the conversion of a temple partly damaged by fire into a school (1563). Such hostility towards religious institutions is not found in McKay though he was an atheist in his early life.

McKay who was aware of Gandhi's experiments in education and politics compares the various systems of education in the East. According to Ray in McKay's *Home to Harlem,* the universal objective of education is teaching something of real decency in dealing with all kinds and classes of people. (272) The leaders of the black community are asked to study the examples of Ireland, Russia and India under Gandhi, observes Amritjit Singh. (52) McKay emphasizes the inseparability of art and race in his autobiography and highlights the link between education and social progress in *Banana Bottom.*

Bharathidasan's concept of art, race and education can be inferred from his lines addressed to the Tamils: Develop arts! Study crafts! Compose poetry! (213) Obviously, he wants the study of both arts and crafts, along with the art of composing poetry. The racial character of the Tamils as conceived by him is well brought out in these lines: "Take up the deadly dagger/To bring to nought/The deeds of the very wicked." (213) Finally he celebrates the formation of a democratic socialist republic. He opposes English education and demands liberal education for the masses delinked from religion.

Barclay, a character in McKay's autobiographical short story "Truant" expresses his hatred for formal education, textbooks and libraries. (*Ginger Town* 54) On the other hand, Bharathidasan who was benefited by a system of formal education praises universities, books and libraries.

McKay in his campaign against the white structured education condemns white power in its guise of materialism, imperialism and education. (Giles 82) In *Banjo,* Ray condemns white education and proposes that black art must have its roots in the masses and be as independent as possible of the imperialistic white culture.

Such a black campaign was needed to counter the white campaign against education for the blacks. In India, Macaulay paved way for English education to the upper classes, which he believed would percolate slowly to the masses. (Santhanam 42) Bharathidasan opposes the study of English for mere employment (1724) and regrets that there is nothing in that system of education for Mother India. (75) In his poem written to celebrate the liberation of Paris, he praises France for making education common to all. (1755)

McKay's hostility towards English education is revealed in a symbolic act of Bita in Banana Bottom. She throws down the photograph of her English College and crushes it under her foot. (212) Kenneth Ramchand observes that such a description of a specific act is a "much more convincing and suggestive process," (208) than Ray's generalization that "civilization is rotten." (*Home to Harlem* 243) In Bharathidasan's "Kadala Kadamaiya" (Love or Duty?) a young girl wants her suitor to be an educated man capable of educating others also. (624) Konrai Nadu, a slave country in the story, may be taken as Tamilnadu (603) and Mazhai Nadu, the British Empire. To emphasize the importance of universal education in a country struggling for liberation, such a scene is introduced by the poet.

Bharathidasan opposes not only the English system of education but also the study of English ignoring Tamil because he thinks that it will be detrimental to the welfare of the Tamils and Tamil (1724). McKay, on the other hand, opposes the English system of education only, not the English language.

Both McKay and Bharathidasan have given importance to the improvement of women's status through education. The status of an educated black woman is portrayed in McKay's *Harlem Glory*. In it, Millinda, a village teacher, goes to Harlem, finds her rudimentary education far below the required standard and becomes the "Numbers Queen" (11) in the under world and outwits the whites as well as the legal authority. When she quarrels with Lotta, another black woman, the latter shouts: "Education. . . . Perhaps that's what's wrong. If I weren't educated, I would fight like a bloody savage." (25)

McKay's hatred for the white man's education can be inferred here, if one can connect this reaction with the simile used to describe the eyes of Millinda preparing herself for the squabble: "Millinda eagerly straightened up on the couch, her eyes big, wild and strange like an excited cat." (24) An educated black woman may "become a postmistress or a school mistress." (*Ginger Town* 239) Bharathidasan, on the other hand, thinks of better jobs for educated women: "To pilot the air plane/To measure fully/The oceans of the world." (495) Tamil women, traditionally home-locked, illiterate and superstitious are shown as university students, moon faced with blue floral eyes who skin Devil Ignorance. (446)

This optimistic attitude of Bharathidasan stands in contrast to the pessimism of McKay. Of all the plans of action, says the Tamil poet, educating women should be given priority. A wise wife will bring peace to the world. If all women enter politics and capture power, there will be no war or death in the world. That he does not want learning to end in school is evident from these lines. If all women have education, knowledge and character, there will be no need for medical care; and disease and old age will not approach. (952)

Education thus should guide a woman in her search for knowledge which in turn should develop her character. Such a chain reaction is not envisaged by McKay in the Harlem milieu with its emphasis on the present. Realising that eradication of illiteracy is a *sine qua non* for racial progress, Bharathidasan threatens to send those rascals who have not imparted education to the illiterates to gallows. (352) McKay, on the other hand, does not go to such an extent to stress the importance of education.

While discussing the relationship between the theory of criticism and the larger humanistic principle, Northrop Frye in his *Anatomy of Criticism* observes that "the freedom of man is inseparably bound up with his acceptance of his cultural heritage." (349) Bharathidasan and McKay have fought against barriers to the freedom of man and the influence of dominant cultures over their native ones. The onward march of humanity is often halted by obstacles man made and multicoloured. A comparison of the cultures of diverse races such as the black and the Tamil will no doubt measure their progress.

Works Cited

Bharathidasan. *Bharathidasan Kavithikal,* Comp. A Tiruvasakam and Suradha Kalladan. Chennai: Arul-Cudar, 1993.

Davis, Arthur P. *From the Dark Tower: Afro-American Writers 1900-1960*. WA: Howard University Press, 1974.

Davis, Thadios M. "A Female Face." *Teaching African American Literature.* Ed. Maryemma Graham et al. NY: Routledge 1998. 98-131.

Frye, Northrop. *Anatomy of Criticism: Four Essays.* NJ: Princeton, 1967.

Giles, James R. *Claude McKay.* Boston: Twayne, 1976.

Kailasapathi, K. *The Relation of Tamil and Western Literature.* Madurai: Madurai Kamaraj University, 1984.

Lechte, John. *Fifty Key Contemporary Thinkers,* 1994. London: Routledge, 1995.

Mannar Mannan. *Karuppuk Kuyilin Neruppuk Kural.* Villupuram: Muthu, 1985.

McKay, Claude. *Banana Bottom.* 1933. NJ: Chatham, 1970

——. *Gingertown.* 1932. NY: Books for Libraries. 1972.

——. *Harlem Glory.* Chicago: Charles H. Kerr. 1990.

——. *Home to Harlem.* 1928. Boston: Northeastern University Press, 1987.

——. *The Negroes in America.* Re-Trans. from the Russian. Robert Winter. Ed. Alan L. McLeod. NY: National University, 1979.

Moi, Toril. *Sexual/ Textual Politics.* London: Routledge, 1985.

Moore-Gilbert, Bart. *Post Colonial Theory.* London: Verso, 1997.

Santhanam S. *Kalviyin Thathuva Samooga Adipadaikal.* Chennai: Palaniyappa, 1987.

Singh, Amritjit. *The Novels of the Harlem Renaissance: Twelve Black Writers.* PA: PAUP, 1976.

The Prodigal Son of the Immigrant Family: Ward Minogue in Bernard Malamud's *The Assistant*

EAMI MATHEW
Govt. College, Madappally

An interdisciplinary approach to a literary character may relate fiction to truth. This approach to life situations through imaginary characters in the light of certain theories of criminology brings law close to literature. Case studies based on actual and official data are the usual methods of criminologists. A critic may supply literary descriptions of a deviant and his delinquent actions. A criminologist may use variables as determinant factors of delinquent behavior. Yet both are important as two distinct approaches to a given situation.

The purpose of this study is two fold: (i) to attract the attention of the literary critics to the necessity of studying the villain as supplementary to the study of the hero; (ii) to examine the explanatory value of variables drawn from three traditional theories of delinquency such as the social control theory of Hirschi (1969), Reckless (1961), the structural strain theory of Cloward and Ohlin (1960), and the theory of Conger (1976) and Zimring (1981). The crucial question to be analyzed is whether Ward is a social criminal or has a psychic problem. And what role the society plays in promoting his deviant nature?

This study of Ward Minogue, the anti-hero of Bernard Malamud's *The Assistant* (1957) is to bring into focus the shadow behind the hero. The novel is often treated as the gradual upgrading of a criminal mind. Still, his fellow criminal Ward Minogue is left unnoticed. All his actions vary much from the traditional patterns of human behaviour. He is the live background against which the hero, Frank Alpine, is projected. He has his counter-parts in Shakespeare, Dostoevsky, and Dickens. He is the best case study in the modern American situation.

Ward is introduced in the novel as a co-criminal of the hero. Frank Alpine an Italian who seeks a better placement and comes to New York meets Ward Minogue. They carry out a hold up on Morris Bober, a poor Jewish shopkeeper. It is mismanaged by Ward though he gets a little profit out of it. He controls Frank, by holding Frank's pistol in his custody. He makes fun of Frank for working for a Jew; vulgarizes the relationship between Helen and Frank, and invites him for more hold-ups and theft. He tries to manhandle Helen. He drinks, smokes and uses filthy language. He runs away from the shadow of his own father. He had been indulging in anti-social behavior that has violated public sentiment in appearance, action, words and thought.

In *Understanding Troubling and Troubled Youth*, Loren M. Warboys and Carole B. Shauffer suggest: "The law grants adults full freedom to make their own decisions. . . . At the same time the law long recognized that certain persons are incompetent to exercise this freedom." (28) In the case of Ward Minogue, he is a child as well as an adult. It is very difficult to determine whether he is in his childhood or whether he is capable of assuming the rights and responsibilities of his adulthood. His actions reveal that his childhood and adulthood are flexible. Thus his father acts like a substitute decision-maker. There was no awareness from father's side: "In some situations and individuals emotional or cognitive maturity is more important than chronological age." (Warboys & Shauffer 28) Unfortunately he fails to understand the appropriateness of his father's decisions which were shaped on existing social norms and father's determination to teach him better ways ended in series of collisions between them. It is stated repeatedly by Malamud that Ward was brought up in a Jewish neighborhood and was treated as a "goim" among the Jews.

As Clifford Shaw suggests, "the delinquent belongs to a social group whose cultural values and moral standards vary widely from those of the larger conventional society." (83) His father, detective Minogue, brought him up. He was a stocky, red-faced detective. He was a soft-spoken, unsmiling man. Criminologists believe that "the origin of the typical criminal is an imperfect child, suffering from some defect.'' (Darrow 58) Ward's neighbors could recollect how much the boy was beaten by his father regularly that created a sense of hatred in Ward who felt later that "what will help me is if my goddam father drops dead." (*The Assistant* 67) His imperfections were unusual, and he exhibited curiosity to know the physical differences of the other sex. Sexual desires originated in him at a very early age. The author records that he was an expert in manhandling girls when they were alone. At school he was a real trouble, as he liked to follow girls going to the lavatory. His old man found only one cure for such malpractices. Most often he used his stick or billy to bring him back to perfection. For he was familiar with that mode of treatment, advised in the police department.

There is no reference anywhere in the novel about Ward's father's attempts to lead him to other fields of attraction or adventure. His sense of beauty or spirit for youthful adventure was not kindled. Totally unaware of the world of art, literature, music, sports and social service, the boy wandered in the poor neighbourhood. Since his peer group belonged to a different race, with their own religion, language, morals, manners and taboos, he could not make adjustments with them. At home, he was lonely, motherless, free, and silent. Outside home, people never trusted him because of the criminal records he had had at school and in the neighborhood. In an age at which the boy was craving for adventure and recognition, he "turned into delinquency because of the pleasurable excitement of the forbidden, of defiance to authority, and because of the prestige value of bravado." (Tappan 136-37) His old man worked as the social eye. So people felt sorry for the detective for he was a strict man and they knew what it meant to him to have such a son" [*The Assistant* 48]. The boy unconsciously developed "fear, hate and guilt feelings but no real respect for authority or identification with him who wields it." (Sutton 162)

Marshall B. Clinard suggests that it happens that "the families of delinquents have been either too lax or too strict in their punishment." (189) Gluccks strengthened this view through the statement that "discipline was either insufficient or too severe for seven in ten male prisoners and for nearly two in three women prisoners." (189) Every time Ward committed a crime, his father, the detective, punished him. Even when he understood that he had grown up as not to be controlled by a stick, he foolishly hunted for him. Therefore, when Ward was canned from his job for stealing from the company, his father beat him sick and bloody with his billy and drove him out of his neighborhood. After that nobody knew his whereabouts. Ward stands a proof that age cannot be "affixed constant determinant for when childhood ends and subjective factors like "experience, education, and intelligence are essential part of the determination." (Warboys & Sauffer 28) Ward's parent and society took his chronological age for maturity, neglecting the type of human experience he had undergone, the incomplete education he got and the lower intelligence he possessed as a boy. Detective Minogue had failed to detect the reasons behind his son's delinquent manners. The actual source of his subculture behaviour is the broken home. Chances for adventure and recognition were none. An exposure to healthy human relationship was unknown to the boy. Under these circumstances he himself found out methods for thrill and excitement.

The biblical archetypes for a promising father-son relationship are the prodigal son and his father. The biblical father is the embodiment of love and patience. The relationship between Morris Bober and Frank Alpine, the two other characters in the novel comes nearer to these biblical characters. Bober is consolation and protection personified. When the prodigal son leaves home with his share, the father never stopped him. He knew that experience, the best teacher, would teach him in the right time. The son who got what he deserved for his rebellion and selfishness, returned to his father with a heart-felt regret. He was well received; a feast was well arranged. To his father it is happiness that he came home once again. To the detective, Ward is a curse to his respectful individuality. He punished his prodigal son on and on to pacify his own egoistic motivations. A man who is more interested in the self, uses every means possible to save his image in the society. As a strict man, he punished his son severely. The society was pleased at Minogue's attitude towards his son. Self-denial of the father was necessary to save Ward but detective Minogue could sacrifice nothing to win a son. Pitiably, he could not even identify his son. He should have acted the role of a parent, though not as a role-model but at least as a protector and supporter to a son who is socially distanced, mentally disturbed and physically tortured. A moral support from any possible source would have effected the refinement of Ward's personality. The father, guided by hatred and the son, chased by fear, are symbolic of the victimizer and the victim. The boy runs away from his own blood relation. He fearfully reveals to his friend: "Somebody tipped my old man I was around here, so I hid out for a while." (*The Assistant* 67) Father whose inquiry always ends in helplessness approaches his Jewish friend Bober with a little hope. He says, "Morris, would you recognize Ward Mingue if you happened to see him again? I hear his been seen around but whereabouts I don't know!" (48)

On his second visit, he reminds Morris of the earlier reference: "Morris, I think I asked you already if you saw my son Ward Minogue around here, have you yet?" (128) He could not stop Ward's desire for alcohol or cigar. Since most of his delinquent activities or crime were committed under the influence of alcohol, it is to be believed that his criminal impulses were channelled by the impact of alcohol. When he conducted the hold-up he was unsteady; when he met Helen in the park, he was stinking of whisky. Whenever Frank met him, he was under the influence of liquor. It was his own desire for a drink that drove him to Karp's late in the night.

> Alcohol nauseated him lately; his thirst for a drink killed him. He thought if he could get a couple swings past the nausea he would feel better. . . . Ward grabbed a bottle of wine from the counter and flung it at Louis's head. . . . Ward snatched a bottle of whisky and ran out of the store. (191)

The end of Ward is tragically designed not by fate, but by his own desire. Malamud's own words narrate the scene as a rabbit hunt. His father hunted for him in the dark for fifteen minutes, just to annihilate him.

He took his pistol and fired a shot into the shed. Ward, out of fear, thought that he would be killed. So he crawled out from under the truck and ran into his father's arms, just as a returned prodigal son. But a sharp contrast between the two pairs is cited. Ward pleaded to his father that he had diabetes, and surely will get gangrene if beaten. But "his father beat him with his billy until Ward collapsed." (191)

Apparently the father uses his mode of severe beating as a trick to save his identity. Therefore he yelled to the bleeding son: "I told you to stay the hell out of this neighborhood. This is my last warning to you. If I ever see you again, I'll murder you." (191)

There is a small sentence, which Malamud inserted in between the father's curse and the son's offence. It goes like this: "He felt so dizzy, he wept." (191) Since weeping shows some kind of turbulence within, it is a good positive sign, a hope for Ward's feeling regretful. His unstable feeling changed immediately into a negative one. He started thinking of a drink, of Karp's liquor shop. Ward tried to trap Karper but he could not. Later he overtook Karper by turning his flourishing liquor shop in to ashes.

The role of society at this juncture is significant though negative and fearfully encouraging what has been done, though unintentionally, by the people. They have widened the crack in to a larger hole until the wall of protection collapsed. Of this role of the society Ward recollects, "I hate that Jew son of a bitch and his pop-eyed Louis. When I was a kid all I had to do was to go near banjo eyes and they would complain to my old man and get me beat up. " (68)

All the time Ward was sobbing within and silently proclaiming to the world what he said to Helen, "Don't be afraid of me, Helen. I'm personally a fine guy—son of a cop." (149) He wanted to raise himself from the abominable use of language and actions but did nothing for that. Drinking and smoking had the drastic result in the form of a pain in the chest. Helen was the last one in the family to be thrown into the street by Ward. By his action the immigrant Jews suffered a lot. He can properly be called the prodigal son of the immigrant family.

Bober's life, as he adds and subtracts it in his loneliness, is a great loss to him. What is Ward's personal contribution to the suffering of Bobers? Had he not been there to rob the poor Jew, frighten him or hurt him the story would have been another one. Because he attacked Bober made bedridden, Frank took the advantage of his absence and cheated Bober as the store assistant. His attack on Helen forced her to analyze her actions and to decide upon stopping her love affair with Frank. The sudden change of mind caused suffering to Frank. Bober, after Ward's attack, underwent through a series of troubles culminating in his death. This made Ida, Helen and Frank suffer jointly. Once more Ward proved notorious in his anti-Semitic attitudes by bringing endless suffering to his Jewish neighborhood. He was the prodigal son of the immigrant family.

Ward's anti-Semitic attitudes come out of his pangs of isolation. In his neighborhood, his neighbors brought him up with close attention. To a deviant boy, close observation is really suffocating, especially when the rod of Jewish morals measures all his deeds. So the school dropout 'goyim' became a thief first and a womanizer next. Almost all the Jews kept him away from their company. A delinquent boy, whenever he feels sorry and tries to keep contacts with non-delinquent ones, is distrusted by them. Isolation filled his heart with anti-Semitism which eventually resulted in delinquency.

Ward's "delinquent behaviour is the result of frustration, experienced by individuals who are unable to achieve legitimate social and economic success." (Joseph 475-76) His boyish mind yearned for "support and recognition," but got insult, complaint, abuse, curse and punishment, Frank played the role of a mediator between Ward and his society, between his anti-Semitism and philanthropy, between his father and him, but it was too late. So he could not influence Ward any more than his father. What has made Frank's return to life positive, quick, and effective than that of Ward?

The following diagram of the delinquent may chart his growth and fall as a social criminal. The liberation of Frank from delinquency and progress towards self-denial for others is also marked. This kind of an analysis of a literary hero would bring him close to criminology. It would possibly relate him with live criminals drawn from real life situations.

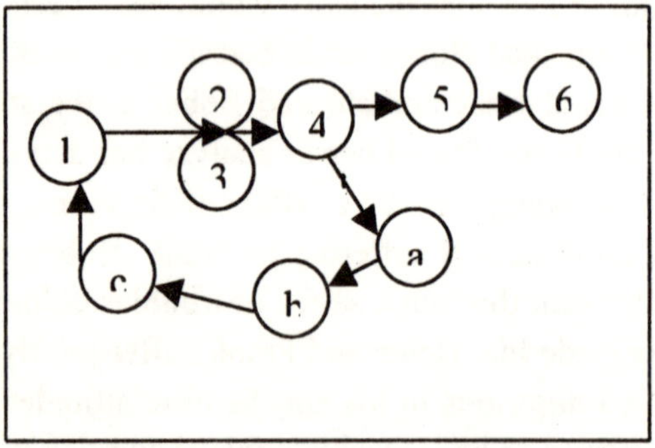

Figure 1: Frank's return to life

1. Life 2. Ward. 3. Frank. 4. Gang 5. Hold ups 6. Death.
a. Job b. Suffering. c.Love and responsibility

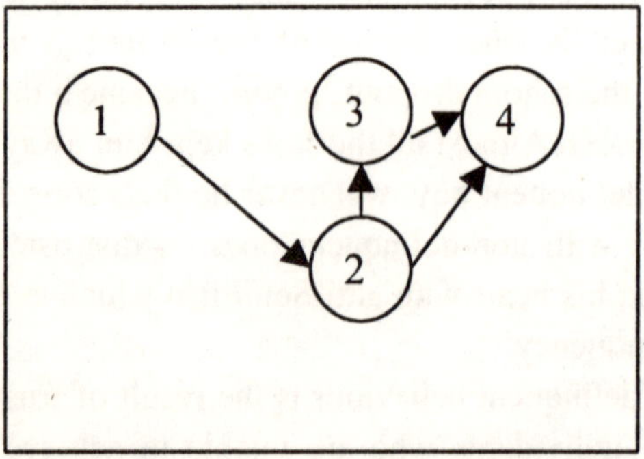

Figure 2: Causes for delinquency

1. No attachment to parent
2. No attachment to school
3. Gang formation
4. Delinquency

The above diagram shows that Ward and Frank are not orphans, but orphaned. They form a gang to conduct hold-ups. Ward continues his negative trends such as rape and theft and keeps on his thirst for liquor and smoking. The negative marks show that there is nothing worth mentioning in his biography. Unlike him, Frank, though misled by Ward, changes at the earliest, his negative qualities into plus points and positive ones. His social responsibility has helped him much to seek human companionship of men and women. Positive feelings of security, stability, satisfaction, consideration, love, responsibility and recognition gradually evoke confidence and self-respect in him. So with Bober, he could be positive and with Helen, he could be confident.

Frank's transformation into a reformed personality by adapting himself to the given environment is superb. He accepted the Bobbers for his family, the library for his school and the store for his dwelling place. Such socializing agents were rejected by the criminal, since he was not ambitious in life. Frank and Ward committed a crime together but Frank alone regretted his having taken part in it. His pricking conscience worked as a constant reminder of his theft. Ward missed all chances for self-analysis because he had no pricking of conscience. Frank's love affair too was advantageous to the development of his personality. Ward's relationship to women was notorious and he was the most dangerous womanizer of that neighborhood.

From the total analysis of his character, beginning from his early boyhood up to his premature death, three findings are to be noted: (a) his father's method of child rearing was not practical in the case of a child like Ward; (b) he was a boy of emotional maturity greater than his chronological age; (c) a child who has no attachment to his parents may fail to show any attachment to school; (d) a child who fails to have any attachment to school shows chances for deviancy; (e) he may develop a tendency to cultivate differential association with boys of the similar behavioral patterns. In the case of Ward, not only his father, but also school and environment had contributed much to his deviant behavior. Nowhere in the novel can one see a loving word spoken by his father or teacher or neighbor to the boy. He is distanced even by the girl friend who could have won him and changed him a lot. The importance of the hero is apparent when one realizes how hardly he strives against the oddities of life and how daringly he survives his limitations. Malamud's Bober takes all the credit for Frank's success in life. His readiness to suffer to win a son should be appreciated. Alder D. Miller says: "Delinquency is a community problem in the final analysis the means for its prevention and control must be built into the fabric of community life; this can happen only if the community accepts its share of responsibility for having generated and perpetuated paths of socialization that lead to sporadic criminal episodes for some youth and carriers in crime for others." (Alder 11)

Works Cited

Malamud, Bernard. *The Assistant*. London: Eyre and Spottiswood, 1975

Clinard, Marshall B. *Sociology of Deviant Behavior*. New York: Rinehart, 1957.

Cloward, R & L. Ohlin. *Delinquency and Opportunity*. New York: Free Press, 1960.

Conger, R. "Social Control and Social Learning Models of Delinquent Behavior: A Synthesis." *Criminology,* 1976. 17-40.

Darrow, Clarence, P. *Crime: Its Causes and Treatment*. New Jersey: Patterson Smith, 1972.

Glueck, S. and E. Glueck. *Unravelling Juvenile Delinquency*. Cambridge: Harvard University Press, 1950.

Hirschi, T. *Causes of Delinquency*. Berkley: University of California, 1969.

Joseph, Janice. "Juvenile Delinquency among African Americans." *Journal of Black Studies*, 25:4. March 1995. 475-88

Miller, Alder, D. *Delinquency and Communality*. California: Sage, 1985.

Reckless, W. "A New Theory of Delinquency and Crime." *Federal Probation*, 25, 1961. 42-46.

Shaw, Clifford, "Juvenile Delinquency: A Group Tradition," *Gang Delinquency and Delinquent Subculture*, ed. James Short. New York: Harper and Rowe, 1969.

Sutton, John R. 1988. *Stubborn Children.* California: University of California Press, 1988.

Tappan, Paul W. *Juvenile Delinquency.* San Francisco: Chandler, 1977.

Weiserg, Richard. "Law and Literature." MLA conference paper, Dec. 1984.

Warboys, Loren. M and Carole B. Shaffer. "Protecting Youths Rights," *Understanding Troubled and Troubling Youth*, ed. Peter E. Leone. California: Sage, 1990.

Zimring, F. Kids, "Groups and Crime: Some Implications of Well-Known Secrets." *Journals of Criminal Law and Criminology*, 72 (3), 1981.

Unmeltables in the Melting Pot: A Study of Huckleberry Finn

K. SAJI
B.P. C. College, Piravom, Kerala

"No one of us is outside or beyond geography, none of us is free from the struggle over geography. That struggle is complex and interesting because it is not only about soldiers and cannons but also about ideas, about forms, about images and imaginings," says Edward Said in his work *Culture and Imperialism.* (6) The story of the peopling of America is precisely the story of this struggle over geography with all its complex dimensions. Its temporal simultaneity with Enlightenment and technological development in printing facilitated the transportation of Euro-centric values, universalized as transcendental moral values, to this new geo-social space as to the rest of the globe.

Since the concepts of morality are historically specific and are fleshed out in different shades to define culture and social propriety, evil or sin, which was central to medieval Christianity, was not totally abandoned in the Enlightenment shift to secular ethics. These concepts were instrumental in bodying forth as evil, the strange peoples, inhabiting strange lands made imaginable by accounts of the voyages of discovery in the 15th century. Media reports and representation of characters in literary works (e.g. Nigger Jim in *The Adventures of Huckleberry Finn*), through their repeated use of terms like nigger, exotic Arab, tradition, indigenous, alien etc. reiterate the existence of a radical cultural alterity which shows in relief the WASP culture as universal. Thus the western imperialistic cultural structure effectively evoked the concept of the 'Other'—an inalienable part of

American subjectivity, in embodying all that is a negation of the 'Universal' standards.

The global political phenomenon of decolonization reverberated in the academic field in the form of vociferous marginalized discourses subverting the classical hierarchy. The peopling of America, therefore can be read subversively as the story of the extermination of the Native Indians, dehumanizing slavery of the Black Americans, marginalization of minor ethnic cultures etc. rather than as the success story of the Pilgrim Fathers who roughed it out in the strange, wild land.

It is in this context that we have to examine Ernest Hemingway's statement eulogizing *The Adventures of Huckleberry Finn*—"All modern American literature comes from one book by Mark Twain called *Huckleberry Finn.*" The drama unfolding the American Mind takes place in a setting remote (only in lifestyle and values, not geographically) from the strait-jacketing influence of the imperial structure of references and attitudes, embodied in the persons of Aunt Polly, Widow Douglas or Mary, all part of the self-legislated civilizers of Huck Finn. Their catechisms, replete with images of evil, hell etc, a necessary counterpoise to the imperial construct of propriety is totally rejected by Huck Finn, "All I wanted was to go somewhere; all I wanted was a change. She said it was wicked to say what I said; she said she wouldn't say it for the whole world; she was going to live so as to go to the good place. Well I couldn't see no advantage in going where she was going, so I made up mind I wouldn't try for it." (4)

Fiercely independent, with his cowboy like scorn for the WASP standards, "I never seen anybody but lied one time or another, without it was Aunt Polly, or the widow or maybe Mary" (3) and again his scornful observation of Colonel Grangerford's lineage, "He was well born as the saying is and that is worth as much in a man as it is in a horse." (101) Huck's insatiable zest for adventure is the true American spirit that has kept America constantly on the move in search of new frontiers. Fathered by a thorough going rogue, fostered by paradigms of social virtue and propriety Huck, thus represents the true American spirit. Though caught between an instinctive affinity for his father's lazy and jolly lifestyle and a qualified respect for the unattainable rectitude of the structure of references, projected as transcendental: "There is something in it when a body like the widow or the parson prays but it don't work for me" (37), it is only Huck's relationship with his sable companion Jim, that really problematises his subjectivity. Both have set out on a daring bid for freedom from 'sivilization.' The Other in Huck's imagination is very exotic and alien whereas Nigger Jim is a constant companion to Huck.

The Huck-Jim relationship is a subversive equivalent of the Prospero-Caliban relationship. To Huck, Jim is no savage to be nurtured into a civilized being, but rather his soul mate. Unlike in the Prospero-Caliban imperial equation, here it is Jim who misses his home and family and forces Huck to unlearn many of the white man's notions about niggers as subhuman. At each juncture of his contact with the civilized world; Huck automatically becomes a detached observer sensitively recounting events, thus making the reader fully aware of the significance of his misspelling the term 'sivilize.' It is only in interaction with Jim that Huck becomes a participant in the movement of events. It is interesting to note how the shift in narrative signifies Huck's way of positioning himself in the imperial structure. Whenever he is among civilized people, Huck positions himself outside the structure but in the company of Jim he is the embodiment of the imperial construct. Hence the resultant stereotyping of Jim as a mere superstitious nigger as niggers are generally shown to be (the instance of the nigger at Phelps' Farm). Huck problematises that image of niggers by showing himself subject to that same frailty of fear that makes man superstitious.

Jim, through a series of instances of shattering of Huck's image of a typical nigger—each of Huck's exasperated comments 'I never see such a nigger' shows how distant the nigger figure is in his imagination—redefines Huck's subjectivity so much so that between them they fix the norms of propriety, after discussing the views of the widow etc. It is worth noting that to both Huck and Jim, it is the same American spirit of pragmatism that informs ethical propriety: "Jim said he reckoned the widow was partly right. . . . But towards daylight we got it all settled satisfactory, and concluded to drop crabapples and p'simmons. We warn't feeling just right before that, but it was all comfortable now. I was glad the way it come out, too, because crabapples aint ever good and p'simmons wouldn't be ripe for two or three months yet." (64)

Huck perceives Jim to be equally sharp in sniffing out the duke and king to be mere rapscallions. In the end, when the duke and the king play the dirty trick of selling Jim, it is his awareness of the fact that Jim can gain specificity as an individual only among his own people, that makes him contrite for helping his benefactor's property sail to freedom. Thus considering Jim as chattel is the direct consequence of acknowledging his human status.

Huck reductively explains away his affinity for Jim, as being due to his own bad upbringing and hence is chagrined to see Tom Sawyer earnest in stealing Jim out of Slavery: "Here was a boy that was respectable and well brung up; and had a character to lose; and folks at home that had characters; and he was bright and not leather-headed; and knowing and not ignorant; and not mean but kind; and yet here he was without anymore pride or rightness or feeling than to stoop to this business." (184)

This piece of thought is an important signifier for it clearly shows that the imperial construct, which informs American norms of propriety, presupposes the dehumanization of the Other (not just the nigger for it could be any of those exotic Orientals who feed the boys' sense of adventure or 'Sick Arab,' the faceless creature that Jim is transformed to, to cheat civilized America), and the moment it is forced to adjust its subjectivity to accommodate the human selfhood of the Other culture, it is bound to crumble. One historic attempt at acknowledging the humanness of the Other was the abolition of slavery as an institution but it was more a political exigency than an empathic act. As Abraham Lincoln said in Springfield, Illinois, on June 17, 1858, "'A house divided against itself cannot stand.' I believe this government cannot endure permanently half slave and half free."

Thus in a single sweeping act of constitutional amendment the White man brushed aside centuries of dehumanization of the Black man. He who had become a social cipher found himself one fine morning, thrust into the struggle for geography even before he could recover his sense of identity (White man, through various stratagems like segregation, racism etc. saw to it that the Other identity remained undesirable.) A century later the same imperialistic structure is looking at them with a chagrined look of 'see didn't I tell you'.

With post-colonialism has crept in a vague consciousness of the unfairness of the historical process, leading to an acceptance of the contingency of old universalism. "Having accepted the contingency of the old universalism the American Right now maintains that 'western values' must be quarantined against those whose cultures are at odds with them—accepting in other words certain key diagnoses of post-colonial analysis, namely that 'western' society stands or falls on the HEGEMONY of a particular 'culture' (the White, Anglo-Saxon culture of its elites)." (Kahn 6)

Thus the White man's authentic rhetoric in conceptualizing the Other, a thorough comprehension of whose otherness is not possible without a negation of his own values and assumptions, has problematized his own cultural identity.

Works Cited

Bodkin, Maud. *Archetypal Patterns in Poetry: Psychological Study of Imagination.* London: Oxford University Press, 1965.

Goldberg, David Theo. *Racist Culture: Philosophy and the Politics of Meaning.* Massachussets: Blackwell, 1994.

Kahn, Joel S. *Culture Multiculture Post Culture.* London: Sage, 1995.

Said, Edward W. *Culture and Imperialism.* London: Chatto & Windus, 1993.

Twain, Mark. *Adventures of Huckleberry Finn.* Bantam Classics, 1884.